Market Drayton in 1851

Aspects of life in the Market Drayton area in and about 1851

Market Drayton U3A
Local History Group

Editor : Peter Brown

© *Peter Brown and Ian Picton-Robinson
and the individual authors*

2013

Cover picture: 'The King's Arms', Shropshire Street,
painted by J Heywood in about 1843, and
reproduced by kind permission of Michael Williams

Cover design by Les Lacey

Published through Amazon

on behalf of TF9 Publishing
34 Waterside Drive
Market Drayton
TF9 1HU

ISBN 978 148115681 3

Contents

1	Introduction: The 1851 Project	*Peter Brown & Ian Picton-Robinson*	4
2	Britain in 1851	*Ian Picton-Robinson*	5
3	The development of Market Drayton in the 19th century *David Jenkins*		8
4	The census	*Ian Picton-Robinson*	14
5	Aspects of birth & death	*Meriel Blower & Peter Brown*	18
6	Employment	*Ian Picton-Robinson & Peter Brown*	19
7	Servants living-in	*Peter Brown*	25
8	The enclosure of Little Drayton Common *David Jenkins*		28
9	The Census of Religious Worship	*Peter Brown*	36
10	Churches & chapels: the 1851 buildings and what survives today *Peter Brown*		40
11	The Poor Law & the workhouse	*Chris Sharp & Grace Russell*	44
12	Friendly societies in Market Drayton in the mid 19th century *Ros Wells*		49
13	Education	*Meriel Blower*	57
14	Libraries & the Book Society	*Peter Brown*	61
15	Crime & justice	*Peter Brown*	64
16	Transport	*Peter Brown*	69
17	Inns and beer-houses	*Peter Brown*	73
18	Betton	*Bill Page*	76
19	Lydia Roden's mug: a detective story	*Meriel Blower*	80
20	Gentry houses & their landscapes	*Kunigunda Gough*	83
—	Supplement: The Shropshire Rifle Volunteers, 2nd (Market Drayton) Company, 1860–1908 *David Jenkins*		91
—	Index		99

1 : Introduction — The 1851 Project

Peter Brown and Ian Picton-Robinson

The University of the Third Age (U3A)

The U3A is a self-help organisation for people no longer in full time employment providing educational, creative and leisure opportunities in a friendly environment. Local U3As are autonomous learning co-operatives which draw upon the knowledge, experience and skills of their own members to organise and provide interest groups in accordance with the wishes of the membership. The aim is 'learning for pleasure'.

Market Drayton U3A Local History Group

The Market Drayton U3A has about thirty groups, of which the Local History Group is one. There are about a dozen members, with a wide range of backgrounds and special interests.

Each year the Group has adopted a theme — past ones have included street names, oral history, research into the history of three of the principal streets during the Victorian era, and cataloguing Drayton Museum's archive.

The 1851 project

In the autumn of 2006 the members of the Group decided that a good project would be to research Market Drayton in the year 1851. This year was chosen for several reasons:
- it had the first full census which detailed each member of every household;
- there was the only religious census ever conducted;
- Bagshaw's directory for that year was particularly informative; and
- it was a transitional period in the history of Market Drayton — local public services were on the increase, but the railway had not yet arrived to end the town's relative isolation.

The area covered by the study is that of the old Drayton Union, the mid 19th century Poor Law area. In addition to the town, it embraced the surrounding parishes including those in Staffordshire. In other words it was (and is) the area for which Market Drayton is the natural centre — indeed it was virtually the same area as is now covered by the Market Drayton U3A, sometimes called the 'TF9' area, after the local postcode.

One of the Group computerised a 1-in-5 detailed extract from the census, and this formed the basis of some of the other members' studies. Lessons from the census are detailed in Chapter 4.

Each member of the Group chose a subject or subjects which particularly interested them and conducted their research in their own way, reporting back to the monthly meetings about their progress and there asking for advice or opinions.

This book

It soon became clear that the findings would be of wider interest than merely to the Group members. Two of the Group therefore decided to publish a book in the form of a series of papers on the various topics researched. These have been lightly edited, mainly to minimise duplication and to try to ensure consistency.

David Jenkins' article on the Market Drayton Rifle Volunteers (1860–1908) falls outside the period of study but has been included as a supplement because of its importance.

This book does not pretend to be a comprehensive portrait of the Market Drayton area in 1851. Many relevant topics have been omitted or covered only sketchily — sometimes because the source material was not readily available, sometimes because nobody in the Group possessed the necessary background knowledge or interest.

Nevertheless, we hope the reader will find much of interest — and possibly be inspired to carry out and publish their own research.

[Note: All photographs are by the Editor unless otherwise attributed.]

2 : Britain in 1851

Ian Picton-Robinson & Peter Brown

In 1851 Queen Victoria had been on the throne for fourteen years. The Royal Family then had seven of their eventual nine children.

Prince Albert was active, a principal supporter of the Great Exhibition held that year in Hyde Park. This was a demonstration to the world of the supremacy of British industry, but the more discerning visitor realised that technologically other countries were catching up quickly, particularly the United States, Germany and France, and that in many respects those countries' product designs were superior.

The economy, transport and trade

The economy was booming, having recovered from the banking crisis of 1847. Britain was at the zenith of its industrial lead over the rest of the world, producing over 40% of the entire world output of traded manufactured goods, 60% of the world's coal, 50% of its iron, and 50% of commercial cotton cloth. The steam engine had replaced water as the principal power source for industry, which as a consequence tended to relocate and develop mainly in the areas where coal was abundant: the Midlands, South Lancashire and West Yorkshire.

In 1851 agriculture was in its period of 'high farming', in which the application of science was significantly improving yields which were much needed to feed the fast-growing cities. Almost all farm work was still done by hand or by horse; Clayton & Shuttleworth of Lincoln had built their first portable steam engines for agricultural use, particularly threshing, in 1845 but the first steam ploughs were not introduced until 1858.

These developments were both influenced by and stimulated improved transport links for the movement of raw materials and finished produce. The main canal network was completed by 1810, with a few additions and improvements in the 1830s. The first main line railway was between Liverpool and Manchester, opening in 1830; this line was linked to Birmingham in 1837, and from there to London the following year. Other trunk lines followed. 1845–7 were the years of the 'Railway Mania' with 765 railway Acts being passed in the three years; not all the lines were built, but those which were created the network which substantially survives today.

The railways enabled places to specialise in producing those goods or agricultural products to which they were best suited, and to move them cheaply to other parts of the country. This reduced prices but led to greater uniformity and destroyed many local jobs. For example, areas with hand-made bricks produced from less suitable clays then acquired standard uniform bricks from the main brickmaking centres.

The main roads were all turnpikes (toll roads) but their income had been hard hit by the development of the railway system. Only in the industrial areas were there significant new or improved roads. The lanes could be dusty or muddy, or full of livestock being driven from field to farm or to markets. Nevertheless, they were generally quiet and safe for children to wander, for men and women to walk home from work, for 'mouchers' to collect anything and sell to 'townies' and for itinerants (chapmen) selling wares and their skills.

The railways had killed off the long-distance stage coaches, leaving just feeder services. The long distance carriers had also transferred their trade to the railways, but the local carriers working into the various market towns were thriving. Drivers would often collect goods for others, settle or collect debts and perform other services, often delivering directly to front doors.

Fairs and markets continued to be held for special purposes — horse sales or hiring of servants for example — and brought a wider range of goods than was normally sold locally, plus entertainment.

Science and technology

The most far-reaching scientific development was in electricity, but it had not reached the stage of having a significant commercial impact. Michael Faraday made the first electric motor in 1821, and in 1831 he discovered the reverse effect — movement of a coil near magnets produced electricity. By 1842, practical electric generators were in commercial production. In 1845 Faraday found an interaction between magnetism and light: the turning of polarised light. John F Daniell developed in 1836 the first practical battery. The first electric telegraph was installed in 1838. By 1840 several people worked out the chemistry of electroplating.

Wrought iron was replacing cast iron in many engineering uses, but the bulk production of steel had not yet been perfected. Other technologies which were to become important after 1851 included bulk chemicals such as dyes and dynamite, and oil from petroleum.

The Frenchman Louis Daguerre invented the

earliest photographic process, which was first used by the press in 1840. William Fox Talbot discovered the principles of photography that developed into today's methods, publishing them in 1834.

Although Charles Darwin had published his description of his five year cruise in 'The Beagle' in 1837 and had largely worked out his theory of evolution, 'The Origin of the Species' was not to be published until 1859.

Public services

Most of the limited public services were provided locally. The county magistrates were responsible for justice, prisons and some highways bridges. Some activities devolved to the local community: parish, Union, or ad hoc grouping. The most important local service was administration of the Poor Law following the 1834 Act; relief was financed from the local rates but parishes were grouped into a union, with a local board of elected guardians. Other local services were mainly discretionary rather than compulsory, thus the extent of provision varied widely across the country.

The sense of service to the town and village was strong, with tradesmen, craftsmen, teachers and others taking part, through vestry meetings, as guardians and overseers of the poor, along with appointment as highway surveyors, way-wardens, rate-assessors, parish valuers, parish constables and so on. They kept roads, footpaths, ponds and drains maintained, kept animal pounds for strays, sold lane-dropped manure, ran fire-brigades, maintained burial grounds, built schools, overviewed pubs and alehouses etc. Other services, if they existed, were provided by the churches and chapels (particularly education), by charitable endowments, or by voluntary groupings such as friendly societies.

In the first half of the 19th century Parliament began to regulate the worst excesses of employment. The 1819 Factories Act gave some protection to women and children. This was extended in 1833; and in 1842 it was legislated that women and children under 10 were no longer to be employed underground.

Social issues were beginning to be investigated rationally through the collection of information, hence for example the most detailed census to date and the first and only Census of Religious Worship. Central monitoring and in some cases inspection of local services was initiated, examples included public health, police and factory inspection, and Poor Law Commissioners. The permanent staff in some government departments were becoming recognised as a Civil Service. The Trevelyan-Northcote Report of 1853 recommended various reforms to make the civil service more professional; despite much opposition, their recommendations began to be implemented in 1855.

The home

Labourers' cottages generally had little to recommend them. They often had lime-washed timber and plaster walls and were roofed with thatch, with a garden for potatoes and vegetables.

The brick tax had been abolished in 1850. By the middle of the 19th century they were becoming mass produced and transported by canal or rail in thousands, resulting in the local bricks being ousted by standardised red bricks. Window tax was abolished in 1851, and glass was being mass-produced, so cottages began to be glazed. Rather than curtains, paper, sacking or boarding was used.

Cooking was usually on open fires in cast iron pots. The main meat was pork or bacon from pigs reared outside the door. Baking of bread was done in ovens hot from burnt out faggots of wood. Later coal was used, and grates appeared, then ranges. Few could afford candles for providing lighting, so they used rushes from the meadows steeped in animal tallow.

Rural cottages typically had vegetable gardens for growing potatoes, turnips, carrots, parsnips, beets, onions, cabbages, spring greens, kale, spinach, broccoli, cauliflower, broad beans, runner beans, haricot beans and peas. Fruit trees and bushes included apple, pear, plum, damson, greengages, cherries, medlars, mulberry, gooseberry, currants and raspberries. There was likely to be a pig and perhaps fifty poultry. Food grown for animals included cow cabbage, chicory, swedes, buckwheat and hemp (also grown for its fibre).

Water supply was from rain collected in water butts, from wells up to 100ft deep (which were easily fouled), or from rivers or ponds (with 'multi-use' additions). Consequently the safest drink tended to be home brewed small beer. Excrement was put into pits, though in some towns 'night soil' was removed regularly, then dumped or used for manure.

The arts and architecture

This was not a great period for the arts in Britain.

As the only western country without an 'art music' tradition, it was described in the 1860s as a 'land without music'. Certainly no British music of the period has remained in the repertoire. Nevertheless, foreign musicians were fêted: for example Felix Mendelssohn visited the country ten times before his death in 1847, being particularly welcome at Court; and Charles Hallé settled in Manchester in 1848, ten years later founding the orchestra named after him. The one area of formal musical development was church music; the choral tradition was strong, and the organ was fast replacing the local group of musicians as the provider of music during the services. (This also had its effect on church architecture, with the musicians' gallery being taken out.) Folk music doubtless thrived, but it was to be many more decades before the words and tunes were the subject of research.

For the visual arts it was also a bleak period. Turner died in 1851, having had his last exhibition at the Royal Academy the previous year. The most popular living artist was Edwin Landseer, a master of painting animals. The Pre-Raphaelite Brotherhood was the name adopted in 1848 by a group of young English painters including Millais, Hunt and Rossetti; John Ruskin, the art critic and writer was influential in helping their recognition.

Mid-Victorian architecture has been described (perhaps unfairly) as a 'collapse of taste'. Most of the major buildings were for the public sector or for official organisations rather than private individuals. Birmingham Town Hall, built to a classical design, was opened in 1834.

The architectural novelty of 1851 was the 'Crystal Palace' built for the Great Exhibition — with its cast iron frame and extensive use of glass, its design derived from conservatories such as that at Kew and from railway station roofs such as Tithebarn Street (later renamed Exchange) Station, Liverpool.

A particularly influential architect was Augustus Pugin (1812–52) whose style was the reincarnation of Gothic, highly decorated. He designed four cathedrals, and several churches and large houses. The latter were innovative in that the starting point in their design was the sizes and relationships of the rooms, the exterior being irregular in shape, reflecting the interior requirements. He designed the interior decoration, fittings and furniture of the rebuilt Houses of Parliament (from 1837), probably influencing Barry on the external appearance. He also designed the mediaeval centrepiece for the Great Exhibition.

Foreign affairs

A resurgent France was seen as the major threat in Europe.

Britain's navy dominated the seas. In 1856 Britain renounced the right to stop any ship, neutral or otherwise, and seize its goods in times of war; conversely it now considered itself a protector of all shipping. Merchant ships sailed to all parts of the globe. By 1851, Britain had bases in Gibraltar, Malta, Trincomalee, Mauritius, Bombay, Aden, Singapore, Hong Kong, Sydney, the Sandwich Islands, Valparaiso, Buenos Aires, Rio de Janeiro, Jamaica, Antigua, Bermuda and Halifax. Steam-powered ships started being used commercially in coastal waters in the 1810s; by the end of the 1830s they were beginning to cross the oceans.

In 1849 Britain annexed the Punjab, so ending Sikh autonomy.

The 'Scramble for Africa' was just starting. David Livingstone was exploring from Luanda in the east to the centre and head of the Zambesi and down past the Victoria Falls to the coast, 1841–1856.

William Parry (1790–1855) with John Ross (1777–1856) and his son James Ross (1800–62) explored the Arctic and Antarctic.

In 1850 Henry Rawlinson gave his first public lecture to a London audience concerning Assyrian and Babylonian history, as proved by his (and others') translation of cuneiform scripts. He showed that the Old Testament referred to real people, places and events.

Politics

This was a time of social awareness and debate, and of transition of power from the land-owners to the increasingly wealthy middle class. A North/South divide was emerging between the conservatism of the traditional ruling class and a new pragmatism based on individualism and industry.

It was a politically unstable period, with the parties split into several factions. Lord John Russell was Prime Minister from 1846 until 1852; he was regarded as an irascible, unpopular and weak leader. His was a Whig ministry but the Peelites held the balance of power in Parliament, though Peel himself had died in 1850. The other leading Whig politician was Henry Temple, 3rd Viscount Palmerston, the anti-Radical Foreign Secretary, an advocate of 'gun-boat diplomacy' which was popular with the public (for as long as it worked). He was dismissed near the end of 1851, and a few weeks later brought about defeat of Russell's government. Edward Stanley, Lord Derby (14th Earl from 1851), then became Tory Prime Minister; he was a tepid protectionist reformer.

The major political issues included: protectionism versus free trade; political reform (the Chartist movement had peaked in about 1848); foreign policy, especially regarding France, Russia and Turkey; income tax; Catholics; and Irish immigration into England.

3 : The development of Market Drayton in the 19th Century

David Jenkins

This chapter gives an overview of the town's history in the 19th century. Several of the topics are dealt with in greater detail in later chapters.

The ancient parish of St Mary in Drayton covered an area of some 14,000 acres lying partly in Shropshire and partly in Staffordshire. This parish consisted of the townships of Drayton Magna, Drayton Parva, Sutton, Betton and Longslow in Shropshire and Tyrley and Almington in Staffordshire. In the middle of the 19th century the ancient parish of St Mary's Drayton was reduced by the creation of the parish of Christchurch, Little Drayton, in 1847 and the parish of St Mary's at Hales in 1856.

Population

The population of Drayton in Hales, including both the Shropshire and Staffordshire elements, increased from 3,743 in 1801 to 5,856 in 1901. This increase was steady but not uniform from 1801 to 1881, but the population in the 1891 census had declined and it rose very little by 1901. This decline was attributable to the agricultural depression of the 1880s and 1890s, which was caused by an increase in animal disease, poor harvests and the importation of cheap grain from North America. In 1891 the population of the Shropshire part of Drayton was:

	Population	*Dwellings*
Drayton Magna	2,125	466
Drayton Parva	2,178	486
Betton, Longslow and Sutton	786	156

The growth of industry

Drayton Magna had enjoyed the benefit of formalised market trading since 1245 and this provided an outlet for the grain, livestock, dairy and agricultural products of the countryside. Drayton Magna also provided the service industries that agriculture required. At the beginning of the 19th century the town, or its close environs, provided maltings, tanyards, a bark mill for the tanneries, papermills, cornmills, ropemakers, blacksmiths, ironmongers and horsehair weaving.

During the 19th century, the advance of technology and the economy of scale had their effect in Drayton and the following industrial developments took place.

Maltings, which had initially been associated with inns, as brewing was on a small scale, gave way to independent maltsters but by the middle of the 19th century, breweries were being established in the town and these had their integral maltings. The Crystal Fountain Brewery in Cheshire Street was in production from 1861 until the 1920s. The Market Drayton Brewery was established in 1891, also in Cheshire Street, on a site now occupied by the Library. The Crown Brewery was established in 1880 and this moved in 1899 to a newly-erected, six storey, steel framed building in Station Road, now Cheshire Street.

The tanyards ceased to function in the mid 19th century, as did their bark mill. The town's three water powered paper mills ceased production in the 1840s.

Water-powered corn milling continued at Hinsley Mill and Betton Mill until 1851 and at Victoria Mill until well into the 20th century. William Rogers established a steam-driven roller corn mill in Station Road in 1900. This was an exceptional enterprise since steam driven roller mills were usually built at ports, such as Liverpool, to process imported grain. Rogers Mill building remains to this day, though not in use, and it and the adjacent Crown Brewery are listed buildings.

The trades of blacksmith and ironmonger continued into the 20th century, but to serve the needs of the agricultural community two agricultural implement manufacturers were established in the town. A W Gower and Son of Britannia Works, Stafford Street (now the site of Netto) was founded in 1842 as specialists in the manufacture of corn, seed and manure drills. They sought markets throughout Britain and Europe and claimed the patronage of Queen Victoria and the Emperor of Austria! The firm continued trading until 1941 when it was bought out by F H Burgess. John Rodenhurst and his brother opened a foundry in Cheshire Street in 1856 and this employed 100 hands and functioned until 1926. The Raven Iron Foundry had an arcaded front on Cheshire Street and this was replicated in the frontage of the Rodenhurst buildings erected in the 1960s to replace the foundry.

Horsehair weaving was a substantial industry

in Market Drayton in the 19th century, mainly making sives and cloth. It was done in three factories in Drayton, and was also a cottage industry. A directory of 1856 recorded that 200 people, mainly women, were employed in the hair weaving industry. The demand for horsehair cloth waned in the latter part of the 19th century but horsehair sieves were made in Drayton until the 1930s.

Market Drayton gingerbread or ginger biscuits were made and exported around the world throughout the 19th century.

Building materials could be found locally in Drayton, though of variable quality. A quarry on the edge of Little Drayton Common was used to provide building stone for the town. Some of this was used, for example, in the 19th century restoration of St Mary's Church. Clay for brick making was also found locally, no fewer than fourteen brick kiln fields being marked on Foxall's map prepared from the tithe particulars. However these bricks were of extremely variable quality and local brickmaking ceased after the railways came to Drayton and bricks like Ruabon reds and Staffordshire blues became available.

It is not surprising that Market Drayton, being in the centre of a dairy cattle area, should have become a centre for dairy products produced on a factory scale. Shropshire's first cheese factory was founded in 1878 at Ternhill, just within the parish. In the early 1890s the Maypole Dairy established a butter factory in Stafford Street, next door to Gower's foundry. The Medical Officer for Health protested at the juxtaposition of foundry fumes and dairy products but his protest was unheeded.

Drayton's first venture into the clothing industry commenced in 1884 when the Phoenix Clothing company was established in a former horsehair seating factory near the tanyard but it survived for only a decade.

It is not without significance that Drayton Magna was the location of most of Drayton's industrial development. There was almost no industry in Drayton Parva.

Public utilities

The town's gas works was built in 1850 but electricity generation did not commence until 1902. Both utilities were founded on a site that had been part of the old tanyard.

Surprisingly the town did not get a piped water supply until 1892 and this came by pipeline from the Burntwood at Loggerheads. Prior to 1892 the inhabitants relied on a number of private and public wells.

Transport

The Birmingham & Liverpool Junction Canal, passing by Drayton, opened in 1835. This canal was commenced under the direction of Thomas Telford but not unfortunately completed in his lifetime. It was a late canal and was constructed on the then modern principle of maintaining as straight a course as possible and concentrating locks in flights, even if this meant expensive cuttings and embankments. This procedure was in contrast to the previous technique of following contour lines which minimised 'cut and fill' but at the expense of lengthening the route.

It was said by Gregory in his Gazetteer of 1834 that prior to the introduction of canals 'Drayton had one of the greatest markets in the district'. Since many other towns got their canal connections many decades before Drayton, the coming of the canal to Drayton did not restore the former importance of its market. However the canal did enable South American guano to be made available to the farmers around Drayton.

Drayton featured in at least six different railway proposals made in the 1860s and if all had come to fruition Drayton might have become an important junction. Drayton did however offer an opportunity for the Great Western Railway to gain access to Manchester via Wellington, Drayton, Nantwich and Crewe. The line to Nantwich opened in 1863 and to Wellington in 1867, thus giving the GWR the connection they required. Drayton was linked to Stoke and Newcastle in 1870.

Religious worship

St Mary's, Drayton Magna, followed the changing trends of religious worship through its long life of over 900 years. From the 16th century the lay rectorship was held by a member of the Corbet family and this continued until its abolition in the 20th century. In the 19th century, until 1833, the church was led by a vicar who was not too demanding of himself or his congregation. In 1833 the incumbent died in office and the Reverend James Lee was appointed vicar in his place. Lee remained in office for 23 years and during that time, in addition to managing his large parish and having three services each Sunday, mostly without the aid of a curate, he was able to undertake the following duties:
- eliminating waste and corruption in Poor Law management;
- serving as Deputy Chairman of the Drayton Poor Law Union;
- obtaining funds and arranging the construction of National Schools in Drayton Magna in 1835

and Drayton Parva in 1851;
- being responsible for initiating the construction of Christchurch, Little Drayton and becoming patron of the living in 1848; and
- serving as the self-appointed master of the Market Drayton Grammar School

Lee's living provided a remuneration of £280 per annum, as compared with those of the smaller parishes of Stoke-on-Tern (£878), Adderley (£665) and Hinstock (£530). However Lee was fortunate to become the first occupant of a newly-built handsome vicarage in Church Street. The vicar's glebe land included the near vertical bank below the churchyard and down to Phoenix Bank and the Newtown Road.

When Lee arrived at St Mary's it was a 'Georgian preaching box' with galleries over the north and south aisles and at the west end. The pulpit was a 'triple decker' — ground floor for announcements, first floor for the lesson and the top floor for the sermon.

The Congregationalists or Independents were the first non-conformist sect to take root in Drayton. They arrived in 1778 and their chapel, which could seat 600, was built in Church Street within sight of St Mary's church. The Wesleyan Methodists came to Drayton in 1807 and the Baptists in 1815. Primitive Methodism arrived in Drayton in 1828, services being held in a chapel off an alley between Cheshire Street and Frogmore Road; this first chapel was succeeded by the chapel in Frogmore Road that is now the Festival Drayton Centre.

Roman Catholicism had few adherents in Drayton and their church, in Great Hales Street, did not open until 1886.

In the latter part of the 19th century, St Mary's moved towards formal high church practices. This promoted a division amongst Anglicans in Drayton, which led to the construction, in 1882, of the Emmanuel Church in the Burgage. This church was subsequently demolished in the 20th century.

As a simplified generalisation, it can be said that the Congregationalist and Wesleyan Methodist denominations tended to be middle class Whigs. The Baptist movement and Primitive Methodism appealed more to the working class. The Anglican Church was supported by the gentry and middle class Tories. There was thus a division in the town between Whig non-conformity and Tory Anglicanism but this was a common characteristic of 19th century market town life. The town had a multiplicity of shops and even the owners of these were divided in their loyalties to the Whigs or Tories, and they were patronised or shunned by the public on political/religious grounds.

The cattle market

Up until 1871 the street market included trading in live animals. Cheshire Street had the alternative name of Horsemarket Street. Stafford Street was also known as Sheep-market Street and there is still a side road off Stafford Street known as Lamb Shutt. Cattle were traded in the Beast Market, which was later called Great Hales Street. (The writer has been unable to discover where pigs were traded.) All the animals were walked through the streets of the town into their respective market places, no doubt requiring a considerable following of street cleaners. This practice was substantially reduced in 1871 when the Cattle Market opened. This was built adjacent to the new railway station so that most animal movements could be made by rail.

The writer can find no evidence as to the function, if any, of Shropshire Street on market day. Since Shropshire Street contains the greatest proportion of the town's listed building dwellings and was thus the most affluent street, it is possible that the citizens of Shropshire Street combined in the distant past to ensure that their street was not involved in the street market. They would however still have to have tolerated animals being herded through their street on their way to market.

Schools

The Market Drayton Grammar School was founded in 1555 by Sir Rowland Hill. It was a Free School and was provided with an annual endowment of £22, which was increased in 1622 to £31 19s. This was then sufficient to pay the salaries of a master and an usher (or assistant master) and provide some maintenance of the building. However the endowment did not increase with inflation; by Queen Victoria's reign it was insufficient to properly remunerate one master. Recourse was made to taking and charging for boarders but education remained free. By this means the school remained functioning until the beginning of the 20th century. The school building was small; being wedged between the churchyard and Phoenix Bank it had no room even for a playground, let alone a playing field. When the Shropshire County Council took responsibility for secondary education in 1902, it was soon to realise that it was impractical to retain the old grammar school. A new substantial grammar school was built in 1911 in the Mountfields to the west of Frogmore Road.

A National School was opened in Drayton in 1817 in a rented building but it had an insecure existence. The Reverend James Lee, as previously noted, obtained a site and raised finance for the construction of a purpose built National School in Mount Lane that opened in 1835. This school accommodated 340 children from the age of six upwards. The children were separated into two classes — boys and girls — and they were taught on the monitorial system, whereby the schoolmaster and schoolmistress trained older, brighter children to teach a row of younger children, sitting on a form, a simple lesson in numbers or reading, which they learned by rote. Several of these 'forms' would be reciting their lessons in the same room at the same time. The school was subsequently enlarged and remained in use under the management of the Shropshire County Council until the opening of the Grove Comprehensive School in 1957. The Mount Lane School building survives to this day and functions as a day nursery.

Little Drayton National School was founded by the Reverend James Lee in 1851 and, after being taken over by Shropshire County Council, remained in use until 1914.

Since National Schools were promoted by the Church of England, not all nonconformists were happy to entrust their children to such teaching. The Wesleyans, for example, provided lessons from 1867 to 1891 in the original Wesleyan chapel in Shrewsbury Road.

There were several private schools functioning in Drayton at various times in the 19th century. These were run by one or two teachers, usually female, and often in their own homes. They were not required to keep records but they had to advertise to attract their pupils, so evidence of their existence can be found in newspaper advertisements and directories and indirectly from national census returns. In 1833 there were no fewer than fifteen private schools in Drayton.

The following are some of the better known and longer lived private schools in Drayton in the 19th century:
- Cottons House   Shropshire Street
    Day and Boarding   1840–1851
- Salopia House   Shropshire Street
                        1865–1895
- Rylands House   Great Hales Street
    Girls Boarding   1871–1905
- Beech Tree House   Shropshire Street
    Day and Boarding   1885–1909

Local government

Local government evolved slowly from the feudal system and in particular the Court Leet, which was concerned with the good behaviour of the community, one to another, and to the community at large. One of the last duties the Court Leet undertook was the naming of the following streets in 1885: New Street (later to become Victoria Road), The Burgage and Prospect Road.

The regulation of the market was also a function of the Court Leet, in regard to weights and measures, quality of foodstuffs and fair trading. The market having been established by the then Lord of the Manor, the Abbot of Combermere, in 1245, as a business venture, was in the 19th century still in the control of the Lord of the Manor, then the Corbet family. It was Sir Corbet Corbet who was responsible for the provision of the Buttercross market hall in 1824.

In 1865 the Market Drayton Cattle Market Act created the Market Drayton Cattle Market Company, which bought out the financial interest of the Corbet estate in the sale of animals, which were then still being traded in the town's streets. However the Corbet estate maintained its financial interest in the street and indoor market until 1921, when it was bought out by the Market Drayton Urban District Council.

The Corbet estate integrated all butchers' stalls into one shambles in 1842, but in 1852 they provided a purpose-built Shambles, at the eastern end of Shropshire Street. This building survived until 1964.

At the end of the reign of Elizabeth I, the Crown realised that parishes had the authority and knowledge to accept responsibility for the management of secular duties, such as poor relief, the provision of constables, fire fighting and maintenance of highways, these functions to be financed by a locally levied rate.

As a consequence of the will of the Reverend Richard Price, vicar of Drayton and rector of Hodnet, who died in 1730, Drayton was provided with a workhouse that was enlarged in 1788. Following the Poor Law Union Act of 1834, Market Drayton was made the centre of a Poor Law Union of twelve parishes. This necessitated a root and branch purge and reorganisation, led by the Reverend Lee, of the administration of poor relief. Lee was also responsible for organising the extension of the workhouse to accommodate 100 inmates. However the provision of drainage to the workhouse was inadequate and in 1849 there was an outbreak of cholera there. This led the Guardians of the Poor to decide to build a new workhouse on a greenfield site on the former Little Drayton Common. This building, which was named Quarry House, from its adjacency to a stone quarry, was opened in 1854 and was to serve the public, in some fashion, for 130 years. The original workhouse was in Shropshire Street and after it ceased to function as a workhouse, the building was used for a number of public functions such as an armoury for the local unit of the Shropshire Rifle Volunteers from the 1860s and as a public library before the building was demolished in the 1960s.

In 1848 the Drayton Sanitary Committee was formed to take responsibility for the town's drainage. This initiative was doomed to failure because the revenue to pay for drainage works would have been raised from both rural and urban parishioners but only the urban parishioners would have benefited. A further attempt to initiate some action on the town's drainage was made in 1865 but the reaction of the populace was so violent that the police had to seek the assistance of the army to quell the ensuing riots. Public drainage initiatives in the 19th century throughout Britain were frustrated by the fact that the technology of sewage treatment was in its infancy.

The Drayton Rural Sanitary Authority was created in 1872 and it appointed both Dr Sandford as the first Medical Officer of Health and also an Inspector of Nuisances. However there was little progress in the matter of drainage. In 1894 the Market Drayton Rural District Council was formed and this had more authority to address the wide subject of public health. Dr Sandford's contract was renewed and a Mr Craig was appointed Surveyor of Highways and Nuisances. Craig had been trained as a sanitary engineer and he was able to commence planning and implementing the solution to Drayton's drainage needs.

Market Drayton Cottage Hospital was built in 1892 by private subscription but this would not admit infectious cases. A tented isolation hospital was erected in 1893 in Little Drayton, on the outer edge of the parish, and this was not made into a permanent building until 1912.

The exercise of law in Drayton

Prior to the creation of a county police force, an attempt was made to exercise the law by the formation of private organisations of landowners of Societies for the Prosecution of Felons. These sought to obtain evidence for the private prosecution of wrongdoers by offering rewards for information leading to the conviction of felons. One such organisation met in the Cheshire Cheese public house near to the Buttercross market hall.

Drayton's first County Police station was built in the early 1840s on a site in Cheshire Street, now occupied by the library. This station was subsequently replaced by another building in Frogmore Road, which remained in use until 1938. Both these early stations contained prisoners' cells and living accommodation for the police sergeant and his family. The present police station was built near the site of the Baptist burial ground in Salisbury Road.

The solicitor's office and former County Court at 46 Cheshire Street was built in 1850 at the expense of Joseph Loxdale Warren, the solicitor who founded the practice later known as Warren, Upton & Garside. Warren was the Clerk to the County Court, which, prior to 1850, was held in one of the town's public houses. Warren's courtroom held 400 people and it was also used for public meetings and lectures.

Drayton's post offices

Drayton has had three post offices prior to the present one in Queen Street. The first post office was in a private house, Rylands House in Great Hales Street and this functioned until 1881. The first dedicated post office was at 15 Stafford Street, which was in operation from 1881 to 1910. This was replaced by the first purpose built post office, which was in Cheshire Street, adjacent to the Rodenhurst iron foundry. This building was demolished in 1972, together with the foundry, to make way for the Rodenhurst buildings, a terrace of arcaded shops with flats above. The new post and sorting office in Queen Street was opened in 1972.

Market Drayton is sometimes accused of being behind in new innovation. Perhaps a good example of this is that the numbering of properties was not ordered until 1908. Victorian and Edwardian postmen must have been very well informed of the names of residents in particular streets but even then the sorting of the post into the order for delivery must have been time consuming. In contrast, the numbering of buildings in cities was well organised by the middle of the 19th century.

Fairs

The first fair to enter Drayton's calendar was St Mary's annual fair on the eve, the day and the morrow of the feast day of St Mary, 7, 8 & 9 September. The licence for this fair was given in the same charter of 1245 that granted Drayton its market. This fair was terminated in the late 19th century owing to the rowdy behaviour of some of the participants.

By the 19th century there were many fairs and special market days, most relating to the sale of agricultural produce and livestock. There was an Agricultural Show in mid September, the Dirty Fair for the sale of horses in the last week of October, and the Dairy Show in early November. The Gawby Market, at the end of the year, was the hiring fair for servants and agricultural workers.

A Cheese Fair was held every three weeks and

the Damson Fair was held in September, from which trainloads of damsons went to the mills of Yorkshire and Lancashire to be used as a dyestuff.

The enclosure of Little Drayton Common

Little Drayton was, up to 1850, a very poor neighbour to Drayton Magna. It had almost no industry and few shops. The lordship of the manor was divided between two families and the manor had always suffered from neglect.

Little Drayton Common was about 90 acres in extent. It had little commercial value and hence was never developed. It was however to benefit from a piece of far-sighted Victorian general legislation: the 1845 Enclosure Act. This sought to release areas of common land throughout the country for the benefit of the poor. The whole procedure was intended to be self-financing.

The enclosure, finally concluded in January 1852, was of great benefit to Little Drayton. It liberated land for building such that the number of dwellings on the common increased by 137% between 1841 and 1861. The enclosure formalised the existence of 'squats', the location of several of which is evident today. It gave a focus to Little Drayton and it enjoyed the benefit of allotments and a recreation ground that Drayton Magna did not get until well into the 20th century.

Conclusion

If population growth is a measure of success, then the following percentage growths of population between 1801 and 1891 shows Drayton to be the leader amongst the market towns of north-west Shropshire.

Market Drayton	61%
Whitchurch	47%
Wem	23%
Newport	16%

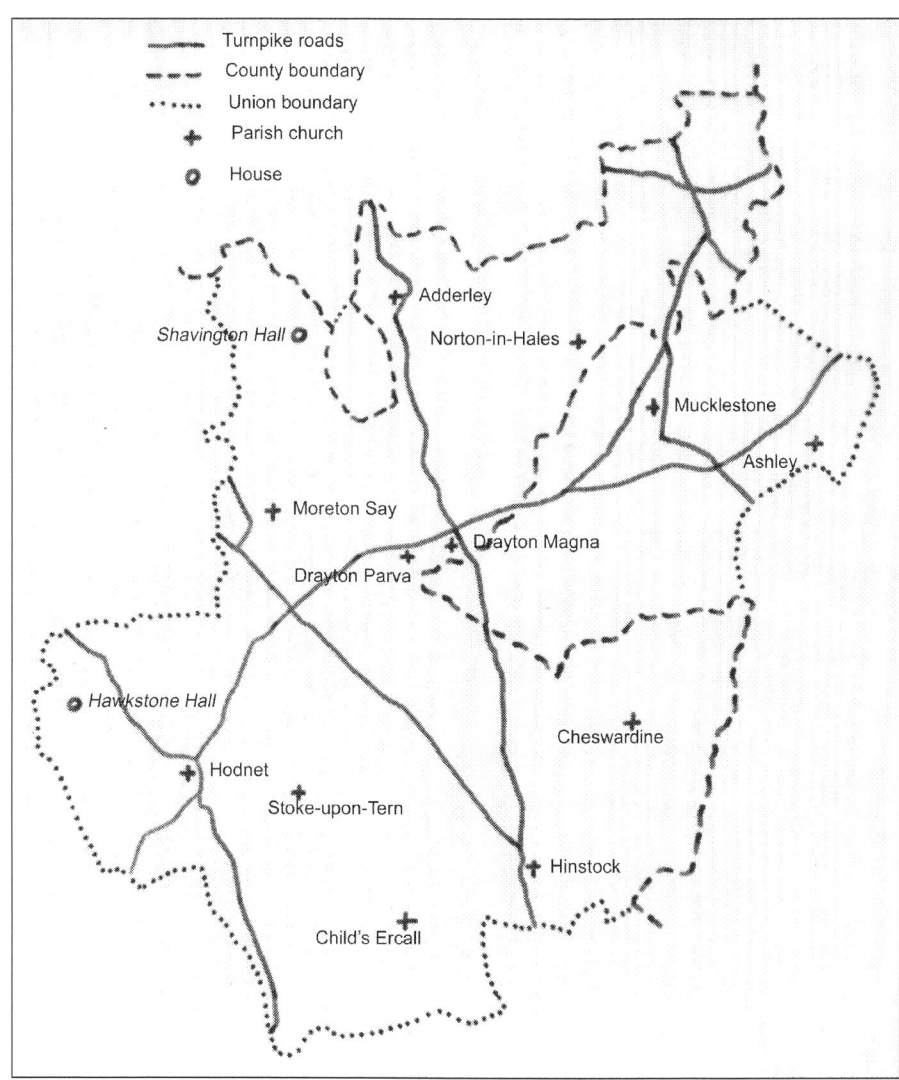

The Drayton Union from 1836 — the area adopted for this U3A Local History project.

Tittenley (to the east of Shavington Hall) was moved from Cheshire to Shropshire in 1895, and the Tyrley area west of the canal was moved from Staffordshire to Shropshire in 1965.

4 : The census

Ian Picton-Robinson

The national census was held on the night of Sunday 30 March 1851. This was the first census where every member of the household was recorded. The details shown are:
- parish and township;
- location of dwelling;
- forename and surname of each person in the house on census night;
- relation to the head of the family;
- married or unmarried;
- male or female;
- age;
- rank or occupation;
- where born;
- whether blind, deaf or dumb;
- for employers, the number of employees; and
- for farmers, the acreage of the farm.

The handwriting is cursive. Although elegant it is often difficult to read and therefore may not have been interpreted correctly. The spelling is also sometimes idiosyncratic: for example, Moreton Say is written as 'Moreton Sea'.

Most locations are not defined precisely enough to be able identify to them today. Street numbering was not introduced until 1908. However some places can be, such as halls, manors, some farms and odd names such as 'Bendles'.

All the entries have been analysed for certain aspects, such as employment. However, most of the analysis is based on a one in five (20%) sample of households. At the end of each section of the census records the next member of the sample has been selected by counting on five from the previous household chosen, so as to avoid the possible preference for an enumerator to start a section with the Grand Gentry. This 20% analysis is robust enough for most statistical purposes, though it will not necessarily show up the extremes.

A copy of the full analysis has been deposited in the archives of the Drayton Museum.

Population

The area analysed was that of the Drayton Union, comprising the urban area of Market Drayton (that is, Drayton Magna and Drayton Parva) and the surrounding rural townships and parishes, including a part of Staffordshire and one small township, Tittenley, which was then in Cheshire. (See box on page 22.)

The population figures for the Drayton area were:

	Urban	Rural	Total
Males	1,616	5,503	7,119
Females	1,782	5,259	7,041
Total	3,398	10,762	14,160
Male:female ratio	0.91	1.05	1.01

As can be seen, less than a quarter (24%) of the population lived in the urban area. These figures can be compared with the 2001 census, where the urban population had grown to just over 10,400 but the rural population was little changed.

One interesting statistic is the ratio of the sexes, where the urban area shows an excess of females and the rural area an excess of males. Possibly there were more opportunities for female employment in the town, whereas farming employment tended to be male.

The age distribution shows that children under 14 years of age formed some 30% of the population, each five year age group larger than any adult group, perhaps an early indication of the coming rise in population throughout the country. Those of working age, 15 to 64, formed about 60% while there were about 120 people over the aged of 80 and 14 over 90.

The following table compares the age distribution with the figures for England & Wales in the 2001 census:

Age	1851	2001
	%	%
Up to 9	22.6	12.3
10 to 19	21.1	12.8
20 to 29	15.8	12.6
30 to 39	11.8	15.5
40 to 49	10.4	13.3
50 to 59	8.8	12.6
60 to 69	5.4	9.3
70 to 79	3.0	7.4
80 to 89	1.0	3.6
90 and over	0.1	0.6

The median age of the population was 24 in 1851 but 37 in 2001. Historically (and internationally) it is the 2001 age profile which is atypical.

Health

The health hazards were primarily of infection, especially pneumonia, arthritis (as now) and risks of childbirth. It may be that Market Drayton was a relatively healthy place to live — on fairly high ground, with good agriculture, so good quality food, clean water from wells, an absence of serious air pollution from industry and, judging by the few vagrants recorded in the census, adequate housing.

So is there evidence in the census for this good health? The age distribution of children throughout the parishes shows that in the households that night the number of children aged less than 1 year (280 approximately) was a little more than those aged 1 to 2 years, the same as those 2 to 3 years, with no consistent trend up to age 9 when numbers drop progressively to age 17. These numbers do not show what the early post-natal mortality was, and is confounded by those away from home, at residential school, with friends or working. The lack of a consistent decline in the early age groups however, encourages the idea that child mortality was not high. Also the spacing of children, at one year or less, seems common.

Families

The Victorians are known for their large families. However that may be more true for the later years of the 19th century as the families of Market Drayton and its surrounds are not that big. Considering just those families with children living at home, the census showed the family size as:

Number of children	1	2	3	4	5	6	7+
% of families	27	23	19	15	9	5	2

While the younger parents had not reached a full complement, and the older parents had children who had left home and were not recorded, this average of three may be representative of the true 'burden' on the parents. However remember that some children were working by age 10 and nearly all were by age 15, so enhancing the family income, or at least removing the cost.

The maximum number of children living at home in the sample was ten. Not all large families were amongst the wealthy; several were of agricultural labourers and some of traders.

With today's increased number of teenage mothers, said to be due to the availability of welfare benefits, it is interesting to see what the situation was in 1851. The youngest mother was aged 12, but 19 was the age for 10% of mothers of first born, with the peak at age 26, quite a few up to the late 30s and 3–5% aged 40+ for first born. The last born peaked at age 33, 20% or more mothers were 40+, and a few in their 50s. Again this suggests a quite healthy population. However, the word 'bastard' is used only once, so it may be that 'old mothers' are in fact grandmothers, their young unmarried daughters being politely protected; such an occurrence seems possible in several census entries, but not all.

Children & young people : education or employment?

Education was not neglected. At a time when it was not compulsory for children to attend school, half of children between the ages of 4 and 10 were registered as scholars, a few being taught at home, but most in day schools. The percentage of those aged under 18 in the various categories were:

	Boys %	Girls %
No activity recorded		
— aged 4 and under	17	17
— aged 5 to 17	23	26
Scholars	38	36
Apprentices	4	0
Working	24	21

Some 17% of those under 5 and 50% of those at 5 to 10 years were recorded as scholars. Older groups were increasingly at work, 50% by age 14 rising to 80% by age 16, boys more than girls. Apart from a few apprentices the remainder had no activity recorded; those on farms or with parents in trade may however, have been learning their craft. There were approximately 1,730 recorded as scholars, a few being in residential schools, of which there were eleven in the area, four in Market Drayton. Education is discussed further in Chapter 13.

The 20% sample contains two girl apprentices, both very young (aged 9 & 11), and nineteen boy apprentices, aged 12 to 17. This equates to just over a hundred apprentices in the whole area.

The youngest working girl in the sample was aged 7; the youngest boy was aged 8.

Migration

With transport very limited in scope by today's standards, it is not surprising that 96% of the population in the Drayton area had been born in one of the three local counties (Shropshire, Staffordshire and Cheshire) and that a further 2½% had been born in the the neighbouring counties. Only some 1½% — that is, about 200 in all — came from further away, with some of the landed gentry and their servants being from London (but most were local), churchmen from Lancashire and Yorkshire, and the Exciseman and his family from Devon. Andrew Gower, who was beginning to create the iron-founding business which was to become the town's major employer later in the 19th century, was born in Suffolk, his brother in Hampshire.

Within the 20% sample, several agricultural labourers and traders were from Ireland. The rest were a mixture of the wealthy, wives of farmers, and labourers and traders, usually married to local folk. One of the sample, an agricultural labourer, was born in Jersey; a shoemaker, though British, was born in France; and Elizabeth Heblethwaite, who was visiting Purney Sillitoe at Pell Wall, was born in the West Indies.

Of course it is not possible from the Drayton data to assess the extent of out-migration to the industrial areas such as Birmingham & the Black Country and Lancashire.

Employment

The overall picture is of a farming community. Drayton, and to a lesser extent Hinstock and Hodnet, show a wide variety of trades, such as shops for everyday goods, tailors and dressmakers, shoemakers and so on, and some millers. There are the beginnings of larger scale industry in Drayton itself. Employment generally is analysed in Chapter 6.

What is noticeable about servants is their generally young age. Only 16% of female servants and 13% of male servants were aged 30 or more. Employment as a servant was likely to have been a favoured way of learning life skills: domestic skills for future wedlock, farming and trade for employment. Living-in servants are discussed in detail in chapter 7.

Farming

There were 462 farms recorded, forming 21% of rural dwellings. Size varied widely, from smallholdings of 20 acres or less (19%), through many farms of 100 to 300 acres, to four farms of more than 500 acres — at Child's Ercall (Dodecote, 780 acres), Almington (Old Springs, 750 acres), Stoke-upon-Tern (560 acres) and Moreton Say (500 acres). The median size of farms was 100 acres. Employment in farming is discussed in chapter 6.

Gentry and landed proprietors

The 'landed gentry' and the 'landed proprietors' seem to be different groups as far as the registers go. Many of the former were recorded as being a magistrate, whereas the latter generally seem not to have been notably significant. Viscount Hill and Algernon Heber-Percy were not at home on census night, so no details of them and their families were recorded here.

Common local surnames

Reading through the register reveals common surnames, of course, but also some recurring names that seem very local, at least to north Shropshire and south Cheshire. The most evident names are Arkinstall, Beeston, Boffey, Boughey, Bruckshaw, Farnell, Grocott, Nagington and Ridgway (and their variants). From a search through the whole local census, and locating these names in the current phone directory, it has been found that all are still current in this area apart from Arkinstall, of which there are only three listed in the Shrewsbury area and none in Market Drayton. Yet Arkinstalls were then found in all walks of society, from governess of a Market Drayton School, to a retired Royal Artillery man, through several trades to the servants and a charwoman. Why have they all gone? The other names listed above covered the widest range of lifestyles, with a Nagginton being a fairly large scale farmer (but not in the eponymous Hall), and many of the Bruckshaws being blacksmiths.

Other quite common local names were Averill, Hockenhull, Millington, Mullinux (and variants) and Ruscoe.

Christian names

About half of people had one of the top three names for their sex. The most popular names were:

	Male	%	Female	%
1	John	21	Mary	20
2	William	16	Elizabeth	16
3	Thomas	13	Ann	13
4	George	9	Sarah	11
5	James	6	Jane	5
6	Samuel	6	Martha	4
7	Joseph	5	Hannah	4
8	Richard	5	Frances	3
9	Henry	4	Harriet	3
10	Charles	3	Emma	3

Closely related names and diminutives have been included in the percentages above.

In 2008, John ranked 84th amongst the boys' names though its informal version, Jack, was 1st. Thomas (6th), James (9th) and William (10th) were still in the top ten.

None of the top ten girls' names in 1851 appeared in the 2008 top ten; the highest-ranking was Hannah in 20th place. Mary was not even in the top one hundred.

Specific addresses

While most residences are shown in the 1851 census by village or, in Drayton, by street name only (the numbers in the entries being the sequence number of the enumerator, not a house number), many of the halls, manors, mills and some farms are quite specifically identified.

Some more curious names can be located on today's Ordnance Survey maps, such as Audley

Brow, Styche Dairy House, Lees, Greaves, the Red Bull at Almington, the Loggerheads at Ashley (as it was then), the Nook, Bendles, and Sillonhurst (Syllenhurst today). The census lists those who were living in these dwellings in 1851; perhaps someone can add more to our knowledge of these people and their descendants.

Change?

While time and technology has changed the nature of British society, somehow the essence of farming and trading remains from past years with only superficial change. Would a Victorian from 1851 be so startled by Market Drayton today?

Note

The information in this chapter is taken from more extensive documents derived from the 1851 Census, documents that will be held in the archives in Drayton Museum in Box 180, 'U3A 1851 Project'.

Drayton Union : parish populations, 1851

Shropshire

Adderley	353	
Cheswardine	1,119	
Drayton-in-Hales (part)	4,163	includes Betton 250, Longslow 70, Sutton 180, Woodseaves 270 (see note 2)
Ercall, Childs	512	
Hinstock	862	
Hodnet	1,755	excludes Weston-under-Redcastle and Wixhill (in Wem Division of Bradford North Hundred)
Moreton Say	701	
Mucklestone (part)	860	comprising Bearstone 110, Dorrington 200, Gravenhunger 160, Woore 390 (see note 2)
Norton-in-Hales	320	
Stoke-upon-Tern	937	comprising Eaton 150, Ollerton 134, Stoke 416, Wistanswick 237

Staffordshire

Ashley	896	
Drayton-in-Hales (part)	784	comprising Almington 198, Bloore with Tyrley & Hales 586 (see note 2)
Mucklestone (part)	876	comprising Aston 252, Knighton 177, Oakley 63, Mucklestone 184, Winnington 200

Cheshire

Tittenley	22	part of Audlem parish
Total	**14,160**	

Notes

1. Source: 1851 Census Report, Population Tables I, Vol I, Division VI, pages 48 & 49.
2. The figures for the individual townships for Drayton-in-Hales and Mucklestone are based on the proportions in the 1841 census. The 1851 Census Report stated: 'The boundaries of the townships are ill defined, a circumstance which accounts for a want of uniformity in the returns for 1831 and 1841, as well as for the population in 1851 being returned in aggregate only.'
3. Because of boundary changes, in some cases the figures are not directly comparable with more recent censuses.

5 : Aspects of birth and death

Meriel Blower & Peter Brown

Illegitimacy

In the 1851 census the number of illegitimate children in the Moreton Wood area of Moreton Saye parish was considerable. Several families had children listed as illegitimate, often grandchildren of the head of the household. Census enumerators were not required to state whether or not a child was illegitimate. It is possible that the Moreton Say enumerator was particularly censorious.

In the parish registers the entries for illegitimate children differ from those of legitimate in two ways. Under the heading 'Parents' only one name, that of the mother, is listed. This is in contrast with entries in the register in earlier centuries where the reputed father is often also listed. Under the heading 'Occupation' the words 'single woman' or 'spinster' are written.

A study of the 1851 parish registers for Market Drayton and the surrounding villages shows a wide variation in the illegitimacy rate.

Parish	Births	Illegitimate
Adderley	10	1
Cheswardine	29	2
Child's Ercall	14	0
Hinstock	31	2
Hodnet	34	2
Little Drayton, Christchurch	54	7
Market Drayton, St Mary's	48	2
Moreton Say	13	2
Norton in Hales	6	0
Stoke-on-Tern	20	2
Woore	27	4

One illegitimate birth in a village where small numbers of births are recorded can give a deceptively high rate. Records would have to be studied over a longer period before we could be sure of trends and patterns.

Overall there were 286 baptisms in the area and of these 24 were illegitimate, an average of 8.4%.

Two villages, Child's Ercall and Norton-in-Hales recorded no illegitimate births — indeed Norton recorded only six births during the year.

The next lowest figure, 4%, was for St Mary's parish, Market Drayton. Of the 48 births only two were illegitimate. St Mary's covered the richer end of town and any lower middle-class girls would perhaps have been sent to the country to give birth. Poorer girls might have had to go the Workhouse, at this time situated in the parish of Little Drayton. This and the fact that Little Drayton was regarded as the rougher end of town probably accounts for the fact that Christchurch, Little Drayton, had an illegitimacy rate of 12%, the third highest. The address given for one mother was the Workhouse.

The two highest figures are for Woore where four out of 27 births were illegitimate giving a rate of 15% and Moreton Saye where two out of 13 births were illegitimate, a rate of 15%.

Life expectancy

The register of deaths at St Mary's Church, Market Drayton, states the name, home township, date and age. Regrettably, the cause of death is not stated.

The area covered includes Little Drayton — although Christchurch had been consecrated a few years earlier Little Drayton was not yet a separate parish — and the surrounding townships like Betton and Longslow. A few entries show locations well outside the Drayton area; presumably one had to register the death with the church in the area in which the person had died.

During the year 79 deaths were registered, but five entries did not show the age at death. The number of deaths for each age range was:

Infant	12	40 to 49	4
1 to 4	12	50 to 59	8
5 to 9	3	60 to 69	6
10 to 19	2	70 to 79	11
20 to 29	6	80 to 89	4
30 to 39	6		

Thus 32% of deaths were in the first five years of life. Survive till then, and one's chances of a reasonable length life were good — the median age at death of those who reached five years old was 55.

Of the 79 registered deaths, 31 were male, only 39% of the total. There does not seem any reason for the number being so far from half the total, so presumably it was a statistical anomaly. (It is always unwise to try to draw firm conclusions from small samples.) Of the twelve infant deaths, eight were boys. Also possibly significant, all six who died in their 30s were female: childbirth being the biggest risk in this age-group.

Behind every entry is no doubt a sad but usually unknowable story. But there is one pair of entries where the story can be guessed. On 16 July the death of Ann Heath aged 39 from Swinchurch near Eccleshall was recorded. Then on 1 August the register shows William Heath, infant, also from Swinchurch. No doubt she died in childbirth and her new-born son died a fortnight later.

6 : Employment

Ian Picton Robinson & Peter Brown

Introduction

The 1851 census allows us to see the type of society that prevailed in the town of Market Drayton and in its surrounding parishes. In many ways it seems to have been fundamentally the same as today — an agricultural countryside with the town acting as a centre of trade.

Almost half the employed population was engaged in farming. What little industry the town had was either dependent on agriculture for its raw materials or was making farming equipment.

A picture emerges of communities which were relatively self-sufficient, with most of the day-to-day needs being provided for locally. Market Drayton was still hardly affected by industrialisation. Its few factories wove horse-hair for a regional market; the iron-founding industry which was to be so important to the local economy in the second half of the 19th century was only just beginning.

A warning about the data

Most of the information is taken from the 1851 census. Respondents were not consistent about how they described their occupations: the same term could mean significantly different jobs; conversely, different terms may have been used for the same job. Some people gave two roles, for example 'victualler & timber merchant' — to keep the analysis manageable they have been included in whichever occupation they put first. The numbers quoted for people employed in various occupations include apprentices and assistants.

Farming

The year 1851 was about the high point for British farming, despite the repeal of the Corn Laws a few years earlier. In the Drayton area it is notable that most of the rural parish populations reached their maximum in the censuses of 1841, 1851 or 1861. The three most populous rural parishes were Hodnet, Hinstock and Cheswardine, the census populations peaking in 1841, 1841 and 1861 respectively.

Demand for farming produce was high because of the rapid urbanisation of the country — Britain was the first country in the world where over half the population lived in cities or large towns. Transport had improved: Market Drayton was connected to the main canal network in 1835, which gave easy access to the conurbations of Birmingham, the Black Country and Manchester from wharfs at Adderley, Market Drayton (two), Tyrley, Cheswardine and Soudley. However, some other agricultural areas had the benefit of railways, a significantly quicker mode of transport, particularly suitable for perishable produce.

Corn imports from North America did not have the economic significance they were to acquire a couple of decades later, and in any case the Drayton area was not a major area for grain production. Then, as now, cattle were the main basis for local farming. Shropshire and Market Drayton in particular were badly affected by the succession of wet seasons and foot and mouth epidemics of the late 1870s and early 1880s, but that lay some time in the future.

Within the Drayton area, according to the 1851 census, 3,172 people were employed in agriculture. This was 21.9% of the total population of 14,560, almost double the percentage for the British Isles as a whole (11.4%). The figure for Shropshire was 17.3%. The numbers are likely to be understated because casual employees, mainly women, who were at the date of the census without a job may not have declared themselves as agricultural workers. Putting it another way, of the employed population, some 48% were involved in farming, compared with 27% in trade, 18% in domestic work and 3% in professions. About a third of agricultural workers lived in the same household as the farmer; this was to diminish rapidly as the century went on.

There were 462 farms in the area, varying in size from cottage gardens to the largest which were Dodecote, south of Childs Ercall (780 acres), and Old Springs, south of Almington (750 acres). Many were in the 100 to 350 acre size and had resident labourers, wagoners, cowmen, house servants, cooks etc. The type of farming is not revealed, but there is no reason to believe that it was different from today's emphasis on dairy farming. Many larger farms had a 'vessel cleaner', some had dairy maids, and the number of wagoners suggests crops to be collected or delivered, as well as moving manure and lime and basic slag fertilizer.

The number of people needed to run a farm was very approximately two plus one extra for every 20 acres. For a farm of 100 acres this formula would give seven people; the actual range for the farms of that size was three to twelve. The farm of 750 acres employed 42 people; the farm of 780 acres employed 39.

Why there was a very wide variation it is not possible to divine; clearly crop or animal farming would affect the numbers required but no distinct pattern can be found. An analysis by location and by size of farm is available but gives no real clues. Land quality, energy and desire for a good living would have varied, and some individuals would not or could not have contributed to the running of a farm.

A curious statement by one entry in the census draws attention to a possible recent change in the employment status of agricultural labourers. In the column for 'Employment' it says 'Farmer employing 2 labourers after free trade'.

In Drayton Magna and Parva there were only ten farms but 220 employed in farming, mainly as agricultural labourers, implying that many people lived in the urban area but travelled to neighbouring parishes to work. This was almost certainly because some of the neighbouring parishes such as Stoke-upon-Tern were 'closed'; in other words, they were owned by just one or two dominant landowners. Until 1865 each parish was responsible for raising by rates the cost of maintaining its own poor, so the landowners in a 'closed' parish had a strong incentive to ensure that as few people as possible who might become paupers were allowed to live there.

Farming-related employment

Curiously there seem to be few involved with the care of horses, the most important non-human source of power on the farms and for transport. Saddlers, yes, and of course the blacksmiths in most villages (often called Bruckshaw, still a very local name), and two Veterinary Surgeons, Joshua Pimlott in Staffordshire Street, Drayton, and William Calow of Hodnet, aged but 22 years, supplementing his living with cordwaining. Presumably, in this age of little formal education, the care of horses was in the hands of those on farms and the carters who had learnt their craft from their elders using their natural talent. There were two colt breakers and a horse breaker in the villages. A cow doctor lived in Knighton and a castrator in Hinstock.

In the census in the rural area, 64 people identified themselves as blacksmiths (or their apprentices or assistants) and two as shoeing smiths; 60 people were wheelwrights; 13 were saddlers. Of course, some horses were used for transport or for pleasure purposes, but most would have been employed in farming. In comparison, the town had 26 blacksmiths, 14 wheelwrights and 10 saddlers. There were also four colt-breakers.

There was just one cattle dealer and two cheese factors, but four pig dealers: perhaps pig-keeping was more of a domestic occupation than a farming activity.

Nine of the villages had mills, with a further three in Market Drayton. At this time milling was still a local small-scale activity; by the end of the century the industry was dominated by large mills using imported flour and roller technology rather than traditional millstones.

The eastern fringes of the area had significant amounts of woodland, and this created employment for woodmen, woodcutters and one 'wood collier', presumably making charcoal.

Building trades

The eastern part of the area has suitable building stone. This is reflected in the trades reported in the census: quarryman (3), stonecutter (1) and stone-mason (39). Other parts had suitable clay, and there were 20 brickmakers and 63 bricklayers. The third principal building material was wood, which was also used for furniture and other purposes, of course. The census shows 31 sawyers, 44 carpenters, 22 joiners, and 16 cabinet-makers. Other trades (sometimes in combination) included glaziers, painters, plasterers, plumbers and one thatcher. Three people described themselves as 'builders'.

In total 296 people were in building-related trades (including furniture), roughly evenly spread across the whole area proportionally to population.

Industries

The only significant industry in the whole area was horse-hair weaving. Being short, if horse hairs were used for both the warp and the weft, it was not possible to produce pieces bigger than about two feet square. This was used for making sieves for potteries, malthouses and dairies, for press cloths for cider makers, and for stiffening the shoulders of garments which were subject to very heavy wear. For other purposes, horse hairs were used for the weft and longer threads of cotton or linen for the warp. The main use for this cloth was for hard-wearing coverings for seats, particularly those in railway carriages. The best horse hair came from the tails of horses, as this hair was both longer and softer.

In 1851 there were three major firms in Market Drayton, employing in total something like 200 people, mainly women and girls. [See also Appendix B.] Looms were installed in factories and in workers' homes. William Godwin, whose factory was off Great Hales Street, employed 70. The other main employers were William Sand-brook at Walk Mill and Joseph Haslam, who had two factories both of which were off Shropshire

Street in Little Drayton. The industry declined as the 19th century went on, partly because of changes in fashion for covering furniture, and partly because the Factory Acts restricted the employment of juvenile labour. By 1885 Haslam's was the only survivor; in 1903 the family sold the business (by then making only hair sieves) to H W Woodcock, who continued to make sieves until about 1922.

The census returns describe five people as weavers, including one specifically as a hand loom weaver: at Aston, Wistanswick, Almington (2) and Drayton Magna. Some or all of these may have been horse-hair weavers, alternatively they may have been the last vestiges of a domestic cloth industry.

Market Drayton's most important industry in the second half of the 19th century, the making of agricultural machinery, had its origins shortly before 1851, both Gower's and Rodenhurst's firms being established in the 1840s.

Andrew Gower moved to Market Drayton from Hook in Hampshire in about 1842. His father, Woodgate Gower, was a son-in-law of James Smyth of Peasenhall in Suffolk, who had been making seed drills since about 1800, marketing them nationally. Andrew Gower improved them further, winning various prizes and also developing a national market — indeed, some of the drills were exported. The firm's products also included ploughs, chaff-cutters, and many other articles for agricultural and domestic use. A number of Gower's drain covers can be seen round the town. The foundry was in Stafford Street, on the site now (2010) occupied by Netto. However, in 1851 he was employing only six men including his younger brother.

William and John Rodenhurst started as ironmongers but in 1849 built a foundry in Cheshire Street, initially called the Eagle Iron Foundry but by the mid 1870s called the Raven Foundry. They too made agricultural implements and domestic equipment, but never attained a national reputation. The business survived until the 1920s.

Samuel Bonell, who lived in Stafford Street, was a 'machine pump maker' and employed two others.

The newly-established gas works employed an engineer, two fitters and a clerk. Presumably it also employed at least one labourer as a stoker.

Paper making had ceased in the 1840s at three sites: Old Mill, Walk Mill and Tyrley Mill. The census records one person living at Child's Ercall as a paper-maker.

In 1851 there was no commercial brewery in the Drayton area, but several of the public houses brewed both for themselves and for others. The census shows just two people described as brewers. There were several small maltings: three or four in the town and eight in the villages.

There was no industrial development in the villages except for milling, malting and some small-scale brick-making, as already mentioned.

Clothing trades

Several problems are encountered when trying to analyse the census and directory information about people engaged in trades and crafts. It is not possible to establish who were principally retailers of other people's work, who mainly sold their own work to the general public, who were 'one-person' sub-contractors working at home, and who were really employees working on someone else's premises.

Almost every village had several shoemakers, about a third of whom described themselves as 'cordwainers'. The census shows 111 people with one or other of these occupations, including 22 at Hodnet, 13 at Norton-in-Hales, 12 at Hinstock and 11 at Ashley. Drayton Parva had 28 and Drayton Magna a mere 14. There is no hint that the trade was an organised industry, but presumably the surplus from the rural area was sold in the town.

Similarly, almost every village had one or more dressmakers. Of the 60 in the rural area, 14 were at Hodnet. Drayton Parva had 25, Drayton Magna 37. These figures are reasonably in proportion to the population.

The third widespread clothing trade was tailor. Although again almost every village had at least one, the biggest concentration is rather surprisingly at Knighton, which had 10 of the 71 in the rural area. Drayton Parva had 19, Drayton Magna 22.

Other clothing trades included milliners (15, almost all in Drayton Magna), hat and bonnet makers (9) and seamstresses (8, all in Drayton Parva). The extreme of specialisation was two people who said they were cap peak makers.

Other trades and crafts

According to the census, at least four people were engaged in each the following trades or crafts:

	Drayton Magna	Drayton Parva	rural area
Basket maker	–	–	6
Besom/broom maker	1	3	8
Clock/watch maker	1	1	4
Cooper	5	3	6
Millwright	1	1	2
Nail maker	3	–	7
Rope maker	2	6	–
Tanner	2	3	–

In addition there were various people some of whom were probably employed by Gower or Rodenhurst, including ironfounders (6), machine makers (4), moulders (6) and pattern makers (4).

Other trades included brazier (3), coachmaker (2), chain maker, cork manufacturer, cotter, cutlery grinder, japanner, lath cleaver, locksmith, scythe pole maker and tin plate worker (1 each).

Shops

In the rural area 37 people recorded their occupation as 'butcher'. Their distribution does not reflect the population of the villages: although Hodnet and Hinstock had four each, both Cheswardine and Childs Ercall had seven.

Most villages had at least one general shop, sometimes described as a grocer. Hodnet had six shops (excluding the butcher), including a baker, an ironmonger, a druggist and a draper. Hinstock had four, including a baker and a fishmonger. (Even Market Drayton did not have a fishmonger.) Ashley too had four, including a fruiterer and a draper, but no baker.

As one would expect, both the number and the variety of the shops was greatest in Drayton Magna. Shops which according to *Bagshaw's Directory* appear to have specialised in bought-in items are listed in Appendix A. It is noticeable that the largest number were in High Street (12), the remainder being in Shropshire Street (10) and Cheshire Street (4). Unlike Stafford Street, Great Hales Street and Queen Street, neither High Street nor Shropshire Street were used for animal markets. Neither probably was the south end of Cheshire Street where its four main shops were likely to have been.

Thus the 'centre of gravity' of the town's main shops has moved a little northwards since the middle of the 19th century.

Six traders were merely described as 'shopkeepers': they were in Cheshire Street, Shropshire Street (3), Stafford Street and Little Drayton. There were also eight butchers, two of whom were in Little Drayton.

As noted earlier, many craftsmen, dressmakers and the like would have had shops, but it is not possible to establish which of them were principally retailers and which were small-scale manufacturers or repairers. For example, George Rogers was described as 'jeweller, silversmith, watch & clockmaker and agent to the Manchester Fire & Life Office', but with that range of products, and with premises in High Street, he was likely to have been as much a retailer as a manufacturer.

Inns and beerhouses

Bagshaw's Directory lists 13 inns (including the Corbet Arms Hotel) and 14 beerhouses in Drayton Magna and Parva. Curiously the census records 15 innkeepers but only 5 beerhouse keepers. Presumably the rest of the latter were combining that activity with another occupation. The inns and beerhouses of Market Drayton are discussed further in chapter 17.

The directory lists 21 inns and the same number of beerhouses in the rural area. Almost every village had at least one or the other. The census shows 20 innkeepers (or equivalent) and only 8 beerhouse keepers. Again, multiple activities for the latter were common.

Transport

Road transport was by foot, horse or cart. There were five toll collectors on the turnpikes. Only seven people put 'road labourer' as their occupation. Apart from the turnpikes, roads were (badly) maintained by the individual parishes using casual labour.

Operation of carts and wagons was represented by eleven carters and ten carriers, many of the latter specifying that they were coal carriers. Most large farms had a wagoner or two.

Seven people were employed on the canal, plus four wharfingers. On the night of the survey, 47 boatmen were moored in the area: 26 at Cheswardine, 18 at Tyrley and just 3 at Drayton. This number was inflated because many boatmen lived on board with their families, and even relatively young children helped work the boats, the youngest leading the horse, the slightly older ones working the locks.

Transport is discussed further in chapter 16.

Health

The reliance on natural skills is very evident in the practice of medicine, or rather in those who supported such practice. There were seven qualified doctors in the area, one each in Woore, Ashley North, Jug Bank, Cheswardine and Hodnet, and two in Drayton, both in Shropshire Street. All except one were both surgically and medically qualified, in accordance with the Medical Acts of the 1830s; one was a surgeon only.

Remember that medicine then was only beginning to emerge from mediaeval ideas, with treatments based on herbs and minerals, many quite dangerous, and few really effective (digitalis and opium derivatives were soundly established as was Jenner's vaccination); a scientific basis for medicine itself was just beginning.

There were four persons describing themselves as druggists (one also a hopman and another a grocer); perhaps they supplied materials to those who had learnt the necessary skills, such as housewives, 'nurses', and others who would not declare on a census their skills as they were not recognised as professional.

'Nurse' is a title often found in the largest houses and seems to be for child care; again their skills are likely to have been learnt from their elders and not from formal training — Florence Nightingale had not yet arrived!

There is no mention of midwifery, another skill learnt by working with others and practised by becoming known as one prepared to assist in what was perhaps not the most elegant of occupations; the profession of 'midwife' did not yet exist except to service the topmost echelons of society.

Nor, at the other end of life, is there any mention of undertakers.

Other professional and administrative

The spiritual needs of the district were met by some twenty clergy. (This excludes the two who were 'without cure of souls', being major landowners.) One was identifiable as Primitive Methodist in Market Drayton, one 'Independent', one Roman Catholic (in Ashley), and one was described as an 'SCC curate'. The rest were Anglican, in each of the villages.

Legal matters were cared for by seven solicitors with their three assistants, all but one in Market Drayton. Presumably their business was related to local trade, but did they or 'big city' solicitors look after matters of land ownership and sale?

A further group provided services to the major landowners. They described themselves variously as land agent (two), bailiff (two), land surveyor, surveyor & land agent, and land steward (one of each). In addition there were two auctioneers, one of whom was an auctioneer & land surveyor.

An architect & builder was recorded at Marchamley. One may speculate that he was working for Viscount Hill on or about Hawkstone Hall.

Somebody described as a schoolmaster could be a graduate, or they could be merely a young person who had substantially completed his education and was now instructing young children. Indeed, a 'teacher' might be little more than a child-minder. In the Drayton area 47 people were described as schoolmaster, schoolmistress or teacher; there was also one 'professor of music'. Education is discussed further in chapter 13.

The 'public sector' was then little developed. The local police numbered but three, with a Superintendent in Marchamley — he was a relative by marriage of Viscount Hill of Hawkstone Hall. Justice there was, but much unofficial? The other central and local government officials in the area comprised three postmasters, the manager of the workhouse and his two assistants. The administration of the local public services was carried out by the town's firms of solicitors.

Seven people were described as clerks. Additionally, there was one accountant, but that would not have had the same professional connotations as now.

Domestic servants

Within the Drayton area 1,161 (8.2%) of the total population were engaged in domestic service — the single biggest group apart from people engaged in agriculture. This compares with Shropshire's 6.4% and the British Isles' 5.4%.

Many were living in at the big houses, of course. But professionals, shopkeepers, tradesmen and farmers — indeed, most people with a reasonable income — had one or two live-in servants.

Living-in servants are discussed in greater detail in Chapter 7.

Servants not living in included 35 laundresses or washerwomen, and 32 charwomen.

Other occupations

The landed estates had 24 gamekeepers, and 65 people were described as gardeners. Two people specialised in mole catching, one in rat catching.

A total of 105 people described themselves as labourers, without specifying what part of the economy they were employed in.

There were eight hawkers recorded (one being specifically a lace hawker), four higglers, one huckster and one pedlar.

Appendix A

Shops which appear to have specialised in bought-in items

Adams & Powell	Shropshire Street	Draper, silk mercer & hatter
Thomas Bennion	High Street	Bookseller, stationer, printer etc
Walter Bradbury	High Street	Draper, silk mercer & hatter
Joseph Brayn	High Street	Draper, silk mercer & hatter
Edward Craston	High Street	Hatter & shoe warehouse
James Davenport	High Street	Grocer, tea dealer & tallow chandler
William Godwin	Shropshire Street	Grocer, chemist & druggist
John Goodall	Cheshire Street	Chemist, druggist & glass dealer
Thomas Heatley	High Street	Draper, silk mercer & hatter
Thomas Hope	Shropshire Street	Provision dealer
John Jones	Shropshire Street	Hatter & provision dealer
Edmund Lloyd	Shropshire Street	Draper, silk mercer & hatter
Silvester & Lockett	High Street	Bookseller, printer etc
Thomas Massie	Cheshire Street	Grocer, tallow chandler & hop dealer
John Moore	Cheshire Street	Baker & provision dealer
Thomas Moore	Cheshire Street	Grocer & tea dealer
Eliza Oldcroft	High Street	Glass & china dealer
William Powell	Shropshire Street	Draper & silk mercer
William Ridgway	High Street	Grocer, chemist, druggist & glass dealer
Samuel Salter	Shropshire Street	Draper & silk mercer
Benjamin Sandbrook	Shropshire Street	Wine & spirit merchant
Harry Sherwin	High Street	Draper, tailor & hatter
Thomas Snow	High Street	Ironmonger, grocer, hop seed merchant etc
Richard Spendelow	Shropshire Street	Grocer, chemist, druggist & hop merchant
Thomas Stevens	Shropshire Street	Hatter, draper & tailor
George Whitfield	High Street	Ironmonger, grocer, hop & seed merchant etc

Appendix B

Employment of children in the horsehair industry

There is evidence from the 1851 census for Drayton Parva (Little Drayton) that a number of children were employed in the horse-hair weaving industry. Twenty-nine children aged between 7 and 12 are described as 'servers'. The server's job was to 'feed' the hairs to the weaver as he needed them. In the case of hand looms, they sat inside the loom. Three other children, aged 6, 7 and 9 are described as 'tiers' [tie-ers]. Presumably, their job was to join hairs on the underside of the fabric. Small size and little nimble fingers would be necessary which probably explains the very young age of these workers.

It is not known if the children were paid directly by the factory owner or whether each individual weaver paid his own server.

Employment of children under 9 was made illegal in 1851 under the Factory Act of 1833.

MB

7 : Servants living in

Peter Brown

In the mid 19th century not only the gentry employed living-in servants. They were also to be found in the households of the clergy, professional men, farmers, manufacturers and the principal shopkeepers, as well as in a surprising number of less wealthy households.

The census data is difficult to interpret as some enumerators did not distinguish between domestic servants and other employees. This is a particular problem for farms, where most of the people recorded merely as 'servants' were probably agricultural workers. (Some enumerators, however, distinguished between 'indoor servants' or 'house servants' and 'agricultural servants'.) A second issue is that relatives were sometimes in effect domestic servants: for example, there are two instances where nieces were explicitly described as 'servant' or 'employed in house'. Throughout the rest of this chapter, 'servants' refers only to people who can be assumed to be house servants, but excluding relatives.

In addition to the living-in servants there would have been others who rented their own home or lived with their parents so appear elsewhere in the census.

The gentry houses

The leading gentry in the area can be regarded as the nine magistrates plus John Tayleur of Buntingsdale Hall, Henry Clive MP of Styche Hall and Sir John Chetwode of Oakley Hall. They occupied twelve of the thirteen largest country houses. (The thirteenth, Shavington, was owned by the non-resident Earl of Kilmorey.) No magistrate lived in urban Drayton.

On the night of the census, 30 March 1851, four of the twelve were away and may have taken some servants with them. Viscount Hill of Hawkstone Hall was at his London house, and it has proved fairly easy to establish that he had taken six servants with him — these have been included in the analysis below.

Algernon Heber Percy of Hodnet Hall was in the Lake District and the census shows no servants had gone with the family, which is a little surprising. It has not been possible to establish where Henry Justice of Hinstock Hall was that night. In both cases, the household may therefore have had more than the number of living-in servants shown in the census. The list for Hodnet Hall looks particularly unbalanced. For example, in neither case is a cook shown; presumably they both had one, so was she with the family, living separately, or taking the opportunity of the absence of her master to visit her own family?

Richard Corbet of Adderley Hall (Lord of the Manor of Drayton Magna) was absent that night, so the number of servants who normally lived in was almost certainly more than the six shown in the census. A further problem is that the enumerator described all six as 'servant', with no indication of their roles. They have been omitted from the analysis, as have the two 'house servants' of the absent Sir John Chetwode of Oakley Hall.

Thomas Twemlow of Peatswood was being visited by fellow magistrate John Baskerville Clegg and his wife, and the layout of the census entry implies that three of the servants present that night were attributable to the Cleggs — these three have been excluded from the analysis.

Number and gender of living-in servants:

House/Hall	Occupier	M	F	Total
Hawkstone	Viscount Hill	15	10	25
Buntingsdale	John Tayleur	6	8	14
Hales	Alexander Buchanan	3	9	12
Tunstall	Peter Broughton	2	8	10
Styche	Henry Clive	2	7	9
Hinstock	Henry Justice	1	6	7
Peatswood	Thomas Twemlow	2	4	6
Peplow	George Hill	2	4	6
Hodnet	Algernon Heber Percy	2	3	5
Pell Wall	Purney Sillitoe	2	3	5

The places with the most servants also had the highest proportion of male servants. A male servant was paid about half as much again as a female servant.

Another way of analysing the numbers is by their role:

House/Hall	A	B	C	D	E
Hawkstone	8	6	4	5	2
Buntingsdale	4	5	3	2	–
Hales	2	6	3	1	–
Tunstall	1	6	2	1	–
Styche	1	4	3	1	–
Hinstock	–	5	1	1	–
Peatswood	1	3	1	–	1
Peplow	1	2	2	1	–
Hodnet	2	2	–	–	1
Pell Wall	2	2	1	–	–

A: butler, footman, usher etc
B: housekeeper, housemaid, ladies' maid etc
C: cook, kitchen maid, dairymaid etc
D: coachman, groom etc
E: bailiff, gardener etc

Only the Buchanans of Hales Hall had a young child at home, so theirs was the only household with a nursery maid (included in 'housekeeper etc' in the figures above).

About a third of the servants at the gentry houses were male; as noted above, the bigger the household, the greater the proportion of male servants, generally. The men were more likely to be married: five (14%) of the men were married, compared with only two (3%) of the women — and they were both aged over 55. (This analysis excludes widows and widowers.) It is also noticeable that over half of the living-in servants were not born in the Market Drayton area; this proportion becomes much higher if house maids and kitchen maids are excluded. The extreme example was Francis Chappuil, Algernon Heber Percy's butler, who was born in Switzerland.

The age ranges were:

	Male	Female
–19	15%	9%
20–29	26%	49%
30–39	36%	22%
40–49	2%	9%
50–59	8%	8%
60+	13%	3%

The average age of the people named as housekeepers was 50, butlers 42, ladies' maids 32, cooks 30, house maids 26, kitchen maids 25, and footmen 25.

The leading townsmen

The Wilson family of The Grove were the richest residents living in the town. Ann Wilson, the head of the household, was the widow of John Wilson, one of Thomas Telford's preferred contractors who, amongst other works, won the contract for the Drayton section of the local canal but died before its completion. His son, John E Wilson, finished the contract and, although described in the census as a 'landed proprietor', employed 37 labourers, which implied he was still an active engineering contractor. The three young children living in the household were his brother's. There were seven living-in servants (four named Mary, which must have been confusing): a cook, a kitchen maid, two housemaids, a ladies' maid, a nurse, and a footman. In the nearby Grove Cottages lived a gardener, a carpenter, a coachman and a groom (the coachman's son) — presumably these were the Wilsons' outdoor servants.

The professional townsmen included the solicitors, of which Charles Warren of The Manor House (Shropshire Street) was the senior. His household of three adults and three children had three servants living in, but the enumerator has not specified their individual roles. His younger brother, Joseph Loxdale Warren of The Lawn (later re-named The Towers, and now demolished) had a large household: himself and his wife, nine children (aged fourteen down to two), his two sisters, his elderly aunt and an elderly female cousin. They had five living-in servants: a cook, two house maids, a kitchen maid and a male house servant (only fourteen years old).

The other solicitors were:
- Creswell Pigott (Stafford Street), who had a cook, a housemaid and a 'toolboy' (aged eleven);
- his son, also called Cresswell Pigot (Frog Lane), with no living-in servants despite having eight children (aged eleven down to four months);
- William Wilkinson, who had three house servants — his younger brother Joseph, who was also a solicitor, lived with him; and
- Henry Gromley (Stafford Street), who had just one servant.

The town's senior doctor was John Hopkins (Shropshire Street). The living-in servants were a cook, a nursery governess, a housemaid and a groom.

At that time the town had no major industrialist. Typical amongst the manufacturers was William Sandbrook, hair seating manufacturer, who had just two servants. Andrew Gower, who was to become the town's leading manufacturer in the second half of the 19th century, did not have any live-in servant, but he could of course have had one or more domestic servants living locally.

Other households

The 20% sample of the census data for 1851 shows that the proportion of the households employing living-in domestic servants was quite different in Drayton Magna compared with Drayton Parva and the rural area:

	Drayton Magna	Drayton Parva	Rural area
3 or more servants	4%	–	2%
2 servants	4%	–	6%
1 servant	19%	2%	8%
Servants not explicitly identified as domestic	–	–	5%
No servants	73%	98%	79%

This highlights the relative poverty of Drayton Parva.

The sample shows that in the rural area many of the farmers with the larger land holdings had two or three domestic servants. The other group which tended to have more than one servant was the clergy: indeed, two of the sample had four servants living in.

In the urban area, three of the sample had three or more house servants: a retired captain, a draper, and the master of the Grammar School. (In the last case, the servants may have been helping with the school.) However, almost all urban households with living-in servants had only one. The occupations of the heads of these households included draper, chandler, milliner, tanner, maltster, ropemaker, builder, plumber, fundholder, retired, and a proprietor of houses (aged 96).

Most of the living-in servants were female; only 7% were male, and almost half of these were aged 15 or younger. The proportion in the various age ranges was markedly different from that tabulated above for the gentry houses; indeed it differed significantly between the urban and rural area:

	urban	*rural*
–19	35%	48%
20–29	55%	33%
30–39	3%	9%
40–49	—	2%
50–59	—	3%
60+	7%	5%

All the men and all but 3% of the women were unmarried, and two-thirds of those who were married were aged 60 or over. (A further 3% were widows.) Unlike the gentry servants, the great majority were born locally.

The Grove

An inventory of the household contents in 1860 shows that the Wilson family was living in style and comfort at The Grove. The drawing room was a fine oval room designed in the Adam style, with a splendid curved mahogany door, ornamental dado, and twin display niches with plaster figures holding oil lamps. Marble tables and numerous rosewood tables were set near couches and a large circular ottoman. A dozen chairs were in rosewood, while five were of African 'Zebra wood'. Fine matching pier glasses (mirrors), a Broadwood grand pianoforte, a Brussels carpet, blue damask curtains and a great number of paintings contributed to the fashionable style.

The house had 17 bedrooms for family and staff. Typically the family bedrooms had mahogany four poster beds with hangings, Marseilles quilts and Kidderminster carpets. The servants' bedrooms had deal or painted furniture, string bedsteads or straw or flock mattresses and usually floor druggets. The Housekeeper's Room and Butler's Pantry contained the numerous dinner services, fine glassware and silverware used by the household. Even the Servants' Hall benefited from decoration: a 'geological map on rollers'.

The large courtyard included many service buildings, kennels and no fewer than 16 stables and two carriage houses. Even these service ranges were ornamented by a fine entrance arch with cupola over it housing an imposing clock and weather vane.

KG

The Oval Drawing Room at The Grove. The photograph was taken towards the end of the 19th century, but judging from an inventory of 1860, it would have looked much like this in 1851.

[By courtesy of Phil Herring]

8 : The Enclosure of Little Drayton Common

David Jenkins

This article is part of a paper originally written for the Certificate of Local History at the University of Birmingham in 1994. The full paper may be consulted in the Local Studies Section of Market Drayton Library or at Drayton Museum.

Market Drayton has for centuries consisted of two townships, Drayton Magna and Drayton Parva. That Little Drayton was perceived in the 19th century to be inferior is demonstrated by contemporary accounts.

Bagshaw, writing in 1851, after the enclosure, which he stated took place in 1850, conveys a clear impression of Little Drayton as follows[1]:

> Drayton Parva is a populous district ..., chiefly consisting of cottage residences, many of which are small, ill ventilated and have a miserable appearance.

James Robinson Lee, who wrote the first history of Market Drayton, remarked of Little Drayton in 1861[2]:

> The name of this hamlet, which was intended to distinguish it from the manor of Drayton, accords well with its history. It was always little and always dependent.

In the context of its medieval past Lee also wrote:
> No effort seems to have been ever made by tenants or by owners to uplift the village from its ancient obscurity.

This comment had some validity prior to the 1840s.

An early proposal for the enclosure of Little Drayton Common

In 1704 an agreement for enclosing the Common was drafted, though this was obviously not concluded. The agreement listed nine parties: Robert Corbet of Adderley and William Church of Tunstall as joint Lords of the Manor, and seven freeholders, only one of whom was of Little Drayton. After naming the parties, the draft left a space and the instruction, 'If there be any more ffreeholders insert them here.'

> The objective of the agreement is made clear:
> If ye sd Comon & Wastground were Inclosed & divided it would turne to much more profit & advantage than now it does.

The draft agreement is novel in that it proposed:
> that a fit & proporcionable part thereof may be also established & seised for ye sole use benefit & reliefe of ye Poor of ye sd town of little Drayton to be occupied & enjoyed by them forever exclusive from ye sd Lords and ffreeholders.

It was proposed that the land to be given for the use of the Poor, the quantum of which was not specified, should be to the south and south east of the Common. This location had the disadvantage of being the low-lying ground near the river and perhaps also the steep slopes up to the scarp.

The agreement set out the arrangements for appointing surveyors, dividing the land, for fencing and for the division of cost. No mention was made of the construction of access roads and paths.

It is probable that this proposal failed to be concluded because of the large and apparently uncertain number of parties involved and perhaps because it was anticipated that the expense of enclosing a relatively small area would be greater than the anticipated 'more profit & advantage'.

Little Drayton in the late 18th and early 19th centuries

The map opposite shows part of an untitled map clearly drawn for the estate of Corbet of Adderley. Little Drayton Common or Heath is shown in the south-west of the township. which it can be seen had vestiges of medieval open fields. There is evidence of the consolidation of strips and of their enclosure but none of any general enclosure. The spread of ownership was wide despite the large amount of Corbet holdings and thus complexity and inertia were probably the reasons for there being no general enclosure of the open fields.

The map shows the growth of Little Drayton westward from the Doublegates, particularly on the south side of the turnpike. There are twelve encroachments on the Common against the parish boundary and there are cottages on the ends of the strips in the Walkmill Field. A road crosses the Heath and the Tern on its way to Buntingsdale Hall. The present stone bridge was not built until 1794 and presumably the river crossing on the map was either a timber bridge or a ford. Otherwise the Heath extended to the Tern at only one place.

The Tithe Apportionment and Map of 1837 show that the encroachments on the western edge of the Common had increased from 10 in 1780 to 26 and there was also one dwelling within the Common. The Corbet estate owned 6 of these plots, the remaining 21 having 14 different owners, 5 of whom were owner occupiers. With one exception the size

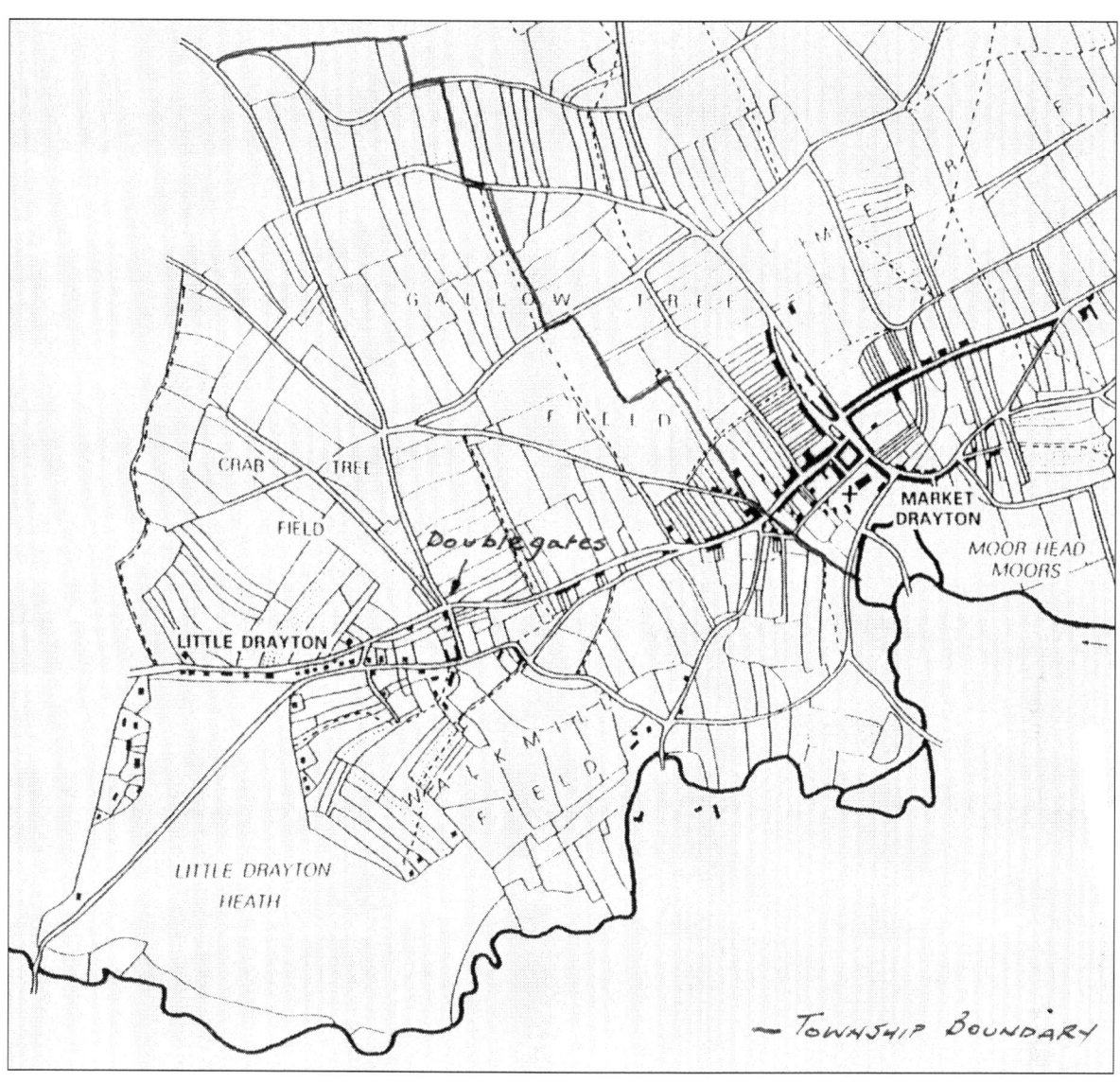

Market Drayton c1780 [VCH Shropshire, Vol IV, Fig 11]

of the holdings ranged from 3 perches (90 square yards) to 1 rood 23 perches (0.4 acres), so that they were no more than kitchen gardens. The complicated boundaries of these plots and the awkwardness of the access to some of them show that their formation was unplanned, though a number of the cottages were built in pairs, either as a joint enterprise or on the 'build two, rent one' principle. There were 20 dwellings lying adjacent to the turnpike on the north side of the Common but these, it seems, were not encroachments on the Common.

The enumerator of the 1841 Census recorded 352 houses and 1,462 residents (including 95 in the Workhouse) in the township of Little Drayton. Enumeration District 5, which listed 539 people in 131 dwellings, embraced all of the township west of the Doublegates and thus included the Common. Apart from the enumerator's general description of his route, there is no indication of the location of any dwelling. However, of the 26 named occupiers of the 27 dwellings (one was void) encroaching the Common in the tithe survey, 15 reappear as occupiers, together with another 4 occupiers with matching surnames, in a group of 22 consecutive entries in the census in a sequence compatible with the relationship of their dwellings. There is thus a close correlation of the tithe and the census, as might be expected with only a four-year interval. There is no evidence that the number of dwellings on the Common had grown during this time.

The occupations of the 22 heads of household and their seven lodgers included eight labourers, four agricultural labourers, three millwrights, two bricklayers, two shoemakers, a sawyer, a stone cutter, a chairseat weaver, a wheelwright, a chairmaker, a tailor and a schoolmistress.

The 1845 Inclosure Act

This Act was introduced 'to facilitate the Inclosure and Improvement of Commons and land held in Common'. It had the objectives of releasing more land for cultivation, of creating productive employment for labour and enabling common land to be made available for spiritual, educational and recreational purposes and for the benefit of the poor.

Administrative and legislative efficiency were obtained by delegating the approval of enclosure proposals to permanent Inclosure Commissioners. Upon the Commissioners receiving a request to consider the enclosure of a specific common, they would, if the proposal had merit, include the project in one of the omnibus enabling Bills presented to Parliament at least annually. In the interim the Commissioners would appoint a Valuer, with whom those who had an interest in the common land could register their claims. After holding meetings, hearing witnesses and considering objections, the Valuer would eventually make a judgement, subject to the Commissioners' approval, of the awards to individuals, in cash or an allotment of land, in compensation for the elimination of their common rights. The Valuer's task was assisted by his being authorised to use the tithe survey and apportionment.

The Valuer was empowered to appropriate part of the common land to provide for:
- public and private roads and paths;
- a gravel pit for the use of the Overseer of the Highways;
- a 'Place of Exercise and Recreation for the Inhabitants';
- 'Allotments or Field Gardens for the Labouring Poor';
- a burial ground;
- sites for a church or chapel and a parsonage; and
- sites for a school and a workhouse.

Since the process of enclosure was intended to be self-financing, the Valuer had, as a preliminary, to sell by public auction part of the common land to meet the costs of compensation payments, road and drainage construction, his own fees and expenses, and the Commissioners' costs. The Lord of the Manor was entitled to an allotment in lieu of his interest in the soil of the common but mineral rights could be treated separately and might be allowed to be preserved. Encroachments of twenty years' standing were to be deemed Ancient Enclosures. All allotments were to be fenced at the expense of the allottee, who was to maintain his fences and any private road or path abutting his allotment. The procedure was thus intended to be fair, cheap and expeditious.

The Little Drayton Heath Enclosure Award 1852

It has not been possible to discover who made the initiative to enclose the Common. That there was an intent to develop the Common is evident from the fact that in October 1845 the Lords of the Manor granted Her Majesty's Commissioners for Building Churches five acres of land on the Common as a site for a church, churchyard and parsonage with extensive grounds. On this site a church, designed by Samuel Pountney Smith of Shrewsbury, was erected in 1847 for the sum of £2,115, mainly from a private benefaction. The living was a perpetual curacy in the patronage of the vicar of Drayton-in-Hales, the Reverend James Lee. It is believed that at least some of the stone for Christchurch came from the quarry within the Common.

Little Drayton Heath was included in the enabling Act 13 & 14 Victoria Cap LXVI, dated 14 August 1850, and in anticipation of this the Inclosure Commissioners had appointed, on 7 February 1850, Samuel Minor as Valuer. Minor was a land surveyor of Moreton Hall, Moreton Say, that is, a man from outside the parish but having local knowledge. The Valuer's first task would have been to insert a notice in the local newspaper announcing his appointment, calling a meeting of interested parties, and requiring those believing that they had rights in the Common to lodge their claims with him: this appeared in the *Shropshire Conservative* on 4 January 1851, the meeting being held on 20 January. A notice in the *Shropshire Conservative* on 25 January stated that a schedule of all claims and objections together with Samuel Minor's determinations had been deposited at the Corbet Arms Inn. Meanwhile, tenders had been invited for the construction of roads and fencing the allotments.

Samuel Minor would next have commissioned a survey of the Common. The map on the previous page is a copy of the essentials of the original survey drawn up in 1850 by Thomas Firth of Macclesfield, which shows the division of the Common.

A public auction was held at the Corbet Arms on 24 January. William Darbyshire Green, the auctioneer, sold 17.5 acres of land in 26 plots to 15 purchasers for a total sum of £1,211 (equivalent to £69 an acre). The Rev James Lee bought one rood (¼ acre) as a site opposite the church for a National School and the Guardians of the Drayton Union bought five acres as a site for a new workhouse. At £50 and £67 per acre respectively, these sites of public benefit had to be bought at near the market price. John Tayleur of Buntingsdale Hall bought 6.7 acres of land (at

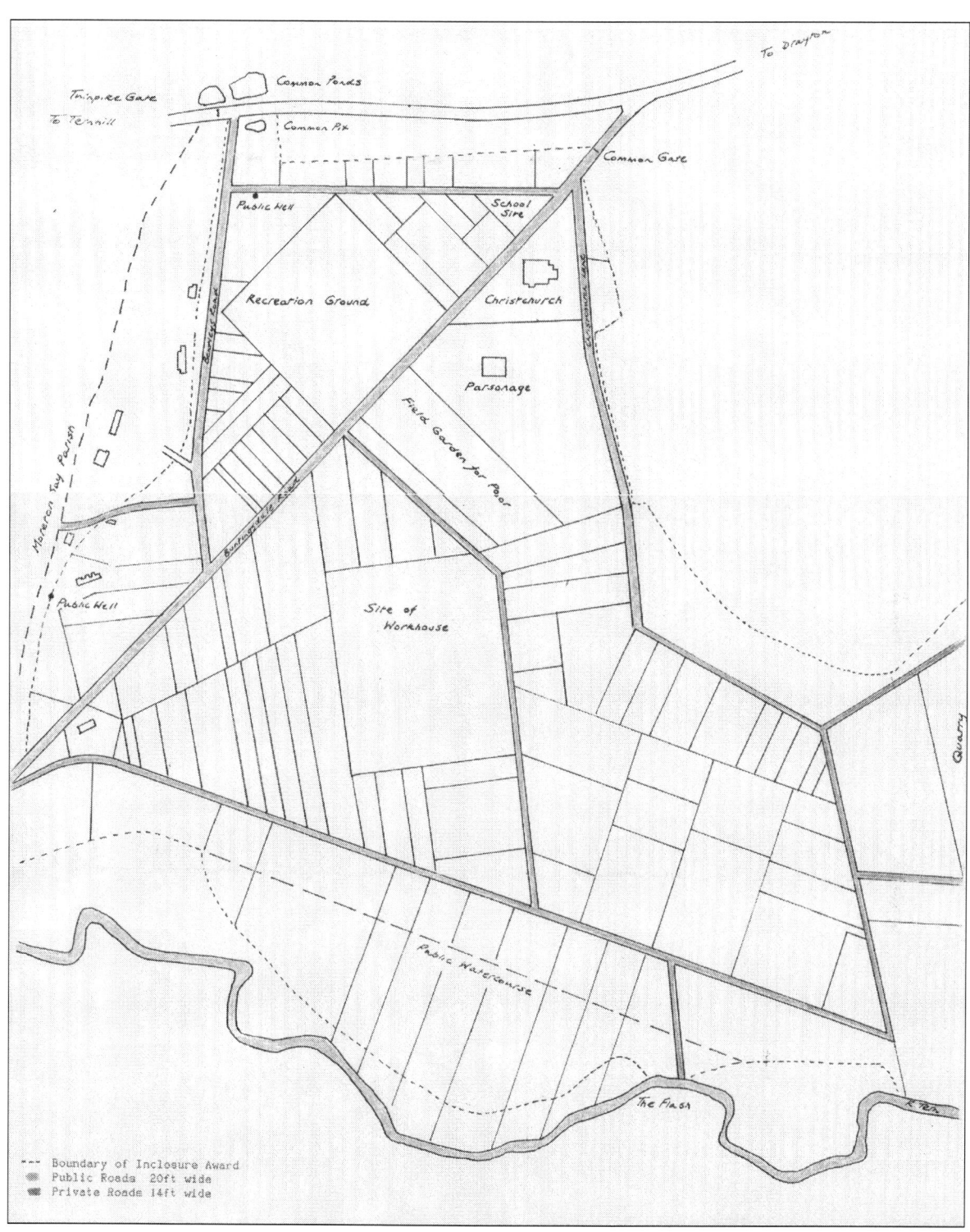

*Inclosure Award map, copied from survey in 1850 by Thomas Firth of Macclesfield
(original scale 1:2,500, rescaled to approximately 1: 4,750)*

£70 an acre), some of which covered the approach to Buntingsdale bridge, no doubt to retain control of the approach to his house. His most significant purchase was of all the land containing the quarry. Apart from two pastures near the Tern, the rest of the sale plots were small and must have been intended for cottages.

In accordance with the discretion available to him, the Valuer gave a perfectly square four acre level plot to the Churchwardens and Overseers of the Poor of the parish 'to be held by them in Trust as a Place of Exercise and Recreation for the Inhabitants of the said Parish and Neighbourhood'. In addition he gave also to the Churchwardens and Overseers a further two acres 'in Trust as an allotment for the Labouring Poor of the said Parish' but this was to have an annual rent charge of thirty shillings to be divided between the churchwardens of Drayton and Hodnet in the ratio of 4:11, perhaps relating to the one-time relationship between the churches.

Prior to enclosure, apart from the road to Buntingsdale, the Common had several tracks leading to dwellings, the quarry, the public pond, two public wells, and the public watering place on the Tern called the Flash where commoners could take their livestock to water. The Common would have been entered through gates at its north-east corner. The proposed enclosure would sever these tracks and therefore Samuel Minor had to provide routes to maintain these accesses. He ordered the construction of three public roads, each twenty feet wide. One was on the line of the track to Buntingsdale, now called Buntingsdale Road; the second, now called Bentleys Road, was adjacent to the west edge of the Common and ran from the common pit near the turnpike toll gate into Buntingsdale Road; and the third road, now called Christchurch Lane, gave access to dwellings on the east side of the church. In addition, Samuel Minor called for nine private roads each fourteen feet wide and eight more of twelve foot width, together with two private footpaths and four public footways which connected with public footpaths external to the Common. The total area of these roads and paths was five acres. The common pit provided gravel for road maintenance.

Samuel Minor awarded the public pond, the Flash and the public wells to the Surveyor of the Highways of Little Drayton with the responsibility for their future maintenance. He also ordered the construction of a public watercourse 6ft wide and 520yds long to act apparently as a drain to the meadows through which it ran. This ditch was not accessible to the public and it effected no improvement from which the public benefited.

The Valuer next had to determine the compensation of the Lords of the Manor for the loss of their rights. The Lordship was divided between Peter Broughton of Tunstall Hall and the trustees of the estate of the late Sir Corbet Corbet of Adderley. They were both entitled to a moiety of the soil and the mineral rights of the Common, for which they were each compensated by the award of one half of one fourteenth of the residue of the Common. Broughton received plots on sloping ground totalling 2.7 acres and the Corbet estate received 1.7 acres of more level land.

There were 54 parties who had such a small interest in the Common, arising from land holdings in the township ranging from one perch (30 square yards) to 1½ roods (3/8 acre), that they were compensated in cash, on a basis which approximated to £14 per acre or 1s.9d. per perch. Authority to make these payments totalling £130 was given by the Commissioners' order of 16 May 1851.

It is appropriate to summarise the Valuer's decisions thus far. He had raised £1,211 (equivalent to £13.4 an acre of the gross area) from the sale of land, out of which he had paid compensation of £130. The balance would have been spent on the construction of nearly three miles of roads and paths and the Valuer's and Commissioners' fees and expenses. Of the 90 acres of the Common (excluding the church and parsonage sites), Samuel Minor had sold 17.5 acres, given away 6 acres and allocated 5 acres for roads, making a total of 28.5 acres. Of the remaining 61.5 acres, the Lords of the Manor were due a total of one fourteenth or 4.4 acres and thus only 57.1 acres, or 63% of the Common, remained to be allocated.

The Common was divided into 165 allotments of which 26 had been sold, 2 had been given away and 3 had been allocated to the Lords of the Manor. The balance of 134 was divided amongst 87 allottees. The largest allotment was almost three acres and the smallest two perches, with an average allotment size of 0.42 acres. There seemed to be no consistent relationship between the area of an allottee's landholding in the township and the area of his allotment, but Samuel Minor no doubt took into account the different values of land, in his view, in different parts of the Common.

The issue of the *Shropshire Conservative* on 13 September 1851 carried the formal notice by the Inclosure Commissioners for England & Wales that a copy of the report of the Valuer acting in the matter of the inclosure of Little Drayton Heath, together with an estimate of the expenses, had been deposited at the Corbet Arms Inn, and that a meeting to hear objections would be held on 2 October.

The award, drafted by Samuel Minor, was sealed by the Commissioners on 23 January 1852; this was a formal conclusion to events that had already taken place.

The changes which the enclosure made to Little Drayton

The table below compares populations from the 1841 and 1861 censuses.

Parish growth	1841	1861	change %
Drayton-in-Hales [A]	3,390	4,428	+12.7
Adderley	404	428	+ 5.9
Moreton Say	770	679	–11.8
Stoke-on-Tern	1,000	961	– 3.9

Township growth

Drayton Magna	1,699	1,970	+16.0
Drayton Parva [B]	1,462	1,659	+13.5
Remaining townships [C]	769	799	+ 3.9

Growth in Little Drayton

The Common: dwellings	27	64	+137
The Common: population [D][E]	115	288	+150
The balance of Little Drayton: population [D]	1,257	1299	+4

[A] Shropshire part of parish only
[B] Including workhouse
[C] Betton, Longslow, Sutton and Woodseaves
[D] Excluding the workhouse inmates
[E] 1841 population based on a known minimum of 103 and an estimated maximum of 126

Drayton's population, which was mostly urban, increased by 12.7% in the period, whereas the adjacent parishes were rural and exhibited a lower rate of growth in Adderley, a slow decline in Stoke-on-Tern and a serious decline at Moreton Say.

Considering next the townships within the parish, it can be seen that Drayton Magna and Drayton Parva, the two urban townships, had a high growth rate, whilst the other four townships combined were rural and hardly grew. Finally the Common area and the balance of the Drayton Parva township are examined. After the exclusion of the Workhouse, which in 1841 was in Shropshire Street and by 1861 was at Quarry House on the Common, it can be seen that the growth of Drayton Parva, excluding the Common, was similar to that of the rural townships and that the higher growth of the township as a whole was due mostly to the 150% growth of population on the Common.

The enclosure of the Common brought the church, the school, the field gardens and the recreation ground together to give the township a compact focus which it had not had before. The creation of these amenities and many potential cottage sites at a time of general population increase and rural population drift, must have made the old Common look very attractive. It is tempting to leap to the conclusion that the migration from Moreton Say was to the Common — the figures fit the argument. However an analysis of the parish of birth of the heads of households on the Common in 1861 shows that 45% came from Drayton, only 6% from Moreton Say, 9% from other neighbouring parishes, 21% from the rest of Shropshire, 15% from Staffordshire and Cheshire, and the remaining 4% from elsewhere.

The following table groups the occupations of the 69 heads of household on the Common in 1861 compared with the 26 previously listed for 1841.

	1841		1861	
Occupation group	number	%	number	%
Agriculture	12	46	26	38
Rural crafts	2	8	3	4
Building	4	15	11	16
Industry	4	15	11	16
Services	–	–	10	14
Retail & clothing	3	12	4	6
Professional	1	4	4	6

It can be seen that the dependence on agriculture and rural crafts declined in the period, that the proportions working in building and industry remained almost constant, and that a category of service workers (consisting of five gardeners, three carters, a groom and a messenger) had appeared. It is to be noted that in neither census are there alehouse keepers on the Common.

The map overleaf, part of the first 1:2,500 Ordnance Survey map of 1880, shows that dwellings had by then been built in the triangular plot around the recreation ground, to the north of School Lane, around the quarry area, and near the workhouse. The map indicates that a large area of tree nursery had been planted south east of the Workhouse and that apart from the pasture adjacent to the Tern, there was little ground remaining for agricultural use, which because of the slope would have had to be pastoral.

The Common today

A recent perambulation of the area of the Common shows that it is very much a palimpsest of its past. The church remains in use, the National School building now serves as a community centre and the recreation ground and field gardens survive to serve their original purpose. Quarry House was demolished in the 1980s and private houses have been built in its place. The quarry is overgrown with trees but its approximate location is identified by adjacent road names. The public pond and the public wells have disappeared but the Flash remains, as does its access track.

The three public roads established by Samuel Minor remain, Bentleys Road still in its original width. His nine private roads of fourteen feet width also survive; four of them are now public roads (Quarry Bank Road, Tern View, Wordsworth Drive and Westminster Drive) and the rest remain in their original form or have reverted to footpaths. School Lane, which now serves many houses, is still an unsurfaced road and because of its narrowness may never be adopted.

A stranger to the area would find no reference to the Common in street names. He or she might perhaps notice the geometrical planning of

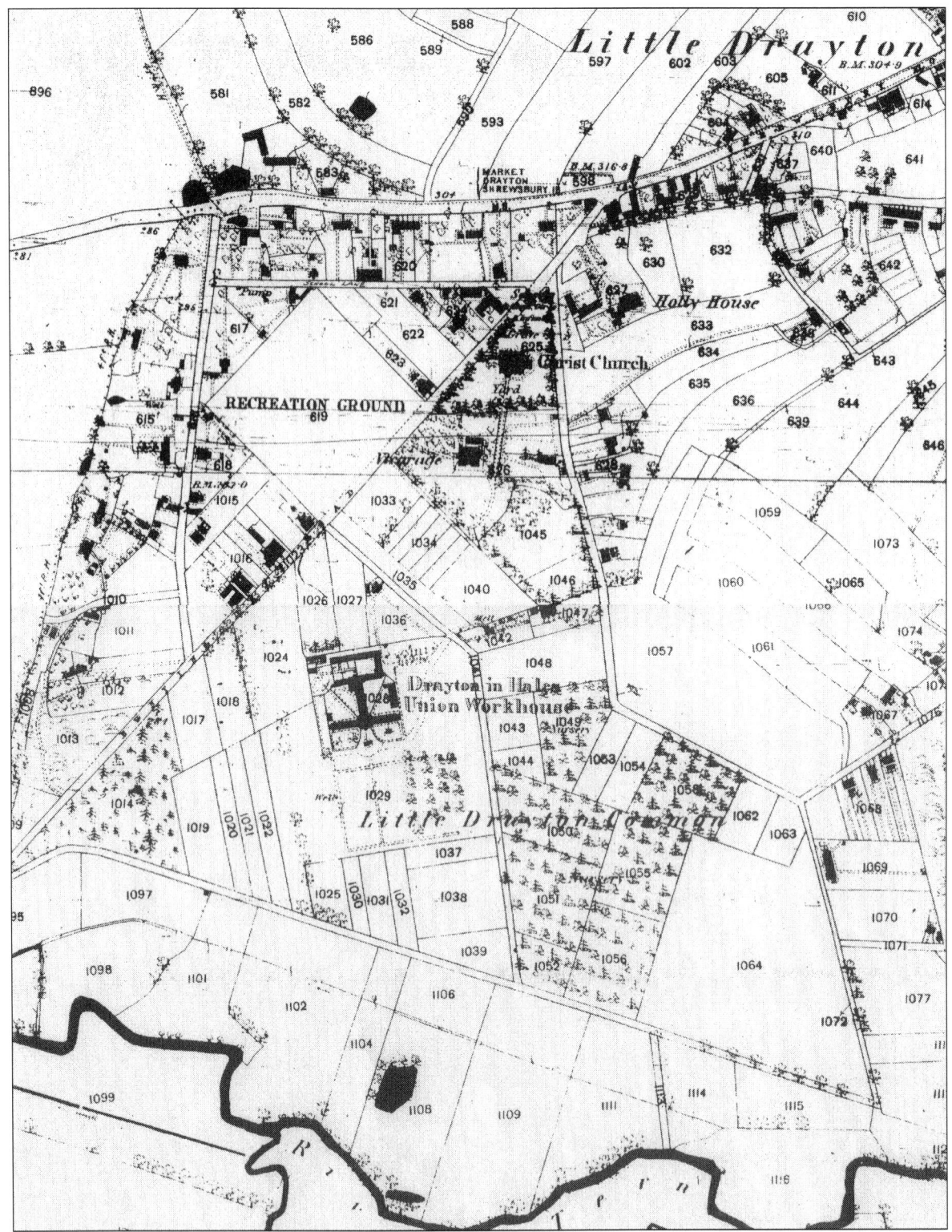

Ordnance Survey 1:2,500 map 1880 (rescaled to approximately 1:4,750)

Buntingsdale Road, indicative of formal planning rather than organic growth. However, observation of the west side of Bentleys Road and the east side of Christchurch Lane would reveal the haphazard orientation of some dwellings and their considerable distance from the road, showing that the sites originated in encroachments before the roads were built, thus suggesting the former presence of wasteland. Some of the dwellings on these old sites may predate the enclosure and some may be timber-framed and subsequently encased in brick.

Conclusions

It is unlikely that the enclosure of Little Drayton Common would have taken place had it not been for the far-sighted legislation of the Inclosure Act.

The Common was relatively small and not potentially valuable as agricultural land and as such would not have justified the expense of enclosure, which was £13.5 per acre.

Little Drayton was especially fortunate in that Samuel Minor used the powers provided within the 1845 Act to allocate recreational ground allotments for the Poor. Tate[3] shows that such provision was rare and that only 6% of common land enclosed after 1845 was allocated to these purposes. The township was indebted to the Lords of the Manor in anticipating the enclosure (indeed they may, perhaps with the Rev James Lee, have initiated it) by granting land for the church and parsonage at a time of Government encouragement of church building. Furthermore, James Lee and the Chairman of the Guardians of the Drayton Union, Thomas Twemlow, saw the opportunity that the enclosure gave to acquire land, respectively, for a National school and a new workhouse designed to the latest principles. Within a period of seven years from 1847, when Little Drayton had no facilities at all, the township thus acquired means of spiritual, educational and recreational care, and an aid to self help.

Turning to the observations made by Bagshaw and J R Lee (who was the son of James Lee) referred to earlier, it is to be noted that they did not criticise the people but only their poverty. Those of the more prosperous Drayton Magna, of whom J R Lee was one, might well deride their poor neighbouring township and Bagshaw could be expected to reflect the views of those he hoped would purchase his Directory. There is no evidence that the commoners were idle, ill-disciplined frequenters of ale houses. They did not acquire the reputation of the residents of Mixen Lane in Casterbridge.[4] Apart from the eight houses erected by the Oddfellows, the houses on the former common have always been privately owned. There were no ale houses on the Common and in 1861 the number of ale houses in Little Drayton was fewer than in Drayton Magna, even after excluding the latter's inns and taverns from the reckoning. Before the enclosure and for some time after, the commoners would have had little need of communication with Drayton Magna. It seems that the commoners were employed mainly on neighbouring farms and poverty would have made them inward looking. Once-removed oral evidence supports this opinion. Such isolation can invite disparagement

It has been shown that consequent upon enclosure the population of the Common area increased rapidly, when the surrounding rural parishes were declining or only growing slowly. Whatever the 'push' factors from the surrounding areas, there is no doubt that the enclosure of the Common and the attendant social infrastructure gave the Common a significant 'pull' factor which enabled the township to throw off its image of inferiority. It must be finally observed that Little Drayton, in having to wait a long time for the enclosure of its Common, eventually received a greater betterment than would have otherwise been the case, which aided the township in overcoming the disadvantage inherent in its medieval past.

Notes

Primary sources

- Inclosure Act 1845, 8&9 Victoria Cap 118
- Inclosure Enabling Act, 13&14 Victoria Cap LXVI, Little Drayton Heath
- Draft agreement for inclosing Little Drayton Heath, 1704:Shropshire Archives (SA), Box 49
- Little Drayton Heath Inclosure Award and Map 1852: Shropshire Archives (SA), A21/58
- Tithe apportionment and map, parish of Drayton-in-Hales, 1837: SA
- Enumerator's returns for the parish of Drayton-in-Hales, 1841 & 1861
- Population totals for adjoining parishes, *Victoria County History of Shropshire*, Vol II, 222

References

1. S Bagshaw, *History, Gazetteer and Directory of Shropshire*, 1851, 262–277
2. J R Lee, *A History of Market Drayton*, 1861, 63–64
3. W E Tate, *The English Village Community and the Enclosure Movement*, 1967, 138
4. Thomas Hardy, *The Mayor of Casterbridge*, chapter 36

9 : Census of Religious Worship 1851

Peter Brown

The Census

In 1851, in addition to the census of population, a census was taken of places of worship. This method was thought to be more accurate than asking people about their religious affiliation in the main census questionnaire.

Clergy completing the returns were asked to discover 'how far the means of Religious Instruction provided in Great Britain during the last fifty years have kept pace with the population during the same period, and to what extent those means are adequate to meet the spiritual wants of the increased population of 1851'. Although it was purely voluntary, most places of worship made returns.

The census returns for the Shropshire parishes within the Drayton Union are summarised in the Appendix at the end of this chapter. The figures exclude the part of the Drayton Union in Staffordshire: the parish of Ashley and the Mucklestone part of Mucklestone & Woore parish.

The census was conducted on Sunday 30 March 1851. The minister or other responsible official was asked to fill in a return, though there was no penalty for failure to do so. It appears that all the churches and chapels in the Market Drayton area complied except for the Primitive Methodists at Little Drayton (who met on Tuesday evenings) and Soudley (Thursdays). The Mormons were recorded as having regular meetings at Market Drayton in 1841 but it is not certain whether they were still meeting in 1851. This is a much more complete record than was achieved in most other parts of Shropshire.

For Anglican churches, the rector, vicar or curate signed the return. Thomas Lewis, Minister, signed the returns for some of the Primitive Methodist chapels, dating three of them earlier than the census date: Market Drayton on 20 March, Norton-in-Hales on 25 March and Stoke Heath on 28 March. The other returns were signed by the 'local preacher', 'steward' or 'deacon'.

The churches and chapels

There were 12 Anglican and 16 non-conformist churches and chapels in the area. Every parish had its Anglican church of course, but the non-conformist chapels were not evenly spread. Thus Cheswardine parish (population 1,119) had just one non-conformist chapel, whereas Stoke-on-Tern (population 937) had five. It is reasonable to assume that many people worshipped in a different parish to that in which they lived.

Although the form asked for 'date erected', the replies were not necessarily consistent: sometimes it was year of the foundation of the congregation, sometimes the date of building the first chapel, or the date of the building of the then current chapel. The consistency of the Drayton data has not been checked.

Only in one instance in the Drayton area did the census return state that the congregation did not have a permanent separate building: the Primitive Methodists at Longford, who met in a house, presumably that of Thomas Griffiths, the local preacher.

There was no Roman Catholic chapel in the town of Market Drayton or its Shropshire hinterland, the nearest being at Ashley. The attendance there can be inferred from the census summary which was published in 1853, which shows the aggregate figures for the whole Union area — 50 people were at the morning service at Ashley and 20 at the afternoon's.

Sittings

The census form did not give any guidance about how the number of sittings (the seats available) should be calculated. Some may have given the number that could be seated comfortably; others may have given the maximum number that could be squeezed in. Sittings described as 'free' — that is, for which no pew rent was paid — could include those currently unlet, as well as those reserved for the poor. Ollerton Baptists managed to have an attendance of 35 with only 32 sittings; Wollerton Independents 50 with 43 sittings; and Hinstock Wesleyan Methodists 62 with 22 sittings. [There is a maxim in statistics that any figure which looks peculiar is probably wrong!]

The number of sittings could have accommodated 81% of the town population and 62% of the rural population (69% overall, compared with 64% for Shropshire as a whole). 46% of the sittings were free, which was the same as Shropshire as a whole.

Attendance at individual services

It is questionable how accurate many of the attendance figures are. Some are very rounded, in particular the Anglican churches at Market Drayton, Hodnet and Stoke-upon-Tern. However, this does

Summary of returns from the 1851 Census of Religious Worship : Market Drayton area

Location	Denomination	Date	Sittings Free	Sittings Other	Sittings Total	General M	General A	General E	General T	Scholars M	Scholars A	Scholars E	Scholars T	Adjusted total G	Adjusted total S	Adjusted total T	
Market Drayton																	
St Mary's	Anglican	1847	300	1,400	1,700	800	600	—	1,800	200	200	—	400	1,466	200	1,666	
Christ Church	Anglican	1815	545	55	600	150	300	450	—	100	100	—	200	400	100	500	Fortnightly; nil on census day
Little Drayton	Baptist	1815	100	50	150	20	—	20	25	40	—	65	20	20	—	20	
Back Lane	Congregationalist	Pre 1800	300	200	500	81	—	194	—	—	—	—	—	—	—	—	
Cheshire Street	Primitive Methodist	1825	80	70	150	—	140	150	290	—	40	—	65	140	40	180	
Shropshire Street	Wesleyan Methodist	1808	115	173	288	152	—	196	348	98	91	—	189	197	197	345	Sunday school usually 90
Rural area			1,440	1,948	3,388	1,203	1,040	859	3,102	423	431	0	854	2,470	438	2,908	Population: 4,163 Estimated attendance: 70%
Adderley	Anglican		170	63	233	100	60	—	160	26	26	—	52	140	26	166	
Cheswardine	Anglican		20	430	450	150	90	—	280	60	60	—	120	250	60	310	
Child's Ercall	Anglican		45	183	228	120	80	—	200	86	86	—	172	173	86	259	
Hinstock	Anglican		100	216	316	250	220	—	470	64	64	—	128	397	64	461	
Hodnet	Anglican		150	450	600	300	200	—	500	120	100	—	220	433	120	553	
Moreton Say	Anglican		54	286	340	150	—	—	150	25	45	—	70	150	45	195	
Norton-in-Hales	Anglican		120	60	180	48	60	100	208	60	60	50	170	172	60	232	
Peplow	Anglican		20	84	104	35	60	—	95	8	10	—	18	83	10	93	
Stoke-upon-Tern	Anglican		500	—	500	400	100	—	500	50	30	—	80	466	50	516	Endowed, not consecrated
Woore	Anglican	1832	227	337	564	50	150	70	270	120	120	—	240	230	120	350	Average
Ollerton	Baptist		28	4	32	35	—	—	35	15	—	—	15	35	15	50	Average
Ollerton	Congregationalist	1838/9	162	20	182	21	48	—	69	18	10	—	28	55	18	73	Average 30/65/-/25/15/-
Wistanswick	Independents	c1805	150	—	150	—	120	60	180	—	50	—	50	140	50	190	
Wollerton	Independents		43	—	43	50	—	35	85	—	—	—	—	62	—	62	
Eaton-upon-Tern	Primitive Methodist	1842	48	40	88	—	30	22	52	25	20	—	45	37	25	62	
Kenstone	Primitive Methodist	1846	60	40	100	41	49	62	152	—	—	—	—	63	—	63	In a house; average 20-30
Longford	Primitive Methodist	1845	—	not stated	—	—	—	25	25	—	—	—	—	25	—	25	
Norton-in-Hales	Primitive Methodist	1835	60	40	100	—	30	36	66	—	33	—	33	46	—	46	
Stoke Heath	Primitive Methodist	1842	60	30	90	—	60	65	125	—	—	—	—	85	33	118	
Woore	Primitive Methodist	1833	80	40	120	—	40	50	90	10	—	—	10	63	10	73	AM & PM: 20-30
Great Soudley	Wesleyan Methodist	1837	60	60	120	25	25	—	50	50	40	—	90	33	50	83	Average AM: 80
Hinstock	Wesleyan Methodist	1831	22	—	22	—	27	62	89	—	—	—	—	71	—	71	
Tern Hill	Wesleyan Methodist	1843	50	14	64	40	—	—	40	—	—	—	0	40	—	40	
			2,229	2,397	4,626	1,815	1,489	587	3,891	737	754	50	1,541	3,249	842	4,091	Population: 7,419 Estimated attendance 55%
Total Anglican			2,251	3,564	5,815	2,593	1,920	570	5,083	919	901	—	1,870	4,360	941	5,301	
	Baptist		128	54	182	55	0	0	55	15	0	—	15	55	15	70	
	Congregationalist		462	220	682	102	48	113	263	43	50	—	93	195	58	253	
	Independents		193	0	193	50	120	95	265	0	50	—	50	202	50	252	
	Primitive Methodist		388	260	648	41	349	410	800	35	53	—	88	516	68	584	
	Wesleyan Methodist		247	247	494	177	92	258	527	148	131	0	279	391	148	539	
	Total non-conformist		1,418	781	2,199	425	609	876	1,910	241	284	0	525	1,359	339	1,698	
Total			3,669	4,345	8,014	3,018	2,529	1,446	6,993	1,160	1,185	50	2,395	5,719	1,280	6,999	Population: 11,582 Estimated attendance: 60%

Source: Clive D Field (editor), *Church and Chapel in Early Victorian Shropshire*, 2004, pp121-8 **Notes**: M - morning; A - afternoon; E - evening; G - general; S - scholars; T- total

not necessarily imply that they were overstated. Concerning the most striking example, St Mary's, Market Drayton, David Jenkins has written:

> The Reverend James Lee had inherited a mediaeval church, which had been converted into a Georgian preaching box with a capacity of 1,700. Thus a peak congregation of 1,000 still left plenty of empty pews. Lee was an evangelical reformer, who came from a humble background, and whose living, at £280 per annum, did not permit absentee indolence. Lee had worked hard to reform the administration of Poor Law relief, he had been responsible for the two National Schools in Drayton, he had aided the construction of the Christchurch district chapel at Little Drayton, and he conducted three Sunday services without the benefit of a curate. He deserved a good congregation.

At the time there were allegations that some returns had been exaggerated. This could happen because, as there was known to be a census, congregations could have been exhorted to make a special effort to attend. This certainly happened in the Wellington area, where the Wrockwardine Wood Primitive Methodist circuit resolved on 22 March:

> That every Local Traveling Preacher use their influence to secure as large a congregation as possible on March 30.

Or it could be falsification, as was suggested by Robert Upton, the perpetual curate of Moreton Say:

> I have seen the enumerator's return of [Tern Hill Wesleyan Methodists] & of another meeting which is held sometimes in a cottage, & I much doubt their correctness.

Indeed, it is evident that in one respect at least the enumerator altered Tern Hill's return as a consequence of what Robert Upton told him — the erection date on the form has been changed from 1837 to 1843.

The Sunday chosen for the census may not have been typical. It coincided with Mothering Sunday, which was alleged to have distorted the figures, being a day for visiting family at a distance; this was given as a factor by some people signing the forms, though not one cited in the Drayton area. The weather was wet and stormy, especially towards the evening, and there had been heavy rain in the previous week, leaving roads very muddy. This could have affected congregations, particularly in rural areas.

Robert Upton of Moreton Say commented on this too:

> As this parish consists of about 140 houses scattered over nearly 5,000 acres of land, many of them far from the church, the congregation depends much upon the weather. March 30 & the Sunday before being stormy, not more than 150 were present, but the usual number is between 200 and 300 in the morning — about 50 in the afternoon in winter and 100 in summer, exclusive of Sunday scholars.

John Parker, minister of the Independent (Congregational) chapel at Ollerton, stated:

> The attendance ... was considerably below the usual number, for the following amongst other reasons: most of the congregation live in the neighbouring villages, and owing to very heavy rains during the last few days, many were unable to attend who usually do so, the roads being very bad.

Whereas the actual general attendances on the census day were 21 in the morning and 48 in the afternoon, he estimated that the usual figures were 30 and 65 respectively.

Others gave special reasons for low attendances. William Godwin, the deacon of Market Drayton Independents, wrote:

> The number of our congregation is but half what it was 2 yrs ago. It was reduced by the conduct of the minister who left 12 months ago — since which time there has been no settled minister.

John Gladstone, rector of St Peter's, Stoke-upon-Tern, noted:

> The parish is very long & narrow, & the church inconveniently placed for the great majority of the parishioners. It is proposed to build schools at the extremities for their better accommodation.

The Baptists at Market Drayton had services every fortnight. There was no service on census day.

Total attendance

The biggest single problem in interpreting the figures is trying to assess the actual number of people who attended church or chapel that day. The real figure could lie anywhere between the maximum number at one service (assuming that all attenders at other services also attended that maximum service) and the total of the attendance at the two or three services in the day (assuming that people attended only one service during the day).

Various methods have been proposed to try to take account of this 'twicing'. There is some national evidence that non-conformists were more likely to attend more than one service in a day. The 'adjusted totals' given in the summary use the methodology proposed by Howard Burrows, as amended by Clive Field: the best attended service plus one third of worshippers at all other services in the case of non-conformists and two thirds for Anglicans. For scholars, the maximum number for any session has been taken as the total number of attendees.

As a further complication, it is also likely that some people attended one Anglican service and also a non-conformist service on the same day. Robert Upton of Moreton Say wrote that some parishioners may attended his service in the morning and the meeting house near their home in the afternoon:

> In this parish there are not 20 who can at all be termed dissenters, for all of this 20 less perhaps half a dozen attend the church services occasionally.

In this context it is interesting to note that three-quarters of non-conformist chapels had evening services, whereas only one-quarter of Anglican churches had them. For the area as a whole, attendance at Anglican services was greatest in the morning. Attendance at non-conformist services was greater in the afternoon than in the morning, and still greater in the evening.

Even more speculative would be any attempt to assess the number (or proportion) of people who regularly attended church or chapel. Many people could have missed attending on that particular Sunday because of infirmity, illness, work, absence from home, the weather or other reasons. Children who were too young for Sunday School are unlikely to have been counted, thus apparent non-attendance could be slightly overstated.

Conclusions

Using the adjusted figures, it is clear that attendance in the urban area was better than in the rural areas, and that the Church of England retained its dominant position in both:

Adjusted attendance as a % of population

	Town	Rural	Total
Anglican	52	42	46
Non-conformist	18	13	15
Non-attenders	30	45	40

Recorded attendance in the town area of Market Drayton was the highest of any of the Shropshire towns. This result is very dependent on how accurate the figures for St Mary's were. Market Drayton town also had a particularly strong Sunday School attendance.

Of the non-conformist denominations, Primitive Methodists had marginally the largest numbers and were stronger in the rural areas; Wesleyan Methodists had only slightly fewer worshippers but were stronger in the town. Most of the rest were Congregationalists or Independents. Fewer than 5% were Baptists.

Sources

Clive D Field (editor), *Church and Chapel in Early Victorian Shropshire*, University of Keele, 2004

Census of Religious Worship 1851, Detailed Table, Division VI, December 1853, 70

David Jenkins, *Market Drayton's Place as a Centre of Worship in North-East Shropshire as Revealed by the Religious Census of 1851*, privately published, 1994

Howard Burrows, *Religious Provision and Attendance in Mid-Nineteenth Century Shropshire*, MA thesis (Wolverhampton Polytechnic), 1983

The two Anglican churches which have changed least since 1851 — Little Drayton (left) and Moreton Say (above)

10 : Churches and chapels : the 1851 buildings
— and what survives today

Peter Brown

Anglican churches

All the places which had Anglican churches in 1851 still have active churches. During the second half of the 19th century most of their interiors were remodelled; some churches were completely or almost completely rebuilt. Three Anglican churches have been built on new sites in the area since 1851: St Mary's, Hales (1856); the Chapel of the Epiphany at Peplow (1879); and the Emmanuel Church in the Burgage, Market Drayton (1882), which ceased to be used in 1958 and has been demolished.

Adderley, St Peter   SJ661395
The present church basically dates from 1801, though the north transept which was built as a burial chapel for the Kilmoreys is from 1635–7 and the west tower was built in 1712. The nave is still used for worship but the rest of the church is vested in the Churches Conservation Trust; the two parts are divided by a plasterboard partition.

Ashley, St John Baptist   SJ763364
The west tower is early 17th century, the rest of the church being rebuilt in 1860–2. Many of the interior fittings were installed in about 1910.

Cheswardine, St Swithun   SJ719299
The tower and north chancel chapel are the only obvious surviving features from the mediaeval church, though the latter was demolished and rebuilt four metres east of its original position when the nave and chancel were built in 1888–9.

Child's Ercall, St Michael   SJ665250
The nave, south aisle and tower are mediaeval. The chancel, north aisle wall and windows are from 1879, though the chancel re-uses a late Norman doorway.

Hales   SJ713340
Parishioners used the small chapel built in 1833 by the Rev Alexander Buchanan, the Lord of the Manor who lived at Hales Hall. He started constructing a new church, the present St Mary's, in 1851. [I do not know whether the chapel survived.]

Hinstock, St Oswald   SJ694263
The nave is early 18th century and the tower dates from about 1800. The church was extended in 1853 with the addition of a south aisle and chancel in the 18th century style rather than fashionable gothic.

Hodnet, St Luke   SJ612286
The present south aisle was the nave of the mediaeval church. The north aisle and chapel were erected in 1846–7. In 1882 the layout was changed, the north aisle and chapel becoming the nave and chancel. The former nave was relegated to being the south aisle; its windows are Victorian. The Heber chapel had been added in 1870.

Little Drayton, Christchurch   SJ663335
Built in 1847, and substantially unchanged since.

Market Drayton, St Mary   SJ675340
Eighteenth century alterations resulted in a church which has been described as 'truly awful'. It was heavily restored 1879–84, making the interior virtually unrecognisable to someone from 1851.

Moreton Say, St Margaret   SJ630344
The walls date from the second half of the 18th century when the previous mediaeval church was encased, hence the survival of the 17th century west gallery and memorials. Overlooked by the Victorian reformers, it still appears much as it did in 1851.

Mucklestone, St Mary   SJ725373
A mediaeval tower, but the rest of the church was rebuilt in 1883.

Norton-in-Hales, St Chad   SJ703387
The tower and chancel, the latter with Jacobean panelling, are mediaeval. The church was much altered after 1851: the nave walls, baptistery and vestry date from 1864–5 and the north transept from 1872. The best feature of the church is the the tomb-chest of Sir Rowland Cotton and his wife (died 1606), the earliest surviving work of Inigo Jones, though in 1851 it was in the chancel and it is now by the western entrance.

Stoke-upon-Tern, St Peter   SJ638279
The present church was built in 1874–5, the previous one being demolished. The only survival from 1851 is the monument to Sir Reginald Corbet (died 1566) and his wife.

Woore, St Leonard
Built 1830–2 but the tiny chancel was reconstructed in 1887 and the west tower added in 1910.

Roman Catholic

In 1851 the only Roman Catholic church in the area was at Ashley. Of the congregation numbering about 100, 18 were from Ashley village and about 50 from Market Drayton.

Ashley, St James & St Mary SJ759363
Built in 1823. Pevsner described it as 'a lovely little building, so naive that you would expect to find it in some *dorp* in South Africa rather than Staffordshire ... May it not be replaced by some fashionable piece!' And it hasn't been (by 2009).

Non-conformist

Most of the 1851 non-conformist chapels had been built within the previous twenty years. There is no simple generalisation about what has happened to them since 1851. Some were replaced later in the 19th century by larger buildings. Others have suffered from dwindling congregations and have been demolished or converted to other uses.

Ashley — Congregational SJ759367
Built in 1841, the gallery being added a few years later. Has now been closed for many years but no alternative use has been found.

Eaton-upon-Tern — Primitive Methodist
A mystery: its exact location has not been ascertained.

Great Soudley — Wesleyan Methodist SJ727288
Built 1837. Now disused, but has planning permission for conversion into a holiday home.

Hinstock — Wesleyan Methodist SJ692269
Opened 1831; later porch. Still open, with weekly services.

Hookgate — Primitive Methodist SJ744353
A small chapel was erected about 1800. In 1860 it was replaced by a larger chapel nearby, itself now pleasingly converted into a house. The original chapel was made into a house with a blacksmith's workshop attached, and was demolished in 1966.

Kenstone — Primitive Methodist SJ596287
Built in 1846. Demolished in the 1990s — no sign remains.

Knighton — Primitive Methodist SJ730402
Built in 1834. It is now privately owned, but has not been converted to a house or any other alternative use.

Little Drayton, Back Lane (Salisbury Road) — Baptist
SJ671339
The congregation met on alternate Sundays in 1851, which is why there is no return for this chapel in the census of religious worship. In about 1870 this was replaced by a new chapel in Shropshire Street (now the Kingdom Hall of Jehovah's Witnesses), the former chapel becoming a schoolroom. The entrance to the police station now occupies its site.

Little Drayton, Shropshire Street
— Wesleyan Methodist SJ671340
The 1851 congregation would have known the small chapel of 1807 which was doubled in size in 1817 and a gallery added in 1842. This remained in church-related use until 1975; four years later the building was sold to the Marker Drayton Amateur Dramatic & Operatic Society, which uses it for rehearsals and storage. A new chapel was opened opposite in 1866; as a result of storm damage this has been replaced by a modern building.

Market Drayton, Church Lane
— Congregationalist SJ675340
Built 1778, a gallery being added in the 1840s. It was extended at the back in 1865-7. In 1895 the chapel was drastically altered internally by the insertion of a floor at gallery level, with the conversion of the lower part to classrooms. The chapel was closed by 1949, and is now converted to housing.

Market Drayton, Cheshire Street
— Primitive Methodist SJ674343
The chapel, built in 1825, was off Cheshire Street in an alley known as 'Ranter's Gullet'. It was 'too

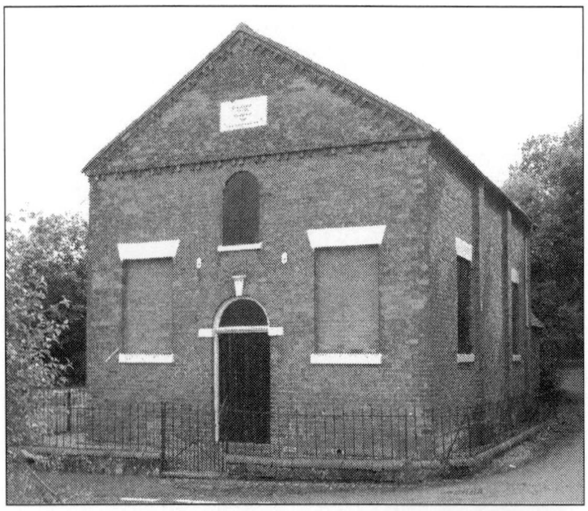
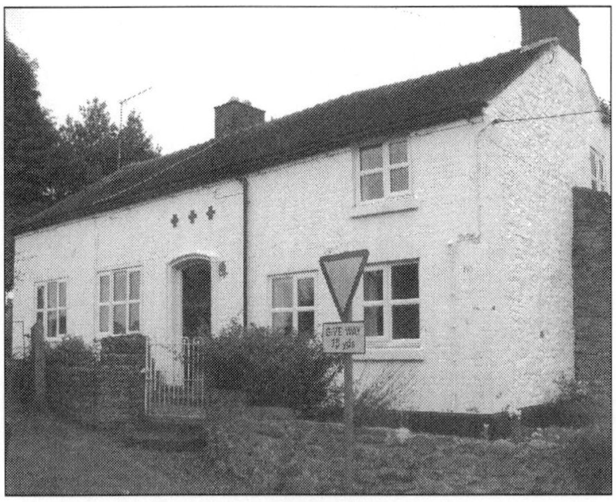
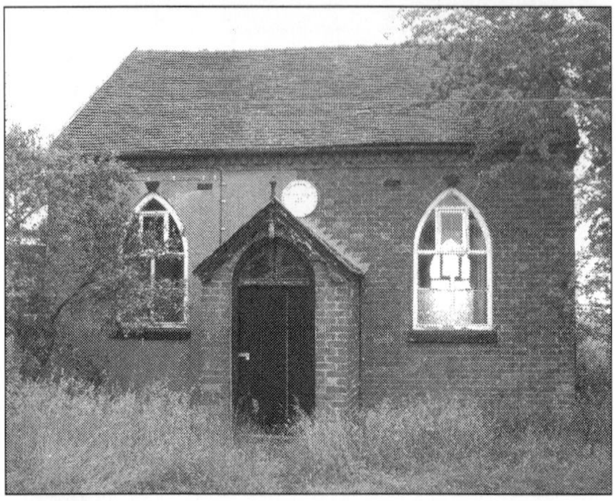
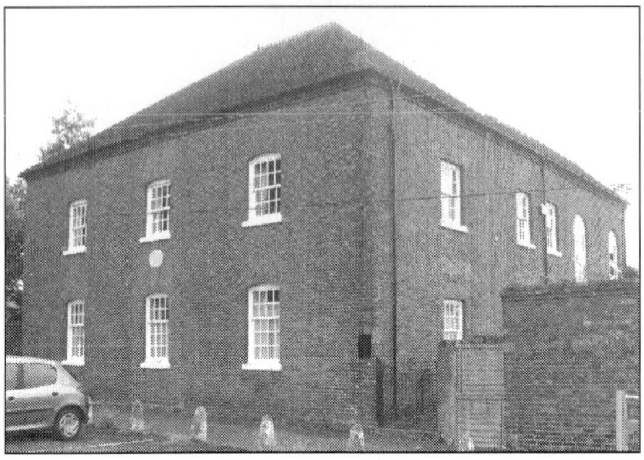
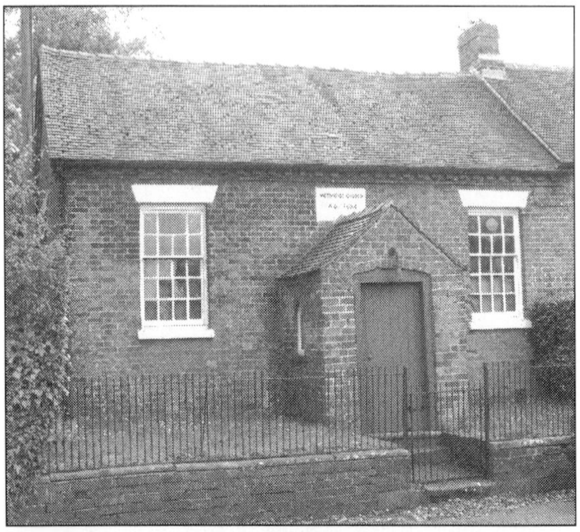
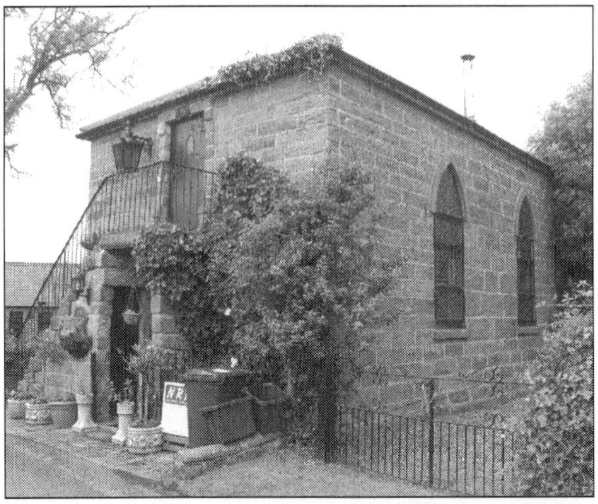
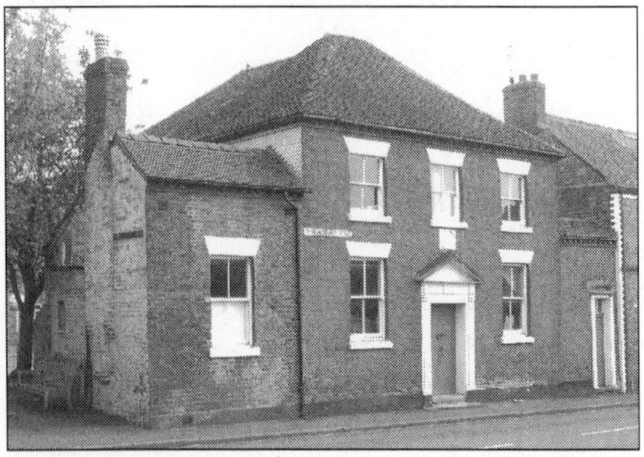
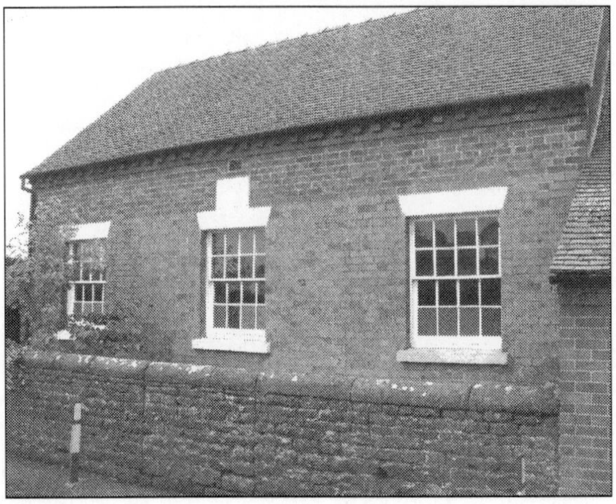

*Opposite: Disused or converted chapels
Left hand column, from top — Ashley, Great Soudley, Knighton and Little Drayton (Wesleyan)
Righthand column, from top — Norton in Hales, Market Drayton (Congregationalist), Ollerton and Stoke Heath*

small for the number of hearers who attend religious service' according to Bagshaw's 1851 directory, so was replaced by a new chapel in Frogmore Road in the 1850s — this is now the Festival Drayton Centre. No vestige remains of the original chapel.

Norton-in-Hales — Primitive Methodist   SJ702385
Built 1835. Now converted into a house.

Ollerton — Baptist
A second mystery: its exact location has not been found. The 1851 religious census return states it had seating for only 32 people, so it was very small.

Ollerton — Congregationalist   SJ650253
A small chapel, built in 1838. After becoming derelict, it has recently (2009) been carefully restored and converted into a house.

Stoke Heath — Primitive Methodist   SJ647294
Built 1841, later extended by about 7½ feet to the left (east) and heightened by about three feet. In the 1990s it was sold to the owners of the adjacent house.

Tern Hill — Wesleyan Methodist   SJ631325
Built 1843. Unsympathetically converted into a house in the 1960s or 1970s.

Wistanswick — Independent   SJ668288
The southern half was built in 1805, the identical northern half in 1860 when the twin east porches were added and the original south entrance blocked. Still in use, with services twice a month.

Wollerton — Independent
A return was made in the 1851 census of religious worship for an independent meeting in Wollerton. No date was given for the building, so it is possible that there was no purpose-built chapel. Further evidence for the absence of a chapel is that Bagshaw's 1851 directory, which usually mentions chapels, does not refer to one at Wollerton. The current chapel, still in use, dates from 1867–8.

Woore — Primitive Methodist
Built 1833. Still in use, with weekly services.

*1851 chapels still in use:
From the top — Hinstock, Wistanswick and Woore.*

Principal sources

John Leonard, *Churches of Shropshire and their Treasures*, 2004

Christopher Stell, *Nonconformist Chapels and Meeting-houses: Shropshire & Staffordshire*, 1986

John Newman & Nikolaus Pevsner, *The Buildings of England: Shropshire*, 2006

Nikolaus Pevsner, *The Buildings of England: Staffordshire*, 1974

Tony Lancaster (editor), *Ashley*, 1980

Directories: *Bagshaw* 1851 (for Shropshire); *White* 1851 (for Staffordshire)

11 : The Poor Law and the workhouse

Chris Sharp & Grace Russell

Until the early 16th century relief of the poor was generally undertaken by the Church and religious charities, along with municipal corporations and guilds, which provided hospitals and almshouses. Funds were generally insufficient, leading to paupers becoming beggars. After the dissolution of the monasteries in the 1530s the poor became the responsibility of parishes. Poor rates were levied to support the one third to one half of the population who were struggling to survive on inadequate incomes. Between 1597 and 1601 various Acts were introduced which became the foundation of the eventual New Poor Law, which came into effect in 1834.

The Drayton Poor Law Union was formed with the co-operation of fourteen parishes covering a population of nearly 14,000 people and extending across the Staffordshire and Cheshire borders. (For a map of the area, see page 13.) A Board of Guardians was assembled comprising local dignitaries and landowners, around fourteen men. They met every two weeks, had a salaried clerk who was a local solicitor, and a salaried auditor. There were initially two Medical Officers, one Relieving Officer, a Workhouse Master and a Matron.

The 'Parish Poor House' was rebuilt in 1839, on the formation of the Union, to enable it to accommodate 100 people. The sexes were segregated. The building was located in Shrewsbury Road, on the right going towards the town, and opposite what is now the Kingdom Hall of the Jehovah's Witnesses. In 1836 the windows bordering the street had been boarded up and all outer doors and walls made secure, so no person could get through or over them.

The Workhouse Master's Daybook was audited at each Guardians' meeting and all costs met. They appeared to be very diligent at getting good costings for goods and services, but did appear to maintain quality, as in the purchase of foodstuffs such as meat. A dietary regime was laid down for all inmates, and special provision made for the sick. (See Appendix B.) There appears to have been a garden to the rear of the Workhouse where fruit and vegetables were grown, and presumably the inmates benefited from this, although we could find no evidence to support it. Those who required particular care, such as lunatics, were placed in a specialist asylum and funded if their family could not afford to pay for them. It also appears that kindness was shown to cripples with extra comforts and expenses on their discharge.

Each district of one or more parishes had an appointed Medical Officer, paid for by the Board at an annual salary, depending on the number of people in their area. Looking at the minutes of the Guardians' meetings several subjects recurred, such as requests from the Education Board to provide maps for the schooling of the children, so there must have been an education system within the Workhouse. Various members of the Board were delegated specific tasks and reported back to the Board at their meetings. (For an example of the contents of one set of minutes, see Appendix C.)

The Workhouse was funded by a Poor Law Rate collected within each parish. The half year cost in 1851 of £1,344 was shared as follows:

Adderley	£60	Moreton Say	£60
Ashley	£80	Mucklestone	£90
Cheswardine	£120	Norton	£36
Childs Ercall	£100	Stoke on Tern	£100
Drayton	£328	Tittenley	£10
Hinstock	£40	Tyrley	£100
Hodnet	£150	Woore	£70

The population of the Workhouse varied seasonally with a high in Spring, recorded in 1837 at 103, and a low of 68 in the late summer of that year, reflecting the rural aspect of the community when work was more plentiful. (The 1851 census record for the workhouse is shown in Appendix A.) Women inmates did the housework, but not those with illegitimate children as it was not considered 'irksome' enough. They, like the men, were set to picking oakum. This was an unpleasant and painful task that involved unpicking tarred ropes to waterproof wooden boats with, although women were not expected to do as much as men in a day. Young people whose parents could not maintain them had apprenticeships arranged for them, although this proved to be quite expensive as clothing and transport had also to be arranged.

Expenditure was carefully audited and Outdoor Relief accounted for more than half of the total. The cost of provision for the poor gradually decreased from 4s.4d to 3s.4d per day per person, and the establishment showed a progressive reduction. There is no evidence to suggest that the treatment of the poor was made more onerous by the 1834 Act. Prior to 1834 there had been an informal executive body, which became more formal after the Act. The members of the Board of Guardians were re-elected unopposed over several years, probably as they had to be people of means as they were not salaried. Thomas Twemlow JP and Mr Crutchley, Chairman and Governor respectively for over 30 years from 1836, seem to indicate a caring dedication rather than an enjoyment of parsimonious discipline. Of course this is only a one sided view of the situation as we have no records of the inmates' thoughts. We do, however, have a written record from a young man who had been in Chell Workhouse, north of Burslem, in 1842 which may be of interest to the reader. (Extracts reproduced in Appendix E)

The Workhouse in Shrewsbury Road was closed in 1854 following a cholera outbreak, and later used as an armoury. The new Workhouse opened in Quarry Lane, previously known as Workhouse Lane, on land given for the purpose. The Board of Guardians of 1851, as shown in the minutes of their meetings, were very involved in the design and building of the property, engaging a builder from Liverpool for the purpose, after receiving several quotes. The design was adapted several times until they were satisfied that it was adequate. They appeared to be very conscientious about their duties, and to have served the local population with more kindness and consideration than was general elsewhere. This was fairly common in rural situations where they were more aware of the local need than those in large towns and cities.

We do have some records from the local press about the situation of paupers in Drayton following the period that we were researching. (See Appendix D.)

Old age in the 21st century can be lonely and depressing, but not in comparison with our Victorian forbears. If you were reasonably wealthy or had a family to support you, you could manage, but for those trying to eke out an existence there were few options, and if you were unable to work there were only private charities, Poor Law handouts or the Workhouse, where they were guaranteed a subsistence but complete loss of independence. Retirement pensions were not introduced until 1908. Many survived on very small annuities, as shown in Mrs Gaskell's 'Cranford', where the phrase 'elegant economy' made a virtue of the never to be acknowledged poverty of the Town's older ladies. For the poor, economy was even more essential — elegant or not. Those who were physically able continued to work into old age, like the men in their 70s described on the 1851 Drayton census of the poor as Agricultural Labourers. Their declining physical abilities put them at a great disadvantage when agricultural employment was scarce as it so often was in winter. Outdoor Poor Relief was both grudging and meagre, often amounting to less than 2s.6d a week, and men found it particularly difficult to claim especially if they were sound of body. Ultimately for a substantial minority of the elderly removal to the Workhouse characterised the last years of their lives.

Principal sources

David Jenkins, *A Comparison of the Administration of Poor Relief in Drayton-in-Hales, before and after the Poor Law Amendment Act of 1834*

Minutes of the Board of Guardians: Shropshire Archives

Articles in *Who Do You Think You Are?*, September and October 2008, January, February and May 2009

Appendix A

Residents in the Workhouse on census night

Joseph	Abbotts	M	81	agricultural labourer	Mary	Jones #	U	30	farmer's servant
Elizabeth	Abbotts	M	64	cook	Thomas	Jones	—	15	scholar
William	Abbotts	U	?	agricultural labourer	James	Jones	—	12	scholar
Daniel	Aconell	—	4	scholar	Sarah	Jones	—	8	scholar
James	Addison	W	45	haircloth weaver	Mary	Leech	U	17	farmer's servant
Alice	Arkinstall	U	75	charwoman	Julia	Leech	U	16	farmer's servant
James	Austin	W	68	coachman	Sarah	Leeds	W?	49	charwoman
Martha	Axon	W	73	[not stated]	Samuel	Leeds	—	13	scholar
Thomas	Axon	W	44	agricultural labourer	Ann	Leeds	—	8	scholar
Thomas	Barnett	W	73	cow man	William	Leeds	—	4	scholar
Mary	Barron	—	24	imbecile	Thomas	Lewis	W	84	agricultural labourer
Joseph	Beech	U	37	waggoner	Thomas	Llewellin	—	4	scholar
George	Bennet	W	71	herdsman	Mary	Lloyd	W	64	dairy maid
Ann	Bickerton	W	53	charwoman	Jane	Madeley	W	28	charwoman
William	Birchall	U	40	imbecile	George	Madeley	—	10	scholar
Richard	Blake	U	18	agricultural labourer	Martha	Madeley	—	8	scholar
Margaret	Braggen	W	46	imbecile	William	Madeley	—	3	—
Abraham	Brown	—	13	scholar	Charles	Murray	—	12	scholar
William	Butch	W	81	blacksmith	Elizabeth	Nickson	U	41	nurse
Sarah	Chinn	U	34	[not stated]	Hannah	Palin	—	4	scholar
Joseph	Clarke	W	47	agricultural labourer	Mary	Pintret	U	25	servant in husbandry
William	Clevose	—	10	scholar	Sarah	Pintret	—	5	scholar
John	Cliffe	U	47	ostler	Ann	Pintret	—	1	—
Thomas	Cooper	W	41	agricultural labourer	Ann	Pool	M	43	farmer's servant
John	Croft	W	66	[not stated]	Margaret	Randles	U	21	[not stated]
Sarah	Deacon	M	78	charwoman	Mary	Roden	W	44	charwoman
William	Edmonds	—	9	scholar	John	Rodgers	—	13	scholar
Sarah	Evans	M?	81	[not stated]	Joseph	Ryce	W	57	miller
John	Farnell	—	2	—	William	Ryley	—	17	scholar
Lawrence	Fletcher	U	75	papermaker	Sarah	Scott	U?	49	vessel cleaner
James	Furnival	W	70	powerloom weaver	Harriet	Scott	—	6	scholar
George	Guilford	W	78	agricultural labourer	Mary	Secker	W	58	seamstress
George	Hancock	W	78	agricultural labourer	William	Simister	M	73	agricultural labourer
Henry	Hapell	—	13	scholar	John	Stokes	—	12	scholar
Mary	Hapell	—	10	scholar	Sarah	Taylor	W	44	charwoman
John	Hewson	W	75	agricultural labourer	John	Taylor	—	6	scholar
Elizabeth	Hinstock	W	30	vessel cleaner	Hannah	Taylor	—	3	scholar
Isaac	Hinstock	—	4	scholar	George	Trevor	W	71	agricultural labourer
Benjamin	Hirchell	—	8	none – fits	Sarah	Turner	U	18	farmer's servant
Ann	Horton	U	77	charwoman	Jane	Walters	U	30	[not stated]
Mary	Ingrams	U	67	house-keeper	Thomas	Webb	—	10	scholar
Mary	Jervis #	U	46	housemaid	Martin	Wesley	—	9	[not stated]
Jane	Jervis	—	11	scholar	Henry	Wilkes	—	11	scholar
George	Jervis	—	10	scholar	Frederic	Wilkes	—	9	scholar
Henry	Jervis	—	4	scholar	Arthur	Wilkes	—	7	scholar
					Therger ?	Wilkes	—	1	—

From the way the census page was laid out, it is unlikely that the children listed with the same surname were hers.

U – unmarried   M – married   W – widow or widower

Appendix B

Diet for the able-bodied

		Sunday		Monday		Tuesday		Wednesday		Thursday		Friday		Saturday	
		m	w	m	w	m	w	m	w	m	w	m	w	m	w
Breakfast															
bread	(ozs)	6	5	6	5	6	5	6	5	6	5	6	5	6	5
porridge	(ozs)	1½	1½	1½	1½	1½	1½	1½	1½	1½	1½	1½	1½	1½	1½
Dinner															
cooked meat	(ozs)	4½	4½	–	–	4½	4½	–	–	4½	4½	–	–	–	–
boiled rice, potatoes or vegetables	(lbs)	1	–	–	–	–	–	–	–	–	–	–	–	–	–
bread	(ozs)	–	–	4	–	–	–	4	4	–	–	–	–	4	4
bread when other veg than pots used	(ozs)	4	3	–	–	4	3	–	–	4	3	–	–	–	–
soup	(pints)	–	–	1½	–	–	–	1½	1½	–	–	–	–	1½	1½
suet pudding	(ozs)	–	–	–	–	–	–	–	–	–	–	16	12	–	–
Supper															
bread	(ozs)	6	5	6	5	6	5	6	5	6	5	6	5	6	5
cheese	(ozs)	–	–	2	2	–	–	2	2	–	–	2	2	2	2
broth	(pints)	1½	1½	–	–	1½	1½	–	–	1½	1½	–	–	–	–

'The aged and infirm are, at the discretion of the Guardians, to be allowed at breakfast and supper, in lieu of the allowance of porridge, cheese and broth at these meals specified in the Table, one and a half ozs. tea, together with seven and a half ozs. butter and seven oz. sugar for a week. Children under nine years of age to be dieted at discretion, above nine and under sixteen to be allowed the same as women. Sick to be dieted as directed by the Medical Officer.' — *m* : men   *w* : women

[Minutes of the Board of Guardians, 16 February 1848]

Appendix C

Notes gleaned from the Minute Book

The Committee appeared to meet every two weeks. The books were updated at each meeting and costs met and paid for. The Master's Daybook was also authenticated at each meeting.

It was also noted that proposed marriages were recorded in the Board of Guardians records. It is thought by Shropshire Archives that this was because the Master of the Workhouse was also the local Registrar.

30th April 1851
It was recorded that William Waring Saxton was appointed Workhouse Medical Officer at £15 and District 1, the Parishes of Drayton and Tyrley at £27.

John Hopkins was appointed Medical Officer of District 2, the Parishes of Adderley, Moreton Say, Norton and Tittenley at £16.

John Allen Wormsley was re-elected Medical Officer of District 3, Hodnet, and Stoke on Tern at £25.

Edward Bayley was appointed Medical Officer of District 4, Cheswardine, Childs Ercall and Hinstock at £21.

Thomas Roberts, Member of Royal College of Surgeons, London, and Licentiate of the Apothecaries Hall, London, was appointed Medical Officer of District 5, Ashley, Mucklestone and Woore at £21.

Mr Barry's amended plans for the new Workhouse were approved.

The price of Beef and Mutton increased from four and a half pence per pound in 1851 to five pence three farthings in 1854.

Appendix D

Newspaper report of pauperism in the Drayton Union in the 1870s

On the 1st of January 1874, the number of indoor poor was 42, of outdoor 217, making the total number of paupers 259, or 1.7% of the population. The cost of maintenance for the half year ending Lady Day [25 March] was £289, and the amount granted in out relief was £354; total £643. ...

On the 1st of January 1878, there were 50 indoor poor; whilst the outdoor poor were 115; the total number of poor being 165, the proportion of papers to the population being 1.1%. During the half year ended at Lady Day 1878, £308 was spent on in-maintenance; the amount granted in out relief was £275. Taken as a whole, the above statistics are very satisfactory, and the Board of Guardians are to be complimented on the fact that, in spite of the comparatively bad times which now prevail, the total number of paupers is much smaller, and the expenditure £60 less than in 1874, when trade was brisk, and the neighbourhood in a more prosperous condition that at the present day.

Appendix E

Memories of Chell Workhouse in 1842

Extracts from *When I was a Child* by Charles Shaw, published in 1884, concerning experiences of the workhouse at Chell, near Burslem. This is included to give a different point of view from that one receives from Guardians' minutes and newspaper reports. However, Chell Workhouse was in a major conurbation; conditions in Drayton Workhouse were not necessarily comparable.

Doors were unlocked by keys and locks and bars. The family taken to a cellar, clean and bare, as grim as a prison cell. There coldly washed and re-clothed in rough clothes, then parted from parents and from the youngest, and then taken to a large room used for dining and schooling. There were hungry looking lads, with furtive glances, speaking in subdued whispers. A stern, military, cadaverous looking man was the schoolmaster. For dinner he said grace, but with no grace in anything he did. He did not join in the repast.

The food — bread, greasy water with a few lumps of something which would have made a tiger's teeth ache to break. In the afternoon, lessons. Those less able could not have got more knocks; however hard he worked a dull boy got nothing but blows. The New Poor Law was to be economical if anything, even to the least quantity of food a growing boy's stomach could do with. Supper — a hunch of bread and a jug of skilly[1] — unutterably insipid. After supper, prayers read by the saintly-looking schoolmaster, flinty and harsh.

The bedroom was a long narrow room with beds in rows on each side of the room, a long narrow passage between them. Bed clothing was scant, the beds hard enough for athletic discipline. At the end of the room was a long narrow tub. The timid boys were frightened by the cruel, with ghostly appearances, especially when seeking the tub at night. Harrowing stories of ghosts, boggarts and murders would keep the nervous awake. Every new boy had to sing a song or tell a tale the first night or be bullied, pulled out of bed and scarified by pitiless mockery. The demons, made so by the cruelty they themselves daily received, were permitted each night to hold their revels, and so long as they kept within their bedroom, were not disciplined by the Guardians or governors. That tub had to be carried downstairs every morning before breakfast by two small boys in turn.

If fever came and took off a lot of inmates, that was a double gain — the parish was relieved and Heaven was enriched. The men who were the 'Guardians of the Poor' were found in later years to be gentleman farmers and large employers, who had a remorseless faculty for 'keeping down the rates'.

[Sundays] Church in the morning, then the clergyman gave grace in the dining room, but did not dine there, gave a long homily about the 'great mercies we enjoyed, of good food provided and comfortable clothing'. On the table, a hunk of bread, a small plate with a small slice of thin, very thin cheese and jugs of water. At least the cheese was appetising. In the afternoon, an hour with their mothers in the women's room. When the bell was rung to tell of time gone, all had to leave the room at once, or have no supper.

1. Skilly: A kind of thin watery porridge, gruel or soup, commonly made from oatmeal.

12 : Friendly societies in Market Drayton during the mid-nineteenth century

Ros Wells

During the nineteenth century, many working people belonged to friendly societies. In return for weekly contributions, friendly societies provided financial and medical support during sickness and a lump sum on death to cover funeral costs. Some friendly societies also provided funds for widows and children. Most friendly societies provided companionship and conviviality through weekly or monthly meetings and occasional feasts and processions. Since they were generally run by working people for themselves, without supervision by the gentry or the clergy, friendly societies are an important example of the development of self-reliance and self-esteem among working people, alongside other 19th century organisations for working people, such as the trades unions, building societies and the co-operative movement.

Membership of friendly societies increased rapidly during the 19th century. It is estimated that in 1818 fewer than one million people were members, but by 1872 membership had grown to over four million. The extent of membership cannot be assessed accurately, because there was no legal requirement for a friendly society to register, nor to state the number of its members.

A system of registration was introduced by the Friendly Societies Act 1793. Passed at a time of social and political unrest, exacerbated by bad harvests and the fear of revolution, this Act sought to ameliorate the conditions of the poor by encouraging the virtues of self help, whilst at the same time providing a means of introducing a measure of government control. The legislation was introduced by George Rose and William Wilberforce. Although registration was voluntary, many societies did register because it provided a number of important advantages. It recognised the legal status and activities of friendly societies, which was important because at that time other working-class associations were normally regarded as subversive and their activities might be unlawful under the common law of conspiracy, even before the Combination Acts of 1799 and 1800. The Act also enabled registered friendly societies to sue to recover misappropriated funds and gave exemption from certain stamp duties. On registration, the magistrates had the right to alter the rules of a friendly society, thus introducing a measure of control.

The importance of friendly societies is reflected in the fact that between 1793 and 1875 some twenty different pieces of legislation were enacted to assist them and to control their activities. One important measure, enacted in 1817, was to allow them to deposit funds in savings banks at favourable rates of interest.

Friendly societies registered themselves by depositing their rules at the local Quarter Sessions. In 1855 the work of registration and record keeping was transferred to the Registrar of Friendly Societies. In 2001 the Office of the Registrar of Friendly Societies was disbanded and its business was transferred to the Financial Services Authority. All surviving records kept by the Registrar were transferred to the Public Record Office at Kew.

A further difficulty in tracing the history of friendly societies is that they were not the only organisations which were allowed to register under the Friendly Societies Act 1793. Other types of society such as building societies (which were regarded with suspicion at first, but were given their own code of legislation in 1836) and co-operative societies (which could register under the friendly society legislation until given their own code in 1852) were also allowed to register in order to take advantage of the legal benefits of registration, even where they did not provide the sort of sickness and death benefits provided by friendly societies. For example, the Cattle Club which was established in Market Drayton in 1849 might possibly have been an insurance group or a co-operative society, rather than a true friendly society. Trades unions often registered as friendly societies until 1824, when the courts put an end to this practice; they did not gain their own code of legislation until 1871.

Friendly societies in Market Drayton

Friendly societies in the Market Drayton area would have registered at the Quarter Sessions in Shrewsbury. The table overleaf has been compiled from two registration books held at Shropshire Archives which record the names of those friendly societies in Market Drayton which registered between 1793 and 1855. In some instances the meeting place of the society was also recorded.

Although the Quarter Sessions lists are helpful, they do not provide a completely accurate picture. This is partly because some societies existed for many

Friendly societies in the Market Drayton area registered at Shropshire Quarter Sessions

Register no	Name of friendly society and meeting place	Date of registration
52	Senior Club	8 October 1793
53	Junior Club	8 October 1793
162	Union Friendly Society, Market Drayton	13 January 1807
179	Union Female Friendly Society, Market Drayton	13 July 1813
195	Provident Annuity Society Phoenix Inn, Market Drayton	23 April 1816
202	Female Friendly Society Independent Chapel, Market Drayton	14 January 1817
232	Wake Monday Society, Market Drayton	10 July 1826
242	Established Church Female Friendly Society Mr Thomas Drury's Shropshire Street, Market Drayton	1827
244	New Union Dividend Society, Market Drayton	14 January 1828
260	Market Drayton Old Midsummer Union Friendly Society	27 January 1832
307	Market Drayton Becher Provident Society	21 June 1841
396	Cattle Club Corbet Arms Inn	27 September 1849
416	Red Stick Club Star Inn, Staffordshire Street, Market Drayton	9 October 1851
473	Court Lord Hill, No 1785 Ancient Order of Foresters King's Arms Inn, Market Drayton	1 April 1853
484	Market Drayton District Branch, Independent Order of Oddfellows, Manchester Unity	11 November 1853
471	Loyal Philanthropic Lodge, No 900, Independent Order of Oddfellows, Manchester Unity Corbet Arms Hotel	9 February 1854

years before registration. Some friendly societies chose not to register due to suspicion of government interference. The local groups affiliated to large friendly societies were not permitted to register until 1850. For example, the Ancient Order of Foresters Court Lord Hill No. 1785, which met at the King's Arms, Market Drayton, was registered in 1853, but we know from the archives of the Ancient Order of Foresters that it was in fact founded earlier, in 1844. Similarly, the Quarter Sessions records show that the Philanthropic Lodge of the Oddfellows was not registered until 1854, but we know that it was already established in Market Drayton before that time, because Market Drayton Museum has a copy of an invitation (reproduced on page 54) inviting the local gentry to a tea party to be held by the Lodge on 16 August 1847 to raise funds for widows and orphans.

The wide variety of friendly societies in Market Drayton during the nineteenth century is typical of that time. Some of the societies would have been quite small and would have been restricted to people living in Market Drayton. Others were local groups affiliated to a large and prestigious national organisation, such as the Ancient Order of Foresters or the Oddfellows. Unlike the trades unions, the friendly societies did not normally restrict themselves to people in a specific trade. For example, William Gladstone was a member of the Ancient Order of Shepherds.

Friendly societies' aims

The main purpose of a friendly society was to provide financial benefits and medical services during sickness and to pay for a funeral when a member died. It must be remembered that there was no social security at that time. Without insurance to cover times of unemployment through sickness, a family might have to go into the workhouse. The workhouse was dreaded because the husband and wife would be split up and the children separated from their parents. These miseries were often compounded by poor living conditions, inadequate food and a harsh regime of work. A further worry created by poverty was that if someone in the family died and there was no money for a funeral, the body would be buried in an unmarked pauper's grave, or the body might be dissected by medical students.

During the 18th century, many working people tried to guard against the misfortunes of poverty by joining a box club, which would normally operate from a public house. Public houses often served as a house of call where workmen looking for work would congregate. The box club would be run by the workmen themselves who would collect small weekly contributions for sickness and funeral payments. Many of these early box clubs survived into the 19th century, when they generally became known as friendly societies.

A serious difficulty faced by the box clubs and early friendly societies was that at first there was no reliable actuarial knowledge to enable them to fix realistic amounts for contributions and benefits, nor to fix a minimum age on entry. If the contributions were too low or the financial entitlements too high, the society would inevitably become insolvent. Female friendly societies suffered from financial difficulty due to the frequent pregnancies of younger members, which was one of the reasons for the decline of female friendly societies. Another problem for women was the lack of suitable premises for meetings: female friendly societies were increasingly criticised in the mid-Victorian era for meeting in ale houses.

A further difficulty in the early days was the lack of education amongst working people, which meant that small local societies often found it difficult to find members who were capable of keeping proper records and accounts. A danger for the members was that if the society collapsed, they would lose all the money which they had paid over the years, and if by that time they were middle-aged they would probably be too old to be eligible to enter another friendly society.

The result of these various difficulties was that during the 19th century many working people were increasingly drawn to their local branch of a large national friendly society, such as the Ancient Order of Foresters or the Oddfellows. These larger organisations kept proper records relating to contributions and benefits, patterns of sickness and statistics of death, in order to build up increasingly accurate actuarial principles.

Market Drayton Becher Provident Society

Although all friendly societies enabled the working classes to make provision for sickness and death, the ethos of a parochial friendly society, such as the Market Drayton Becher Provident Society, would have been quite different from that of other friendly societies. The parochial friendly societies were established and controlled by the local gentry and clergy, who were honorary members and who provided financial support without taking any of the financial benefits available to the ordinary members. They had a paternalistic desire to help the poor, whilst at the same time endeavouring to reduce the poor rates and to establish a measure of control and supervision.

The Reverend Thomas Becher (1770–1848) was a clergyman and magistrate in Nottinghamshire who was influential in promoting his views relating to friendly societies and workhouses.[1] He was an active supporter of the Southwell Friendly Society, publishing three books between 1824 and 1826 setting out details of its constitution and of its tables of contributions and allowances, based on the actuarial principles of the day. These books became the model for many friendly societies which were established by magistrates and clergymen.

The Market Drayton Becher Provident Society was established in 1841 and covered Market Drayton and the surrounding villages: Tyrley; Hodnet; Stoke; Cheswardine; Hinstock and Child's Ercall; Adderley and Moreton Say; Norton, Mucklestone and Woore; and Ashley.

Its rules provided that the society was to be run by a board of trustees and directors. The trustees had to be substantial householders. The trustees at its inception in 1841 were drawn from the local gentry, such as magistrates, clergyman, lawyers and substantial landowners:

    Sir Rowland Hill Bart MP (also Patron)
    Sir John Chetwode Bart MP (also Patron)
    Peter Broughton Esq
    Colonel Dawes CB
    The Rev A H Buchanan
    Henry Justice Esq
    Egerton W Harding Esq
    The Rev Willoughby Crewe
    The Rev S H Macaulay
    William Church Norcop Esq
    Purney Sillitoe Esq
    Thomas Twemlow Esq
    John E Wilson Esq
    Thomas Hudson Esq

The directors were to be chosen from honorary members who were required to contribute towards the funds of the society and were excluded from taking any benefits.

The rule book makes it clear that the society's activities were to be restricted to the business of providing for medical services, sick pay and funeral benefits. The rules state sternly that the objects of the society were 'to encourage among the working classes, habits of industry, forethought and self support, by affording them the best means of support in old age and sickness' and that there would be 'no waste of time and no expense at meetings'. The business of the society was managed in monthly meetings of the directors, held in the National School Room, and so the traditional friendly society customs of feasts, processions and drinking in public houses were firmly excluded. Benefits could be withheld due to drunkenness.

Contributions and benefits

The contributions which were paid by friendly society members and the benefits to which they were entitled varied considerably from one society to another. Even the national friendly societies did not standardise their scales of contributions and benefits until the late nineteenth century. Unfortunately the tables of contributions for many friendly societies have not survived as it was the policy of the Registrar of Friendly Societies to destroy the manuscript returns of friendly societies every ten years.

However, the tables of contributions and benefits for members of the Market Drayton Becher Provident Society have survived.[2] Here the members could choose between four different classes of sickness benefit: 5s, 7s.6d, 10s or 12s.6d per week. Members could choose between funeral benefits amounting to £4, £6 or £10. The benefits included a pension of 2s weekly after the age of 65 years. The Market Drayton Becher Provident Society was open to women members, but made no separate provision for widows and children. The entrance fee payable by new members varied from 1s for the lowest class of benefits up to 2s.6d for the highest class. The monthly contributions varied according to the age of the member as well as to the level of benefits secured. Extracts from the Society's table of contributions and benefits for the lowest class are set out below.

These contributions were similar to those typically paid by members of other friendly societies in the mid-nineteenth century. Whilst the records of the contributions for the Ancient Order of Foresters in Market Drayton have not survived, other Foresters Courts typically required a contribution of 2s.3d a month to secure sick pay of 14s a week for 26 weeks, followed by 7s a week for a further 26 weeks and thereafter 5s a week. These contributions normally covered £12 funeral benefits on the death of a member and £6 on the death of his wife. The entrance fee for new members was normally about 15s.

Medical assistance

In addition to financial assistance, many of the larger friendly societies provided medical services to members during ill-health. Local societies affiliated to the large national friendly societies such as the Ancient Order of Foresters and the Oddfellows would have employed local doctors who were contracted to provide medical attendance and medicine to their members at so much per head per year. By the 1860s the *Lancet* and the *British Medical Journal* were urging doctors to insist on a minimum payment of 5s per head per year instead of the 2s.6d which was the normal friendly society rate. Despite conflicts over the rates of pay, the system of providing medical assistance at a rate per head per annum was later followed in the provisions for medical treatment in the National Insurance Act 1911. The affiliated societies usually made arrangements for a member to be treated by the doctor employed by another lodge if the member had become sick whilst travelling away from home to look for work. (Under the Friendly Societies Act 1793, a member of a friendly society could obtain a certificate to enable him to travel to look for work; this exempted him from the poor law provisions of legal settlement under which workers might be returned to their home parish.)

The rules of the Market Drayton Becher

Market Drayton Becher Provident Society : contributions and benefits

Age next birthday	Assurance of 5/- weekly in sickness	Assurance of 2/- weekly after 65 years	Assurance of £4 on death	Total monthly contributions
15 years	4d	2½d	2d	8½d
25 years	5d	4½d	2½d	1s
35 years	6½d	9d	3d	1s.6½d
45 years	8½d	1s.7½d	4d	2s.8d
50 years	11d	2s.7½d	5d	3s.11d

Provident Society provided for the employment of a surgeon and a physician. Its members were entitled to medical attendance and medicines if certified to be too ill to work. Its rules also provided for a medical examination for prospective members, stating that no one could join the society without a certificate of good health signed by the physician or surgeon. Smaller societies could not afford to employ doctors and instead appointed stewards from amongst their own members to visit the sick to ascertain whether they were entitled to claim sick pay from the society. The advantage of proper medical attendance for members of the largest societies was an important factor in the gradual decline of the smaller friendly societies.

Social activities

As stated earlier, although all friendly societies enabled the working classes to make provision for sickness and death, the ethos of a parochial society, such as the Market Drayton Becher Provident Society, would have been quite different from that of other friendly societies. Its constitution ensured good organisation and financial stability. However, many working people were more attracted by friendly societies which provided not just health and funeral insurance, but which also provided its members with social life and a welcome degree of independence from the gentry and the clergy. Many friendly societies met monthly at a public house and paid rent to the publican in the form of an agreed amount of ale to be purchased by the members at the weekly meetings. In addition there would normally be a yearly feast, which might be preceded by a procession and followed by sports or a fair.

Most of the larger friendly societies had special badges and sashes to be worn at regular meetings and had elaborate banners to be used in processions.[3] Many friendly societies had secret rituals, including passwords and secret initiation ceremonies. Rituals and ceremonies would have fostered a sense of belonging amongst the members.

Moreover, the responsibility of organising the society and managing its funds would have increased the self-esteem and self-confidence of the elected officers of the society. The sums involved are surprisingly large: Bagshaw's Directory of 1851 records that a total of £1,706.2s.6d was deposited in the Market Drayton Savings Bank by ten friendly societies.

The secrecy surrounding the rituals and ceremonies of friendly societies tended to fuel suspicions that they were subversive organisations threatening to overturn the hierarchical structure of society. There was also a continuing criticism that friendly societies wasted their funds on feasts, processions and drinking in public houses. However, by the mid-19th century, friendly societies had become more acceptable to the influential classes. This was partly due to the fact that the work of all friendly societies in alleviating poverty became more clearly distinguished from the activities of other working class organisations, such as trades unions, which were perceived to be dangerously subversive. The widening gap between trades unions and friendly societies is indicated by legislation in 1846, which declared that the law forbidding seditious meetings not did not apply to friendly society meetings, and by legislation in 1850, which recognised the sociable use by friendly societies of passwords, secret signs and regalia. Such matters continued to be illegal if practised by trade unions.

During the mid-19th century, many friendly societies took steps to emphasise their loyalty to the Crown and to stress that they had no desire to subvert established orders in society. An example is provided by the printed invitation (reproduced overleaf) by the Oddfellows to a tea-party on 16 August 1847 to raise funds for the widows and children of its members. It states that it is addressed to 'all those who by their station in society will add weight to our humble endeavours' and declares that 'we are associated for no other purpose than our mutual benefit and the general good: being solemnly pledged to revere the established religion of our country, to promote virtue, suppress vice and to inculcate principles of morality and peace'.

Another example which illustrates the desire of the friendly societies to be regarded as respectable and loyal organisations is *The Odd-Fellows' Harmonia*. This is a collection of songs and poems to be used at Oddfellows' meetings. It begins with 'God Save the Queen' and includes 'God Bless the Prince of Wales' and 'Rule Britannia'. The book also contains anti-Methodist songs and songs deriding the Pope, which were presumably included to demonstrate loyalty to the established Church of England. A number of loyal toasts are printed at the back of the book, including toasts to Queen Victoria, the Prince and Princess of Wales, the government and the armed forces. The songs also include many references to good fellowship amongst working people, which might not have been quite so acceptable to the influential classes. An example of a song which extols the virtues of Oddfellowship is set out in full in the Appendix.

The respectability of friendly societies was later reinforced when their resources enabled them to acquire premises, so that they no longer had to meet in public houses. An example of such a meeting

Philanthropic Lodge, Odd Fellows, M.U.
Market Drayton, August 1847.

The Members of this Order beg respectfully to inform you, that there will be a Public Tea Meeting in the National School-Room, Market Drayton, on Monday, the 16th instant, when the favor of your presence and patronage is earnestly solicited.

We are aware that, by those unacquainted with our principles, we are deemed a "secret Body"; nevertheless it is an easy matter to see the good effected by the fraternity of Odd Fellows, which stands pre-eminent in an age remarkable for its philanthropy. On the present occasion we invite all those who, by their station in society, will add weight to our humble endeavors to establish a Fund for the benefit of the **Widows and Orphans** connected with this Lodge; and we take this opportunity to declare publicly that we are associated for no other purpose than our mutual benefit and the general good: being solemnly pledged to revere the established religion of our county, to promote virtue, suppress vice, and to inculcate principles of morality and peace, we confidently appeal to your best feelings on our behalf; and are assured that as you would lend your influence to promote the public good, so will you afford us your countenance and encouragement; and by so doing to assist us in working out the great principles we profess—"Friendship, Love, and Truth."

I have the honor to be,

For the Members of the Philanthropic Lodge,

Your very obedient Servant,

John Allen, N.G.

Furnival, Printer, Drayton.

Fraternity of Odd Fellows: invitation to a 'public tea meeting' called to establish a fund for widows and orphans, 16 August 1847. (Drayton Museum)

hall is the Oddfellows Hall in Ashley.[4] The availability of meeting halls enabled many friendly societies to make important contributions to the provision of adult education. During the 1840s and 1850s many friendly societies provided evening classes and lectures. This was sometimes in conjunction with a local Mechanics Institute or with other organisations, such as Mutual Improvement Societies. In Birmingham the Oddfellows built an Institute in 1845 with a lecture hall and a library containing 1,500 volumes.

The Oddfellows and the Ancient Order of Foresters also provided members with journals. In addition to giving friendly societies' news these also contained poetry, short stories and essays on a variety of topics including history and natural science. A further illustration that friendly societies were becoming accepted as respectable organisations is provided by the fact that they were allocated special visiting days to visit the Great Exhibition in 1851.

Later developments

The later history of the friendly societies is beyond the scope of this essay. However it is important to note that many friendly societies suffered financial difficulties towards the end of the 19th century. This was partly due to the drain on their resources caused by rising unemployment and a gradual increase in life-expectancy. Other factors included the rising popularity of commercial insurance companies. Furthermore, the social activities provided by the friendly societies could not later compete with the more widespread availability of popular entertainment, such as music halls and pleasure gardens; whilst this development did not directly affect friendly societies in country areas like Market Drayton, the decline in friendly society membership in the large cities contributed to the general reduction of friendly society funds.

During the late 19th century, it was gradually becoming accepted that health services and provision for the unemployed and the elderly were beyond the resources of private endeavour, though at first the friendly societies opposed proposals for state intervention. The modern welfare state was gradually introduced by a series of measures including the Old Age Pensions Act 1908, the National Insurance Act 1911, the National Insurance Act 1946 and the National Health Service Act 1946. The friendly societies continued to have a role in administering the state sickness benefit scheme introduced by the National Insurance Act 1911, but they lost this role under the National Insurance Act 1946. In 1945, there were approximately 18,000 friendly societies with a total membership of about 18 million.

Nowadays there are over 50 friendly societies. Their main functions centre on private insurance schemes, serving the interests of all sections of society, managing funds totalling £18 billion on behalf of 6 million people.

Ashley Oddfellows Hall

Notes and references

The help of the staff at Shropshire Archives and of Roger Logan, the Hon Director and Secretary of the Foresters Heritage Trust in Southampton, is gratefully acknowledged.

Bibliography

- J M Baernreither, *English Associations of Working Men*, translated by A Taylor, Swan Sonnenschein & Co, 1891
- S Cordery, *British Friendly Societies* 1750–1914, Palgrave Macmillan, 2003
- W R Cornish and G de N Clark, *Law and Society in England 1750–1950*, Sweet & Maxwell, 1989
- P H J H Gosden, *The Friendly Societies in England*, Manchester University Press, 1961
- Charles Hardwick (ed), *The Odd-Fellows' Harmonia, Songs and Recitations for the Use of the Order*, George Walker, 1866
- Ralph Parker, Aaron Green and others, *Truth versus Falsehood*, H Roberts, 1854

1. The Rev J T Becher founded a workhouse at Southwell in 1808 and a workhouse at Upton in 1824 which later became the workhouse of the Southwell Union (Thurgarton Hundred Incorporation), Nottinghamshire. The latter is now owned by the National Trust. The layout of the Southwell workhouses, in which men and women were housed in separate wings, even if they were married couples, and children were separated from their parents, provided the model for approximately 700 workhouses built across the country. In 1824 he published a treatise *The Anti-pauper System* which included the plans of his workhouses and set out his views on the importance of making the workhouse regime as difficult as possible for the 'idle, profligate, immoral and improvident'. He worked closely with George Nicholls at Southwell in Nottinghamshire during the 1820s and their work resulted in a reduction of the parish's poor rates by more than 50 per cent. The success of the Southwell regime was influential in shaping the harsh regime of the 1834 Poor Law. George Nicholls later became one of the three Poor Law Commissioners under the 1834 Poor Law.

2. The surviving records of the Market Drayton Becher Provident Society are kept at the Shropshire Archives.

3. A number of museums have collections of friendly society ceremonial regalia, together with cups, medals and certificates; examples include the Foresters' Heritage Trust at Southampton, the People's History Museum in Manchester and the Museum of Rural Life at Reading University.

4. The Oddfellows Hall in Ashley is now owned by the Roman Catholic Church.

Appendix

The Oddfellows Hymn

The Oddfellows Hymn set out below is reproduced from *The Odd-Fellows' Harmonia, Songs and Recitations for the Use of the Order*. The rhythm of the verse indicates that it was probably sung to tune of God Save the Queen.

God save our wide spread band
Long may our Order stand,
Cov'ring the earth!
Its aims are glorious;
Make it victorious;
Send, to rule over us,
True men of worth!

Oh Lord! our Order bless,
That strives to make sin less,
That helps the weak.
If any there should be
Who is our enemy,
We pray he soon may see
What's right we seek.

Upon Odd-Fellows all,
Thick Let thy favours fall –
Like manna drop.
Widows and orphans guard,
Make them Thy special ward;
Thee let them aye regard
As their best prop!

With us let virtue reign;
Teach us how to restrain
Our passions strong.
Our tongues let reason guide;
Free us from envy, pride,
And everything beside
That's mean and wrong.

Let no dissensions rise;
Beware such enemies,
Odd-Fellows all!
Unguarded words beware,
Bespeak each brother fair;
Sharp words, fruits bitter bear –
Their sap is gall.

Let smitten brothers find
Their prosperous brethren kind,
In deed and word!
Lord! when Fortune flees us,
When afflictions seize us,
O succour and ease us,
Be with us, Lord!

The earth's ends fraternise!
O make the whole world prize
Odd-fellowship!
Let us be temperate;
Each frugal in his state;
The low shall then be great,
While high fools slip!

God save our world-spread band,
Firm may our Order stand,
Ne'er may it fall!
Its aims are glorious,
Make it victorious;
Ever watch over us,
God save us all.

13 : Education

Meriel Blower

In 1851, there was no compulsory education. For the children of the poor or the labouring classes the choice was limited. They received a rudimentary education, if they received any at all, from charity schools, Sunday schools, 'Dame' schools or the 'National' or 'British' schools. It was calculated that in 1810 only one third of the children of the poor had any education at all.

In 1808 two Quakers, Joseph Fox and William Allen, adapted and expanded Joseph Lancaster's monitorial school and formed 'The British System for the Education of the Labouring and Manufacturing Classes of Society of Every Religious Persuasion'. In 1814 the title was shortened, mercifully, to the British and Foreign Schools. In 1811, the SPCK formed 'The National Society for the Education of the Poor in the Principles of the Established Church throughout England and Wales'. Its aim was heroic: nothing less than shouldering the whole burden of national education. Each society was able to channel nationally raised charitable funding to provide grants for schools and paced each other in the establishment of schools, usually in the rapidly expanding industrial towns. However, the National Society had the advantages of a diocesan and parish organisation, a formidable number of charity schools to start with and the support of the Archbishop of Canterbury. By 1814 it had 230 schools and 40,284 scholars. These advantages were to be resented by the Nonconformists for decades and played a large part in delaying the provision of a national education system.

There is evidence that in some places the British School, with its Nonconformist background, became the school favoured by the Nonconformist lower middle class while the Anglican National School became the school for the working class.

In 1833 there was a Royal Commission on Education and a census was taken of schools in England. As a result the Government made its first education grant. The princely sum of £20,000 was to be shared between the two societies.

'Dame' schools, run by private individuals, usually in their own home, were often no more than child-minding establishments with a little teaching of reading thrown in. Some villages had schools founded and funded by philanthropic landowners. Sunday Schools, organised by churches and chapels took place, of course, on a Sunday and concentrated on reading and the catechism.

The middle classes, the small landowners, farmers, tradesmen and small manufacturers relied on other forms of education. They were usually ambitious for their children but they also appreciated value for money. They were anxious for their children to acquire an education but an education that would fit them for their future station in life. Girls needed the accomplishments that would help them to obtain a husband — if possible from a slightly higher social stratum than their own — and to run a household. Boys needed the knowledge and skills to help them in commercial, agricultural or industrial futures.

Many middle-class children in the early years of the 19th century would have begun their education in either a 'Dame' school, run by either a man or, more usually, a woman with no formal training and usually held in their own home. Alternatively they could have attended one of the small 'day and boarding' schools which educated a small number of young boys and older girls. Such schools, often kept by pairs of unmarried sisters in the family home they had inherited, were very common in small market towns and larger villages and often the boarders came from no further afield than the area which were served by the local carriers' cart network. Mrs Tulliver, the wife of a miller, in the novel 'The Mill on the Floss' was anxious that her beloved son Tom should not be sent to school beyond the reach of the carrier's cart. She wanted to be able to do his washing and send him parcels of food in case they did not let him have extra helpings!

Boys would have progressed from this type of school at about the age of nine to either one of the Endowed Free Grammar Schools which were a feature of many market and county towns or to a 'Commercial' Academy, set up as a private venture to provide instruction in the non-classical subjects which were outside the curriculum of the Grammar schools. A third route for boys was to become a pupil of a local clergyman to receive a classical education in preparation for going to Oxford or Cambridge — just as Tom Tulliver did in the 'Mill on the Floss'.

Education for middle-class girls followed a different pattern. Even by 1864 there were only thirteen endowed schools for the secondary education of girls in the entire country. The vast majority of middle-class girls were therefore educated by staying on at one of the small 'day or boarding' schools or by attending the more expensive, exclusively boarding establishments in the larger market or county towns. A third choice for girls was a governess, a cheaper alternative to boarding school if there were several daughters in the family.

The children of the aristocracy were educated at home by governesses or tutors or, if they were boys, in the nine great 'public' schools. If they were girls, they remained at home with a governess or went to one of the exclusive or extremely expensive 'Ladies' Seminaries' in London, Bath, Brighton and similar places.

The Drayton picture

The 'Abstract of Education' returns shows that in 1833 Market Drayton, with a town population of 3,882, had seventeen daily schools. The Grammar School had 16 male pupils and the National School 66 pupils. Another school (established 1825) had 44 male and two female pupils (this was probably Joseph Collier's school in the Horsemarket — now called Cheshire Street). Another school (established 1832) had 18 female pupils, and 43 males were educated in another. The remaining twelve schools educated 99 male and 110 female pupils between them. The total school population in 1833 was 398 — 247 boys and 151 girls.

School Log Books and admission registers were not mandatory until 1863 so there are few records surviving from 1851.

Schools for the working classes

As a result of the 1833 inquiry a grant was made to the National School Society; a new building was erected at Mount Lane in 1835. The school taught 340 children from the age of six upwards. They were taught on the monitorial system, which involved the teacher imparting the knowledge to be taught to a small group of older pupils who, in turn, passed it on to small groups of younger children. This took place in one large room with the teacher overseeing the room from a raised platform. The teacher in 1851 was William Scott.

A second National School was started in Little Drayton in 1851, part of the improvements to this poorer end of the town brought about by the enclosure of Little Drayton Common. The first teachers were Charles Miles and Judith Ford. John Bill's Charity, founded in the eighteenth century for the purpose of a charity school in Little Drayton, was one of the charities used to fund the school. The school buildings, situated opposite Christchurch, consisted of two blocks, one slightly larger than the other. The boys were educated separately from the girls and the infants.

There were National Schools, of various sizes, in most of the surrounding villages. In 1851 Child's Ercall had a National School for 104 pupils. The 23 year old schoolmaster, George Hewitt, was born in Middlesex. The schoolmistress, Elizabeth Higgins, was 38 years old, born in Drayton and recorded as unmarried with two sons! Hinstock also had a National School for 75 pupils. The master was also 23, born in Baschurch, Shropshire, and lodging with Thomas Winstanley, who was described as a butler.

At Cheswardine the National School appears to have been for boys only as there was also a much older school for girls dating from at least 1738. In 1851 the teacher of the Girls' school was Maria Green, the daughter of the local wheelwright. The National School at Woore had been built in 1832 by voluntary subscriptions and a grant from the National Society. In 1851 100 children attended, 15 being educated free; the master was paid £15 per annum. The children of cottagers paid 1d a week but farmers' children paid more.

There were also National Schools at Norton-in-Hales, Hodnet and Ashley.

The Grammar School

Drayton had an endowed Grammar School that had been founded in the reign of Queen Mary by Sir Rowland Hill and which had had a chequered history. Between 1800 and 1851 it had been through various vicissitudes. The buildings had fallen into disrepair; its numbers had dropped to two pupils, one the headmaster's son, and the headmaster, the vicar, the Rev James Lee had been the subject of a scurrilous anonymous attack in the local papers. There is evidence, from a letter, that part of the Grammar School premises were, in 1844, used as a girls' day school by Mrs or Miss Watts, a relative of Isaac Watts who was the master at the National School.

After Rev James Lee resigned the post was advertised and a new headmaster, Dr Cooke from Cannock Endowed School was appointed and was urged to provide a wider curriculum. He was allowed to charge for boarders. The 1851 census shows that Dr Cooke had been successful in attracting more pupils to the Grammar School. A 19-year-old assistant had been appointed and there were seventeen boarders, the eldest aged 14 and the youngest 6. Six pupils were born in the villages surrounding Drayton and eight from the area of South Staffordshire from where Dr Cooke had come in 1848.

The report of the National Survey of Grammar Schools in 1869, known as the Taunton Commission, reveals something of the conditions at the Grammar School. There was *no* entrance requirement, not even the ability to read; the boarders had four meals a day — with meat only once; they slept two to a bed in the master's house, rose at 6am and went to bed at 9pm. There was no playground and even the day-boys were expected to go to the parish church twice on Sundays. School work began and ended with prayers and the cane was very rarely used.

Sunday schools

Most Sunday schools taught some writing as well as reading but there was considerable reliance on the Catechism and Bible study. It has been said that attendance at Sunday School was equivalent to one day's school.

The 1851 Census of Religious Worship recorded the number of those attending Sunday Schools at the various churches and chapels in the area. Figures were given for both morning and afternoon sessions but for most Anglican churches the numbers at each were remarkably similar and probably involved the same children. (See page 34 for the detailed figures.)

In Market Drayton, St Mary's, the main Anglican church, had 200 children listed for both morning and afternoon sessions and the other Anglican church, Christchurch in Little Drayton, had 100. The Wesleyan Methodists declared 98 in the morning and 91 in the afternoon, and Independents or Congregationalists 25 in the morning and 40 in the afternoon. The Primitive Methodists stated that they usually had 90 at a morning session, though no Sunday school was actually held on the day of the census. The small Baptist congregation had no Sunday School.

All the Anglican churches in the rural Shropshire hinterland had Sunday schools in the morning and afternoon, as did the little chapel of ease at Peplow; Norton-in-Hales had an evening Sunday school too. The Non-conformist congregations with Sunday schools were: the Primitive Methodists at Eaton-upon-Tern, Stoke Heath and Woore; the Wesleyan Methodists at Great Soudley; the Independents or Congregationalists at Ollerton and Wistanswick; and the Baptists at Ollerton.

The numbers of attendees are given in the table in Chapter 9, 'Census of Religious Worship'. The Rev Robert Upton, the Anglican vicar at Upton Say, cast doubt in his return on the accuracy of the numbers provided by the Non-conformists.

Small boarding schools

The 1851 census showed four schools in Market Drayton town taking boarders. The Misses Arkinstall's in Shropshire St (now Cotton's House) had nine boarders — mostly older girls. The school run by Mrs Bratton in 1841 in the Beast Market (now Great Hales Street) was in 1851 run by her daughter with the help of two assistants, one of whom had been a pupil in 1841. Of the eleven boarders, five were boys aged 7 or 8, the remainder girls aged 9–15. The number of assistants suggests that the school also catered for day pupils. Wigley's Commercial School had ten boarders aged 9–15. Two of these were born locally, the remainder in Staffordshire and Cheshire. It is probable that more locally born boys attended the school as day pupils as it was described as 'day and boarding' in Slater's Directory. Two other Wigley brothers ran Commercial Schools in other towns in Shropshire. The school run by Mrs Elcock, the widow of a paper maker, was listed as day and boarding but had only one boarder, a nephew.

In Cheswardine there is an example of the type of tutoring establishment often kept by clergymen. Charles Miller, the curate of Cheswardine, had ten boarding pupils, all boys, aged between 6 and 15. He employed Frances Jones, a 26 year old London born woman, described as a teacher. Seven of his pupils were born locally, one in London, one in Oxford and one, aged 6, in Bangalore, India.

Two other boarding establishments were found in the villages. At The Hooks near Hinstock, Elizabeth Hand with the help of her sister and niece educated eight boarders — five girls and three boys. At New Street Lane, in the Styche and Woodlands area of Moreton Say parish, Sarah Tillery, the mother of an agricultural labourer, taught nine boarders between the ages of four and ten with the help of her granddaughter.

There was a small private day school at Woodseaves run by Mrs Elizabeth Palmer and a small boarding school at Adderley in which Hester Burrows is described as a 'governess'.

Other day schools mentioned in the directories are those run by George Eaton who went on later to keep a china and fancy goods shop, one run by Mary Whittingham, the Liverpool born wife of a carpenter and another by Mary Bratton aged 62 and born in Market Drayton.

The transient nature of some of these private venture establishments is illustrated by the case of Susan Ray. She is listed in Robson's Directory of 1840 as running a day school. She appears in the 1851 census, aged 40, as a teacher; in 1861 she is listed as a laundress; in 1871 she 'keeps a mangle and a school' (in that order) and in 1881 she derives her 'income from mangling'.

Attendance

Attendance was not compulsory at any school and although many parents recognised its value, some resented or could not afford the charges. Poorer parents also relied on the earnings, however small, of quite young children. In the villages this was usually in service for a girl. They would go to their first job, their 'petty place', usually for a year at the age of twelve before they applied for a more permanent place further afield. Boys often left school even earlier to work on the local farms. There are several rural areas, namely Hodnet Heath, Moreton Wood and Norton Heath, where the majority of children were not in school. This may be because they lived some distance from the school or because the areas were the abode of 'squatters.'

In the town, particularly in Little Drayton, the poorer end of town, only 63% of the children aged between 5 and 12 were described as 'scholar', 20% were not in school and 16% were in employment. There were a number of younger children described as 'scholar': one was a 2-year-old, four were aged 3, and 10 aged 4. There were also several 13-year-olds. Of those in employment, the majority were employed in the horsehair weaving industry. The two youngest, aged 6 and 7, were employed as 'tiers' and the slightly older children as 'servers'. There was also an apprentice chimney sweep aged 10, a 7-year-old 'sales' girl and two girls described as 'servant' aged 10 and 12. There were three other apprentices to a tailor, a baker and a grocer.

There were twenty-one children between 5 and 12 listed in the workhouse and all were in education except one who had fits.

Despite education not being compulsory, there is evidence that, even in the poorest areas, well over half the children received some sort of education.

Sources

- 1851 Census
- 1851 Religious Census
- Abstract of Education returns 1833
- National Survey of Grammar Schools (Taunton Commission') 1869
- Directories: *Bagshaw* 1851; *Slater* 1850; *Robson* 1840
- June R Lewis, *The Village School*, 1989
- Michael Drake (editor), *Applied Historical Studies*, 1973

14 : Libraries and the Book Society

Peter Brown

Libraries

During the 19th century the benefits of spreading knowledge wider became to be realised — it could improve productivity and hence prosperity, and would not merely increase discontent as had been feared.

In the 1840s a news room was established 'by the gentry and tradesmen of the town' at Mrs Lydia Barnett's in High Street, whose premises were described in the directory as 'spirit vaults'. The Secretary was Thomas Bennion (who had the same role in the Book Society) and the annual subscription in 1846 was one guinea, which would have been high enough to have excluded most working men.

In 1850 the Market Drayton Society for the Acquirement of Useful Knowledge was established. Premises in Beast Market (now known as Great Hales Street) accommodated a library 'with many valuable and standard works'. A report in the *Shrewsbury Chronicle* stated that this was a circulating library — that is, the books could be borrowed. The Society also had a reading room 'furnished with the principal London and provincial journals and the most popular periodicals of the day'.

One could become an honorary member for life by giving books to the value of ten guineas. The annual subscription for an honorary member was one guinea, and this entitled the member to exclusive use of the reading room from 9am until 6pm. Ordinary members, paying eight shillings a year, could use it after these hours, as well as attend the lectures and classes. The President, Thomas Twemlow, was a founder member of the Market Drayton Book Society; the Treasurer, W Manley Wilkinson, was another member. The first Secretary was William Crutchley, the master of the workhouse.

The 1861 and 1868 directories record a Mechanics Institute with a library in Great Hales Street — this is presumably the same as the Society for the Acquirement of Useful Knowledge. However, it ceased in 1871, the rules being said to be too stringent for the working man. The main demand from the working classes was probably for relaxation and entertainment, rather than self-improvement.

Bennion's, Market Drayton's leading bookseller and printer in the 19th century, had a circulating library by 1851. By 1863 this was provided in association with Mudie's. Established in 1842, by the end of the 19th century Mudie's was one of the two main London-based circulating libraries (the other being W H Smith & Son's) servicing various outlets round the country. Circulating libraries tended to specialise in novels, particularly for female readers.

The County library service was not established until the 1920s.

The Market Drayton Book Society

Book societies were and are a way of sharing the cost of books, and of encountering books that one would not normally choose to read. They were and are also social institutions, bringing together like-minded people.

The Market Drayton Book Society was founded in 1814. Membership was limited in number and was by invitation only. There was an annual subscription of one guinea. Each member nominated a book (or books) with a cost of up to twice the amount of the subscription. The book then circulated amongst the members, starting with the person who nominated it. After a period the books were sold by auction at the Annual Meeting, with the first bid being deemed to be half the original price, and being made by the person who had ordered that book. (The Society is still thriving, operating under rules almost unchanged except that the subscription is now £10 a year, and the book may cost two & a half times the subscription.)

Its initial membership of thirty comprised three main groups: the gentry, the clergy and the attorneys. Other groups were the professional men and the influential gentlemen living in the town. Unusually for book societies at that date, women were admitted as members.

Socially, the membership was virtually unchanged in 1851. The total number of members had dropped to twenty-two, but the proportion of women had increased to 32% from 13% in 1814.

Of the rural gentry, two founder members remained: Thomas Twemlow of Peatswood and John Tayleur of Buntingsdale. Others in 1851 were Peter Broughton of Tunstall Hall and Rev Alexander Buchanan of Hales Hall. Wives of rural gentry were present in significant numbers: Mrs Tayleur of Buntingsdale (possibly John Tayleur's daughter-in-law), Mrs Justice of Hinstock Hall, Mrs Corbet of Adderley Hall, and Mrs Buchanan of Hales

Hall. Mrs Frances Tayleur of The Fields was presumably a relative of the Buntingsdale Tayleurs. These rural gentry were linked in another way: of the seven Justices of the Peace who lived within six miles of Market Drayton, four were either members of the Society or their wives were.

As well as the Rev Buchanan, who had no parish responsibilities, there were two other clergy, the rectors of Hodnet and of Stoke-on-Tern. Mrs Johnson was the wife of the vicar of Childs Ercall.

The third surviving founder member was the lawyer Creswell Pigott. Other members in 1851 who were lawyers were Loxdale Warren, William Manley Wilkinson and Mr Onions. Dr John Hopkins was a surgeon. A number of other town residents were described in the 1851 directory as 'gentleman': George Andrews, Captain John Horner and John Wilson. The last-named, who lived at The Grove was the son of the civil engineering contractor who, amongst many other works, built the canal through Market Drayton.

The one mystery is Mrs Hill of Almington, who appears neither in the 1851 directory nor in the census.

No member lived in Little Drayton though its total population was virtually the same as its twin; this is evidence of the extent to which the power and wealth of the urban community was concentrated in Market Drayton. It is also significant that no member was 'in trade', either manufacturing or retail.

The 1814 rules stated that the choice of books be confined to 'belle lettres and miscellaneous subjects'. 'Belle lettres' meant works of literary criticism or philosophical reflection or, in a more general sense, serious literature which is neither poetry nor fiction. 'Miscellaneous subjects' could mean whatever one wanted it to mean! At some point in the 19th century the rules were changed from positive to negative — instead of what members could buy, a list of what they couldn't. The following were deemed inadmissible: books on professional subjects, books of prints, reprints of old works, periodical publications, and any book which has been published for more than four years.

The list of books purchased by the Society in 1851 is given in the Appendix below. This probably gives a fair impression of what the educated person was reading for pleasure in 1851.

Appendix

Books purchased in 1851
'Single quotes': author's or publisher's comments   "Double quotes": reviews etc

Fiction

Frederick Richard Chichester, Earl of Belfast — *Two Generations; or Birth, Parentage and Education*

A novel concerned with social problems, written when the author was about 20. He died at 25.

Anna Harriet Drury — *Eastbury*

Novel from a writer with high Anglican principles. "Excellently well told, not particularly brilliant, perhaps, but yet a capital thing to put in one's pocket on the eve of starting for the country" — *The Southern Literary Messenger.*

Elizabeth Cleghorn Gaskell — *The Moorland Cottage*

Short story.

Nathaniel Hawthorne — *The Scarlet Letter; and The House of The Seven Gables*

Novels: *The Scarlet Letter* deals with the consequences of adultery and guilt in Puritan New England; *The House of the Seven Gables* is a tale of a family curse and inherited sin. This book was inexpensive because the author was American, hence his works were not subject to copyright.

Charles Kingsley — *Yeast: A Problem*

Reprinted from *Fraser's Magazine*. The first novel Kingsley started, described by him as 'a parable'. 'I have given my readers Yeast; if they be what I take them for, they will be able to bake with it themselves.' The author explains in the Preface: 'The young men and women of our day are fast parting from their parents and each other; the more thoughtful are either wandering toward Rome, toward sheer materialism, or toward an unchristian and unphilosophic spiritualist Epicurism which, in my eyes, is the worst evil spirit of the three, precisely because it looks at first sight most like an angel of light.'

Hon Caroline Sheridan Norton — *Stuart of Dunleath: A Story of the Present Time*

"What, therefore, middle-aged, sobered readers may call too harrowing to the feelings, too distressing in its truthfulness of description, in the touching tale of 'Stuart of Dunleath', will be precisely the charm to attract the younger part of the community." — *New Monthly Magazine.*

Margaret Oliphant — *Merkland: A story of Scottish Life*

"A quietly portrayed domestic environment, and a temptation to over-ingenious melodramatic plotting"

Catherine Sinclair — *Lord and Lady Harcourt; or, Country Hospitalities*

"Exceedingly attractive, skilfully-contrived, well-balanced story ... sportive, pointed, sparkling" — *Bentley's Miscellany*

Eliot Warburton — *Reginald Hastings; or, A Tale of the Troubles in 164–*

'A fictitious autobiography' "As an historical romancist, Mr. Warburton takes a first wrangler's rank" — *Literary Gazette*

Poetry

Agnes Strickland — *Historic Scenes and Poetic Fancies*

'My earliest literary productions, written when the vivid feelings and perceptions of a young heart and ardent imagination found their natural language in poetry.'

Non-fiction

Hans Christian Anderson — *Pictures of Sweden*

A travel book.

John Hervey Ashworth — *The Saxon in Ireland; or, The Rambles of an Englishman in search of a Settlement in the West of Ireland*

'The design of the work is to direct the attention of persons looking out either for investments or for new settlements, to the vast capabilities of the Sister Island, and to induce such to visit it, and to judge for themselves.'

William Henry Bartlett — *Forty Days in the Desert, on the Track of the Israelites, Or, A Journey from Cairo, by Wady Feiran, to Mount Sinai and Petra*

Bartlett was a widely-travelled artist and illustrator of his own and other authors' books.

William Henry Bartlett — *Walks about the City and Environs of Jerusalem*

With 20 large engravings, and other illustrations and maps in the text.

Richard Bentley — *Romantic Biography of the Age of Elizabeth; or, Sketches of Life from the Bye-ways of History*

Thomas Beven — *Sand and Canvas: A Narrative of Adventures in Egypt; with a Sojourn amongst the Artists in Rome*

L F C — *Extracts from the Diary of a Living Physician*

'Startling truths told by everyday experience.'

Edward S Creasy — *Memoirs of Eminent Etonians*

'With notices of the early history of Eton College.'

? Thomas Davies — *Life of Curran*

Biography of John Philpot Curran, lawyer and Master of the Rolls in Ireland. There was another book of the same name by William Henry Curran which had been published in 1819.

Henry Benjamin Edwardes — *Year in Punjaub*

"Stirred up by a rebellion of the Sikhs, it was the courage and skill of Lieut Edwardes that saved the British power in the Punjaub" — *American Cyclopaedia*, 1874.

Mary Anne Everett Green — *Lives of the Princesses of England from the Norman Conquest*

This is volume 3, covering the period from Edward I to Edward IV.

Captain Albert H A Hervey — *Ten Years in India; or, The Life of a Young Officer*

'... intended to instruct, advise and amuse' young officers intending to join the army in India.

William Howitt — *The Year-Book of the Country; or, The Field, the Forest and the Fireside*

'The result of many years delightful enjoyment of the country, and observation of life and scenery'

William Hurton — *A Voyage from Leith to Lapland; or, Pictures of Scandinavia in 1850*

'The Lapps [now called Sami] are exceedingly phlegmatic in temperament, greedy, avaricious, suspicious, very indolent and filthy, and by no means celebrated for strict adherence to truth ... The countenance of most of the Lapps present a combination of stolidity, low cunning and obstinacy, so as to be decidedly repulsive.'

James Finlay Weir Johnston — *Notes on North America: Agricultural, Economical and Social*

Canada and the United States. Johnson was Professor of Chemistry at Durham University.

Thomas Babington Macaulay — *The History of England from the Accession of James the Second*

This is the first two of the five volumes eventually published.

Alexander Mackay — *The Western World; or, Travels in the United States in 1846–47*

'Exhibiting them in their latest development, social, political and industrial, including a chapter on California.'

Edward Newman (editor) — *The Letters of Rusticus on the Natural History of Godalming*

Extracted from the *Magazine of Natural History*, the *Entomological Magazine*, and *The Entomologist*.

Mary Roberts — *Annals of my Village: Being a Calendar of Nature for Every Month of the Year*

First published anonymously in 1831. The village is Painswick in Gloucestershire.

Arthur Penrhyn Stanley — *Memoir of Bishop Stanley*

Brief biography of the late Bishop of Norwich by his son.

Rev Charles Benjamin Tayler — *Thankfulness: A Narrative Comprising Passages from the Diary of the Rev Allan Temple*

Dedicated to Viscountess Hill of Hawkstone. 'The gracefulness and happiness of a thankful Christian. ... Whether the history of the Revd. Allan Temple is that of a real individual, I do not intend to disclose. The truth and reality of the principles, and the experience of the person whom I introduce to my readers, must not, however, be doubted.'

Rev Charles Benjamin Tayler — *Earnestness: The Sequel to Thankfulness*

'The volume, though it be considered as a work of fiction, is not so, either as to persons or circumstances; no portion of it is personal, no locality could be pointed out, but almost every part is drawn from observation.'

William Cooke Taylor (editor) — *The Benedictine Brethren of Glendalough*

'Anecdotes respecting persons and events omitted during ordinary histories.'

Rev George Townsend — *Journal of a Tour of Italy in 1850, with an Account of an Interview with the Pope at the Vatican*

'Submission to Rome is the worst evil that can befall the Church of God.'

Rev Francis Trench — *Scotland: Its Faith and its Features; or, A Visit to Blair Athol*

Eight of the twenty-three chapters are about religion, the rest is a travel diary.

Wilhelmina, Baroness Von Beck — *Personal Adventures during the Late War of Independence in Hungary*

Presented as fact but actually invented by a woman who had entered Birmingham society purporting to be a Baroness with a history. Eventually found out, she was arrested and died in the court anteroom. She certainly knew Hungary, and may have been an Austrian Government spy. The case was discussed in Parliament on 28 May 1852.

Samuel Warren — *The Lily and the Bee: An Apologue of the Crystal Palace*

'In the nature of a Lyrical Soliloquy, supposed to be the meditative utterance of a devout Poet-Philosopher, musing under the guidance of an attendant Spirit, first by day, and then by night, in the Crystal Palace of 1851.' Two examples of contemporary critical opinion: "The Milton of the Exhibition"; "The raving of a madman in the Crystal Palace".

Annie Webb — *The Martyrs of Carthage: or, The Christian converts, a tale of the times of old*

'The author of this work begs to state that her primary hope ... is that the narrative may be permitted, in some small degree, promote the glory of God, and further the cause of Christ, by calling the attention of her readers to the power of Christian faith, and the beauty of Christian practice, as both were exemplified and set forth in the lives and deaths of the primitive believers.' Based on fact, but some 'trifling' enhancements 'for the sake of increasing the interest of the narrative'.

15 : Crime and justice

Peter Brown

The courts

Indictable offences were those where the guilt or innocence had to be decided by a jury; the judge (in Assizes) or bench of magistrates (at Quarter Sessions) decided the sentence. They included all serious offences, but also some minor ones, such as theft of small value items.

The Assizes were held in Shrewsbury twice a year, presided over by a circuit judge. It dealt with cases where the death penalty could be imposed, those where a first offender could be transported for life, and certain specific offences including blasphemy, perjury, forgery, bigamy, libel and bribery. Examples of cases dealt with by the Assizes were murder, burglary, rape, robberies with violence and assault accompanied by wounding.

The Quarter Sessions, also held in Shrewsbury, dealt with the other indictable offences — indeed it tried the majority of them. These were the less serious but more common offences such as larceny (theft), housebreaking, assault, robbery without serious violence and fraud. The Quarter Sessions had two other principal roles: dealing with appeals against the decisions of local magistrates, and various administrative affairs. In effect, although comprising the magistrates in the county and therefore unelected, it was the precursor of the county council. Its administrative duties included prisons, asylums, and highways and bridges. Much time was taken up with supervision of the Poor Law system, in particular, determining which parish was responsible for people who were destitute.

Summary offences, that is, ones which were not indictable offences, were dealt with by two or three magistrates sitting without a jury at Petty Sessions. On the whole, summary offences were the less serious ones such as common assaults, breaches of the peace, drunk and disorderly conduct, vagrancy, breaches of the licensing laws, and breaches of the local by-laws. The distinction between indictable and summary was not absolute: if the local magistrates felt that a case was particularly serious or they felt their sentencing powers were inadequate, they could commit the accused for trial at the Assizes or Quarter Sessions. For example, in examining people who had participated in the same fight or riot, they could choose to commit some of them for trial on indictment (because they felt their offences were more serious) and try others summarily.

In the late 1840s there were a number of significant reforms in the system of local justice. The Petty Sessions Act 1849 formally recognised the Petty Sessions, that is the grouping of magistrates into divisions within each county, although the process had been commonly used for some time as a matter of convenience. The Indictable Offences Act 1848 required magistrates to see whether there was adequate evidence for committal to trial at Assizes or Quarter Sessions for the more serious offences, thus all cases started in the Petty Sessions. The Act also transferred responsibility for dealing with certain less serious offences from the higher courts to the Petty Sessions. The Summary Jurisdiction Act 1848 was a lengthy enactment dealing with the judicial work of magistrates out of sessions, including pre-trial procedures, summonses, warrants and bail. It also required cases to be heard openly in places to which the public had access; this led to the construction of courts and courtrooms.

At Drayton, the Petty Sessions met on the last Saturday of each month. Its jurisdiction included all the parishes near Market Drayton, so crossed the county boundary. The indictable offences were referred to the Assizes or Quarter Sessions in Shropshire and Staffordshire, depending where the alleged crime was committed.

At Market Drayton the Petty Sessions were held in the Corbet Hotel until 1850. A court room was then provided in the Cheshire Street offices of the Clerk to the Magistrates, Joseph Loxdale Warren. (It was also used by the Society for the Acquirement of Useful Knowledge for lectures and by the Harmonic Society for musical evenings.)

The magistrates

The magistrates were appointed by the Crown on the recommendation of the Lord Lieutenant, who in Shropshire was the 2nd Duke of Sutherland from 1839 to 1845 and Viscount Hill from 1845 until 1875. They were unpaid, though the responsibilities were extensive and, if done conscientiously, very time-consuming..

The nine magistrates in the Drayton division were all members of the local gentry, three of them resident in Staffordshire. None lived in the urban area, which was typical of shire counties outside the boroughs at this date. The nine were (*Stafford-shire):

Richard Corbet	Adderley Hall
The Rt Hon Viscount Lord Hill	Hawkstone Park
Henry Justice	Hinstock Hall
Algernon Charles Heber Percy	Hodnet Hall
Thomas Twemlow	Peatswood *
Purney Sillitoe	Pell Wall *
George Staveley Hill	Peplow Hall
Peter Broughton	Tunstall Hall
Rev Alexander Buchanan	Hales Hall *

The most active amongst them appear to have been Henry Justice, Peter Broughton and Purney Sillitoe. Henry Justice was also a member of the County Constables' Committee.

The Court Leet

The Court Leet which, together with the Vestry, was the traditional form of local self-government, was virtually obsolete by 1851; indeed it did not meet between 1853 and 1862. Its remaining functions principally concerned aspects of the administration of the market, such as weights & measures and cleanliness. When revived in 1863 it seemed little more than an excuse for a social get-together with a good meal.

Detection and prosecution

Traditionally, communities had to be self-policing. Parish constables were elected but were largely ineffective.

In 1826 an Act was passed which permitted the payment of the costs of prosecution and of witnesses' expenses in all criminal cases, and the Quarter Sessions were obliged to publish their scale of allowances. The following extracts are from the scale of payments to parish constables which applied in Shropshire in 1851:

For each summons served	1d
For each warrant executed	2d
For appearing before the magistrates, per case	1d
For each day when on duty	not more than 5d
For going to serve a summons or execute a warrant	4d per mile
If travelling by railway	Third class fare

'Such fees and allowances to be paid by ... such party ... as the magistrates ... shall direct.'

If no such direction was made, these costs would be met from the county rate.

Sometimes a local solicitor would organise the action against criminals, as when in 1828 Charles Warren's efforts brought about the arrest and successful prosecution of Joseph Pugh, Robert Cox and Ann Harris for the murder of James Harrison. A particular problem was where the offender was an outsider who had absconded — following them was difficult, time-consuming and could be expensive.

Even after the establishment of the Shropshire police force in 1840, many prosecutions were brought by other parties. The statistics for people charged before the magistrates in Shropshire (excluding the Boroughs of Shrewsbury, Oswestry and Ludlow) in 1851 were:

	Brought by the constabulary	Brought by other persons	Total
Felony	327	63	390
Misdemeanour	911	2,266	3,177
Drunkenness	218	8	226
Vagrancy	148	32	180
	1,604	2,369	3,973

Felonies were generally the more serious offences; apart from some specific statutory exceptions, all felonies were indictable offences. The reverse was not true, as some indictable offences were categorised as misdemeanours. The real significance of the distinction between felonies and misdemeanours lay in the details of the processes — the means that could be employed in making an arrest, the payment of expenses for prosecution, and the rights of counsel to address the jury, for example. (The distinction was abolished by the Criminal Law Act 1967.)

Of the 3,973 cases, 643 (16%) were discharged, 70 (2%) were dropped because the complainant refused to prosecute, 258 (6%) were committed for trial by a higher court, and 3,002 (76%) were summarily convicted.

The total number of prosecutions for the County as a whole would imply about 250 in the Drayton area for the year, after making some allowance for the higher incidence of crime in the East Shropshire industrial area.

The figures show that only 40% of cases were brought by the constabulary, the majority being brought by other persons. Most of the latter were in respect of misdemeanours. The conviction rate was similar, regardless of who had brought the case.

Groups of concerned people took joint action, forming associations for the prosecution of felons. They rewarded anyone, including tollgate-keepers, if they helped to secure convictions for offences against any members or their property. The rewards varied from ten shillings to ten guineas. They also met the costs of pursuing and arresting criminals and of the attendance of witnesses at the trials.

Two such associations were formed in Market Drayton early in the 19th century. The one based on the Cheshire Cheese Inn gave the highest rewards in connection with breaking and entering at night and conviction of any capital offence. The other association, the name of which is not known, included the lawyers Thomas Dicken and J L

Warren, William Furber (the steward of the Lord of the Manor) and Peter Broughton of Tunstall Hall. Its members were expected to ride a hundred miles or more in pursuit of thieves. There were also various rural associations, including one at Almington and one at Tern Hill. Further associations were created in the 1820s and 1830s, including the Tradesmen's at the Lamb Inn and one at Adderley.

By 1851, following the creation of a police force funded from the rates, the surviving associations had become little more than dining clubs.

Policing

Shropshire was one of the first rural counties to establish a police force when in 1840 approval was given to the appointment of a Chief Constable, six Superintendents and forty-three constables; by 1851 the number of constables had been increased to 50. The Chief Constable was Dawson Mayne (1799–1872) who later in 1840 married Elizabeth Hewitt, a cousin of Viscount Rowland Hill of Hawkstone Hall.

Clothing was provided by the constabulary. The tenders for constables' clothing which were accepted in 1851 had the following prices, which indicates the quality was reasonable:

Great coat	£1.14s.0d
Coat	£1.10s.0d
Trousers	18s.0d
Hat	8s.6d
Boots, pair	8s.9d
Shoes, pair	7s.9d

There were six Divisions — the Boroughs of Shrewsbury, Oswestry, Bridgnorth and Ludlow then had their own police forces — the Market Drayton area coming within the Second Division, later known as the Whitchurch Division. The Superintendent appointed to this Division was Richard James (from Chalford, Gloucestershire, though born in Shropshire), and he was required to reside at Hodnet; he was still at Marchamley, a township in Hodnet parish, in 1851. Two years later he was promoted to Deputy Chief Constable.

The 1851 census recorded three Shropshire police officers in addition to Richard James, two in Market Drayton and one in Hinstock. In the Staffordshire part of the Drayton area there were two police officers: one in Aston and one in Ashley.

In 1848 the Constabulary Committee considered requests for a police constable to be stationed at Woore because it was so far from the nearest town and close to the Staffordshire and Cheshire borders. The committee was sympathetic, agreeing that it would be desirable to have one there, but they considered that the present number in the Force was not enough to allow it. However, the Chief Constable added that he had directed the constables stationed at Market Drayton to visit Woore as often as their other duties would permit.

The lock-ups and police house

The Drayton police had the use of a lock-up in Cheshire Street. In the summer of 1849 a prisoner attempted to escape, though Edward Haycock, the County Surveyor who investigated, considered that he must have had outside help. He reported:

> To warm and ventilate the cells there is a small fireplace. The opening is only one foot wide and over it is placed a stone two feet long and one foot thick. This stone was removed and a portion of brickwork forming the flue, but strong iron bars being placed across the same prevented any possible escape that way.

He concluded that he was not aware how the building could be made stronger, but recommended that it would be very advisable to have a small dwelling attached to it for a constable. His report continued:

> There is a court in front of the present building bounded by a brick wall. I propose forming it into an entrance kitchen and scullery, and above two rooms, one to be used at times as a cell, and the other a bed room. I also propose warming and ventilating the cells from the back of the fireplace … . The cells will have light from above near the new building. The expense of this addition will be £200.

The new dwelling was completed by 1850, after a short delay caused by a dispute with the building's neighbour concerning light. The 1851 census recorded William Hemming as the police officer living there.

The lock-up had been supervised by a civilian keeper who was paid £13 a year on the basis that the average number of prisoner-nights had been 117 in the four years 1843–6. In the county constabulary area this had been exceeded only by Wellington with 312 and Whitchurch with 131. However, in 1849 the magistrates recommended that instead one of the Force should be put in charge of the lock-up. Presumably building the dwelling made this possible despite a resolution of the Committee only two years earlier, 'That it will be very undesirable to have any more policemen appointed as lock-up house keepers'.

Hodnet also had a lock-up but the average number of prisoner-nights was only 13, less than a quarter of the number incarcerated at the next most little used lock-up, at Cleobury Mortimer. An agreement was made in 1852 with Mr Heber Percy to lease the building for 21 years for 1 shilling a year; before that the arrangement had been informal. The keeper was paid £6.10s a year. Unsurprisingly, the Committee discussed closure in 1852 (despite having only recently formally agreed its lease); they decided to continue with it, but the following year reduced the payment to the keeper to one shilling for every day that there was a prisoner there.

Crime in the Drayton area

At first sight it seems that there was remarkably little crime in the Market Drayton area in 1851. However, meaningful crime statistics, even today, are particularly elusive. Perceptions of crime usually greatly exceed the reality. The most reliable statistics are those based on peoples' personal experiences of crime, as opposed to their impressions gained from the media. However, nobody recorded such data in the mid 19th century, so no comparison can be made between then and now.

Nor were there figures kept for reported crime. Even if there had been, they would probably be unreliable. The victims or witnesses of crime do not report it to the police if they feel there is no chance of the perpetrator being apprehended and convicted. On the other hand, the police themselves may record detected offences which are trivial if it is thought (possibly unconsciously) that it helps justify their own existence or effectiveness.

When trying to compare crime statistics over long periods, it must be borne in mind that legislation has created new offences, and technology — particularly motor vehicles — has created new opportunities.

Then, as now, there were certain regular offenders. For example, the following were nicknames of regular offenders brought before the courts at Market Drayton in the mid 19th century:

Richard Biggs	alias	Cinder Dick
William Farnell	alias	The Bear
Eliza Farnell	alias	The She Bear
Arthur Hudson	alias	Sergeant Shee
Mrs Neild	alias	Frying Pan

Court cases

The only firm sources of information we have about details of crimes in the Drayton area in 1851 are the newspaper reports of trials in the Assizes and Quarter Sessions and, for less serious crimes, the Petty Sessions, and the Calendar of Prisoners at Shrewsbury Assizes.

The *Shropshire Conservative* and *Shrewsbury Chronicle* have reports of just 13 cases involving 25 defendants in the Market Drayton area in the whole of 1851. Of course not all cases were reported; indeed on one occasion it was stated, 'A number of other cases of drunkenness, breach of peace, and bastardy, were afterwards disposed of, but none of any particular interest.'

These press reports have been supplemented with the records of prisoners convicted at the Assizes.

Unsurprisingly, the largest group is theft:
- John Hunt (24), attorney's clerk, found guilty of having forged an order for the payment of money, with intent to defraud the Independent Order of Odd Fellows — sentenced to one year imprisonment with hard labour. (As he was in a position of trust, it is surprising that the sentence was not greater. This case was not reported in the newspaper, despite being one of the most serious of the year.)
- Thomas Simon was found not guilty of stealing four fowls from Thomas Peplow of Moreton Saye. (A couple of weeks later there was an editorial comment deploring this verdict.)
- Ann Lloyd (72) was found guilty of stealing a pair of boots from Hannah Jones of Hodnet — sentenced to one month's imprisonment.
- Thomas Hoben, Thomas Fullwood and Thomas Henry were found guilty of stealing two hats at Drayton, the property of Thomas Brown, and of unlawful riot and assault — sentenced to 10 weeks, 8 weeks and 14 weeks imprisonment respectively.
- Elizabeth Dod found guilty of stealing four loaves of bread and one pound of bacon belonging to John Moore at Drayton — sentenced to three week's imprisonment with hard labour.
- George Bratton pleaded guilty at the Assizes to breaking into the dwelling house of George Butler at Childs Ercall and stealing two loaves of bread, two cheeses and other articles — sentenced to be transported for fifteen years.
- Thomas Griffiths (21), labourer 'who can neither read nor write', found guilty of stealing two and a half pounds of veal and one table fork belonging to Thomas Churton Goodhall of Drayton-in-Hales — sentenced to fourteen days imprisonment with hard labour.
- Maria Baggaley (20), servant ('can read & write imperfectly') was found guilty of stealing a pair of stockings, a pair of shoes and other articles belonging to Thomas Churton Goodall of Drayton-in-Hales — sentenced to three months imprisonment. (As these last two cases share the same victim, one wonders whether there is a link between them.)
- John Efford (10), umbrella maker ('can read') found guilty of stealing six shillings and six pence from Mary Ann Taylor of Drayton-in-Hales — sentenced to seven years transportation.
- The case of Andrew Gower v John Wright, 'for taking toll for a corn drill, claiming to be exempt', was adjourned. (There is no report of it being heard at a later Crown Court session.)

There were a couple of cases of poaching or trespass:

- 'At the Magistrates' Office, John Beech, Edward Cooper and John Gee were charged with night poaching on land belonging to Sir J N L Chetwode, Bart, at Oakley, and were committed to the Assizes. Edward Cooper and John Gee were also charged with night poaching with others, to the number of four, in the month of May last, on the land of Peter Broughton, in the Staffordshire part of Drayton-in-Hales, and they were also committed to take their trial on that charge.' (Peter Broughton was an active local magistrate. The outcome was not mentioned.)
- William Reynolds and Richard Montford were found guilty of trespassing in pursuit of game at Adderley — they were each fined 10s.6d plus 9s.6d costs.

The other reported crime was assault in various degrees:

- Thomas Porter (35), a gamekeeper, was indicted for shooting with intent to kill at John Crutchley at Drayton. With the agreement of both parties the charge was reduced to 'shooting with a loaded gun ... with intent to disfigure or disable' — sentenced to three months' imprisonment. (The *Shropshire Conservative* stated the sentence was three weeks' imprisonment, but the Assizes record is the official version.) The newspaper reported that Peter Broughton of Tunstall Hall said the defendant was a peaceable man; the Assizes record show that Broughton was the chairman of the court on that occasion. The census records Elizabeth Porter ('married', thus not a widow) as the head of a household at Betton Moss, with her younger brother living with her and employed as an under-gamekeeper. It's a reasonable assumption that Elizabeth was the wife of Thomas Porter, who must then have been in prison. Betton Moss is in the same parish as Tunstall Hall — most likely Porter was William Norcop of Betton Hall's gamekeeper.
- John Whittel, George Simmonds, William Webb, Samuel Highfield and Henry Bickerton were found guilty of assault at Soudley — 'convicted in costs only'.
- Richard Johnson, William Johnson, John Palmer and John Wainwright were accused of fighting and causing a breach of the peace — Palmer and Wainwright were discharged but had to pay expenses; the Johnsons were bound over to keep the peace.
- 'Case of assault dismissed.' (No details given.)

Sources

- Calendar of Prisoners at Shrewsbury Assizes: Shropshire Archives, QS/10/8 (1849–53) (With thanks to Judith Hoyle for identifying and transcribing the entries.)
- Constabulary report books, 1839–53: Shropshire Archives, QA6/2/1
- Return of persons charged before the magistrates during the year ended December 20th 1851: Shropshire Archives, QA3/3/1
- Douglas J Elliott, *Policing Shropshire 1836–1967*, 1984, pp254–5
- David Philips, *Crime and Authority in Victorian England: The Black Country 1835–60*, 1977, pp298–300, 176–9
- Norman Rowley, *The Story of Market Drayton*, 1987
- Sir Thomas Skryme, *History of the Justices of the Peace*, Volume 2, 1991, pp78, 82,
- *Shropshire Conservative* and *Shrewsbury Chronicle* (Unfortunately the Shropshire Archives do not have copies of *Eddowes Salopian Journal* for 1851.)

16 : Transport

Peter Brown

By 1851 Market Drayton had a well-developed road system. The canal had opened sixteen years earlier. Although there was not to be a railway station in Drayton for a further twelve years, the rail network was already influencing both passenger and goods transport in the town and its surrounding area.

Roads

The Roman road from the Midlands to Chester left Watling Street (the present A5) a mile west of Gailey. From Hinstock through Tern Hill to Bletchley it followed roughly the line of the present A41. By the 13th century much of the Roman road had become disused but the Hinstock–Bletchley section was known as the Longford.

No doubt there were other roads of more than just inter-manor importance, for example, Shrewsbury to Newcastle, and a 'salt route' south from Nantwich through Audlem and Drayton to Hinstock and beyond, but there is little surviving evidence.

Generally roads were the responsibility of the parish, which could be very unfair if the road was a busy long-distance route or if the parish population was small in relation to the length of its roads. In 1663 Parliament passed an Act allowing the justices of Hertfordshire, Cambridgeshire and Huntingdonshire to levy a toll on users of the Great North Road in order to pay for its upkeep — this was the first 'turnpike' act, so-called because the money was collected at a tollgate with a bar ('pike') set across the road which could be turned to allow traffic to pass. Starting in the early 18th century various acts were passed giving the powers to turnpike trusts, non-profit-making organisations usually run by the local worthies. The trustees were able to borrow money at fixed rates of interest in order to make improvements. Sometimes this meant altering the line of the road, often to avoid a steep gradient; sometimes it meant engineering works such as cuttings and embankments; and sometimes it merely meant putting in proper drainage and improving the road surface. The Acts gave the powers for twenty-one years, and if the debt had not been repaid at the end of that period, or if further improvements were needed, a further application had to be made to Parliament — in practice this almost invariably happened.

Users may have grumbled about paying tolls, but there is no doubt that generally the resultant roads were much more satisfactory than their predecessors. The speed of both passenger and goods vehicles increased, and the roads were passable in all but the most extreme weathers.

The earliest turnpike Act in the Drayton area was in 1760, to improve the 'A41' from Newport through Hinstock and Tern Hill to Whitchurch. Between Bletchley and Whitchurch two routes were authorised: via Sandford and Prees Heath, and via Calverhall and Ightfield. In the Drayton area there were tollhouses at Hinstock, Tern Hill and Bletchley.

Drayton was bypassed to the east by an Act of 1763 which turnpiked a group of roads in the Staffordshire/Shropshire border area, including Eccleshall via Loggerheads to Irelands Cross.

An Act of 1767 turnpiked the Whitchurch – Audlem – Woore – Madeley Heath road (now the A525), and also the Hinstock – Drayton – Audlem – Nantwich (A529) road. Tollhouses on the Shropshire section of the latter were located at Hinstock, Sydnall, Spoonley and Adderley.

The other Act affecting Drayton was passed in 1769. This turnpiked what is now the A53 from Shawbury to Newcastle-under-Lyme; west of Shawbury the road had been turnpiked by an Act of 1756. In the Drayton area there were tollhouses at Hodnet, Wollerton, Tern Hill, Market Drayton (at the junction with Betton Road) and Audley's Cross.

None of the records of the local trusts have survived, but the degree of improvement can sometimes be inferred from the line of the present road. For example, where the A53 crosses the end of the Maer Hills between Baldwin's Gate and the A51 junction the cuttings and even slope imply these were turnpike improvements; and the continuation between the A51 junction and the top of the hill above Loggerheads may have been a totally new line of road, judging by the way the byroads and field boundaries seem to ignore it. On the other hand, the twisting course of the A529 between Market Drayton and Nantwich implies that the trustees did little except improve the road surface.

Tolls were usually 'farmed' — in other words, instead of employing toll staff, the trust let the right to collect the tolls to the highest bidder. In 1851 the Tern Hill to Newport tolls were advertised as having produced £260 in the previous year, and the Drayton to Tern Hill tolls as having produced £201.

In the years after 1851 the various roads were de-turnpiked: Tern Hill to Whitchurch in 1854; Shawbury to Market Drayton in 1866; Newport to Tern Hill in 1867; Market Drayton to Newcastle in 1872; and Nantwich to Hinstock in 1875. The County Council took over the responsibilities for these major roads.

The town streets remained a local responsibility. At that time they were unpaved, and street lighting (by gas) was not introduced until 1861. Not only was there a weekly street market for provisions as now, in addition the livestock markets were in the main streets: cattle in what is now Great Hales Street, sheep in Stafford Street, and horses in Cheshire Street. The cattle market by the station did not open until 1872.

The plans for the enclosure of Little Drayton Common were drawn up in 1851 and formally approved in January of the following year. The new public roads included what are now Buntingsdale Road, Bentleys Road and Christchurch Lane; several private roads were also created.

Road passenger services

Unlike Shifnal or Whitchurch, Market Drayton was never on an important stage coach route. Most Birmingham to Chester coaches passed along what is now the A41 through Tern Hill. For example, in 1835 the *Albion* (which was the name of the service, rather than of the vehicle) passed Tern Hill at about 12.45pm on its way north from Birmingham to Chester via Walsall, Weston, Newport and Whitchurch, the southbound coach having passed at about the same time. The *Fair Trader* went from Birmingham via Wolverhampton, Newport and Whitchurch to Chester, then on to Liverpool — the northbound and southbound coaches both passed Tern Hill at about 12.15pm.

A coach from London to Chester passed close to the other side of Drayton: this was the *Royal Mail*, its route being London – St Albans – Dunstable – Northampton – Lutterworth – Hinckley – Tamworth – Stafford – Eccleshall – Woore – Nantwich – Chester. Northbound it passed Loggerheads about 2.30pm, southbound about 11.30am.

Market Drayton gained a stage coach service in 1835, the *Emerald*, which operated from Birmingham to Liverpool via Wolverhampton, Brewood, Newport, Drayton, Audlem, Nantwich and Chester. Northbound it left Birmingham at 7.15am, stopped at Market Drayton at 1pm, and arrived at Liverpool about 7pm. Southbound it left Liverpool at 7.45am, stopped at Market Drayton at 2pm, and arrived at Birmingham about 7.15pm. There were lunch breaks of about half an hour at Audlem northbound and Nantwich southbound. At Market Drayton the horses were changed at the Corbet Arms.

However, this service was short-lived. The opening of the Grand Junction Railway from Birmingham to Stafford, Crewe, Warrington, Liverpool and Manchester on 4 July 1837 altered the pattern of passenger travel in north Shropshire. Almost immediately, all coach services from London and the Midlands to Chester and Liverpool were withdrawn, the rail services being cheaper (though not cheap), quicker and more comfortable.

A new daily coach service, the *Victoria*, was introduced from Shrewsbury to Whitmore Station, advertised as 'to London, Manchester, Liverpool, Birmingham etc'. This left Market Drayton for the nine mile journey to the station at 11am and returned through Market Drayton at 2.45pm. The service was retimed in later years and the Sunday service ceased. It survived the opening of Shrewsbury's first railways — to Chester on 12 October 1848, to Stafford on 1 June 1849 and to Wolverhampton on 12 November 1849 — but was cut back to a Hodnet – Drayton – Whitmore Station service on 12 May 1851.

The approximate timings were then: Hodnet 8.45am, Market Drayton 9.45am, Whitmore Station 11am — meeting the 11.10am up train to Birmingham (arriving at 1.35pm) and London Euston (7pm); the 11.50am train to Crewe (12.20pm) and Manchester (1.50pm), with connections to Chester (1.35pm) and Liverpool (2.15pm). The return coach journey left Whitmore Station after the arrival of the 1.38pm from London (departing 6.15am) and Birmingham (10am). The up train arrived at 1.30pm from, or with connections from, Manchester (11.40am), Liverpool (11.15am) and Chester (11.50pm). The coach reached Market Drayton about 2.45pm and Hodnet about 3.45pm.

This truncated service was operated by Thomas Sandalls, the licensee of the Unicorn Inn at Market Drayton. At Hodnet it commenced at the Bear Inn.

Carriers

Less well-known but perhaps more important than the stage coaches were the carriers. These can be divided into two categories: those that were part of a national or regional network, and those which provided a service into Drayton from the outlying areas on market days.

In 1834, all the longer distance carriers were using the Phoenix Inn at Market Drayton: Pickford's 'fly wagon' went to Stoke on Tuesdays; Thomas Beardsmore's service from Shrewsbury to Newcastle passed eastbound on Wednesdays and westbound on Mondays; and Wakeman & Robins had a Stone to Whitchurch service once a week.

The opening of the canal in 1835 did not mean the end of the longer distance carrier services. In 1844 the Newcastle to Shrewsbury service was being operated on the same days as Thomas Beardsmore's had been a decade earlier, but now Jeremiah Machin ran it, using the Crown as its base. Presumably it could resist canal competition because it ran east–west across the grain of the canal system. More surprisingly, Samuel Foden was advertising a service to Nantwich and Manchester, leaving the Royal Oak every morning; however, this is likely to have been short-lived.

The 1851 directory does not mention carriers by road though the census records eleven carters and ten carriers as well as the waggoners employed on farms. There would almost certainly have been a service on the Newcastle to Shrewsbury route. At the end of the decade George Dawson is recorded as being a carrier from the Royal Oak to Stoke and Tunstall on Wednesdays. The London & North Western Railway would have arranged a delivery service for parcels and other goods using their trains; in 1859 the carrier was Adam Roden from Little Drayton.

Nor does the 1851 directory mention the carriers' services in from the surrounding villages on market day, yet it is probable that someone in almost every village would have been delivering and collecting parcels from a particular inn in the town, and carrying passengers if needed. Often such services were provided by a local farmer who would have been coming into town in any case, so could earn a little more money by offering his facilities to his neighbours. The first directory to refer to such services was in 1901; the inns then used were the Red Lion, Stag's Head, Unicorn, Crown, King's Arms, George and Dun Cow.

The canal

According to a directory of 1834, much of Market Drayton's market trade transferred to Stone when the Trent & Mersey Canal opened there in 1771. Market Drayton was not on the canal network until 1835, the Birmingham & Liverpool Junction Canal being one of the last canals built. This was designed as a short water link from Birmingham, the Black Country and Wolverhampton to the Mersey port. The fact that it passed close to Drayton was a fortunate accident — although it was the only significant town on the route of the canal, no Drayton people were on its committee, indeed none were significant investors. This canal became part of the Shropshire Union Railways & Canal Company, which was created in 1846 by the merger of various canal companies in Shropshire and the adjacent counties.

In time for the opening of the canal, a rectangular basin was constructed adjacent to the turnpike road to Newcastle. This served two wharves. The southern wharf was occupied by Hazledine & Co, the coal being brought from their mines in the East Shropshire coalfield. Within a few years this site had a warehouse, stable, outbuildings, machine house and a dwellinghouse. The northern wharf was rented to William Tomkinson, who dealt in guano, corn and salt. He constructed two warehouses, a shed, a stable and a crane. Both Wilkinson and Tomkinson were still in occupation in 1851. (Even today there are two separate wharfs by the one basin.)

In 1838 Messrs Sandbrook and Ryley, horsehair seating manufacturers described in the canal company's minutes as 'two spirited individuals of capital', constructed a wharf with a rectangular basin (now filled in) and a warehouse just north of Drayton: Victoria Wharf in Maer Lane. From here they operated a coal business which continued until well after 1851 — indeed a coal merchant was still using the site more than 150 years later.

The wharfingers also acted as agents for national and regional canal carrying firms. However, with the construction of so many railways in the 1840s, the pattern of canal trade substantially altered. Many of the larger firms withdrew their boats, some (like Pickford's) transforming their business to become sub-contractors for railway companies. The Shropshire Union, recognising the threat to its toll income, created a carrying subsidiary and this came to be the main canal carrier in the region. In 1851 they advertised themselves as being 'general carriers to all parts of England'. One of the older firms, Crowley & Co, still had a presence at Market Drayton, but this was not to last much longer. William Tomkinson was agent for both companies.

In 1851 the main trade of the canal was bulk loads, principally coal for domestic use and such industries as Gower's (established 1842) and Rodenhurst's (by 1851) iron foundries. The gas works would become a major customer in the following year. Bricks are likely to have been a significant traffic although there was small-scale brick-making around Drayton. Lime and fertiliser would have been brought to Drayton; agricultural produce would have gone out to the conurbations of the West Midlands and Lancashire. Smaller, less bulky and more valuable goods would have gone by road to the railheads.

The canal through Market Drayton never had a significant passenger traffic.

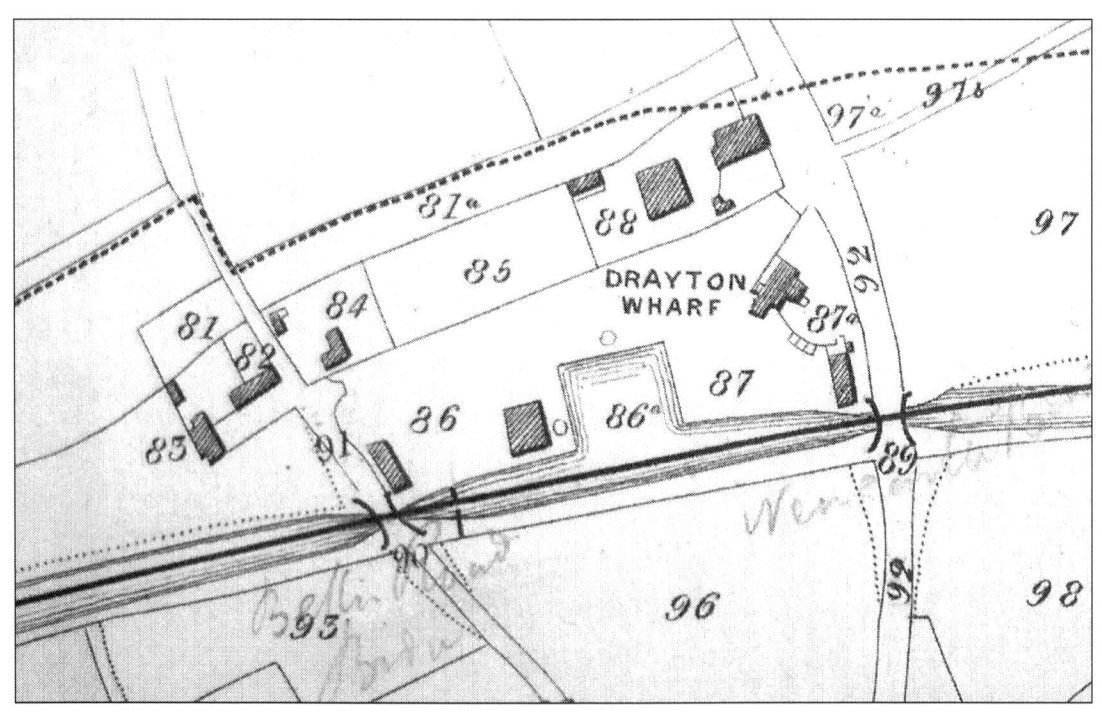

Market Drayton wharf in 1851, showing the proposed railway following the line of the canal.
[Shropshire Archives: DP326]

Railways

As at most of Shropshire's market towns, the railway came relatively late, opening to Nantwich in 1863, Wellington in 1867 and Stoke in 1870.

The earliest proposal for a railway through Market Drayton was a product of the 'Railway Fever', as it was called, of 1824/25. Nationally a number of schemes were put forward for tramroads or railways using the horse as motive power, though some visionaries foresaw that steam power would become a practicable proposition. One of the most ambitious schemes was for a railway from Birmingham to the Mersey, passing through Market Drayton. It provoked a rival scheme for a canal on almost exactly the same route, and it was the canal which was able to gain enough public support to obtain its Act of Parliament and be built.

In the 'Railway Mania' of 1844/45 more than 800 railway bills presented to Parliament — and many more that never got to that stage. Several involved Market Drayton but only one proposal got as far as receiving its Act: this was for the conversion of the canal into a railway. With its direct route, tall embankments and deep cuttings this would actually have been a relatively easy conversion but after intense negotiations the Shropshire Union lost its independence, being leased to the powerful London & North Western Railway, but remained as a canal.

However, although Market Drayton did not have a railway in 1851, the patterns of both its passenger and goods traffic were being strongly influenced by the growing railway network. Market Drayton was ceasing to be relatively economically isolated: cheaper transport meant that it was becoming part of the free trade area of Britain. It could 'export' its products more easily, but it could also 'import' items which could be produced at less cost or with a better quality elsewhere. These changes were to have a profound effect on the town's development.

Principal sources

- Directories: *Pigot* 1834 & 1835; *Slater* 1851 & 1859; Kelly 1900
- Newspapers: *Shrewsbury Chronicle*; *Shropshire Conservative*
- Timetables: *Bradshaw* 1851
- Charles Hadfield, *The Canals of the West Midlands*, 1969
- A D M Phillips & B J Turton, *The Turnpike Network of Staffordshire, 1700–1840*, 1988
- Barrie Trinder, *The Industrial Archaeology of Shropshire*, 1996
- A C & E Waddelove, 'The Roman Road from Pennocrucium to Mediolanum: its role in the early Conquest', *Shropshire History & Archaeology*, Vol LXXIX (2004)

17 : Inns and beerhouses

Peter Brown

Justices' responsibility for alehouses began in 1503, when an Act authorised them to suppress disorderly houses. The Licensing Act 1552 required ale-sellers to be licensed once a year by any two Justices of the Peace, in order to prevent drunkenness and unlawful games. Ale-sellers naturally applied to the Justices nearest to them, who found it most convenient to deal with all applications at the same time annually. From this developed the Petty Sessions, the local grouping of Justices. Similar provisions for the sale of spirits were not introduced until 1729. Further regulations were made during the 18th century; for example in 1787 there was a Royal Proclamation against vice and immorality, encouraging Justices to consider not only the character of the applicant but also such matters as their conduct, opening hours, and the number of licensed premises locally. Enforcement was sometimes erratic, but there is evidence that drunkenness and crime was reduced.

However, in the early 19th century there was a reaction against the controls. People who believed in free trade objected to the ability of unrepresentative Justices to deprive an alehouse-keeper of his livelihood. There were also concerns about the acquisition of public houses by large firms of brewers, which it was thought would reduce choice and increase prices. As a consequence the Beer Act 1830 removed entirely from the control of the Justices all premises which sold only beer; any ratepayer could sell beer on payment of a fee of two guineas. Hence the distinction in the 1851 directory between 'beerhouses' and 'hotels, inns and taverns'. This Act was not repealed until 1869, by which time drunkenness and crime had increased substantially and the standard of the premises in which beer was consumed had got much worse.

Drinking beer — in moderation — could have been beneficial in the 19th century, particularly in urban areas. Water was often unsafe to drink but the alcohol in beer would have killed off many harmful pathogens, as would the brewing process itself because it involved boiling the water. 'Small beer' was made by a second or third mashing of the malt used for stronger beers but it still would not have been especially weak by today's standards, being about 3½% alcohol.

The inns listed in Bagshaw's 1851 directory are shown below, together with a couple of others for which there is evidence. It is remarkable how more than half of these inns are still operating well over 150 years later.

High Street / Great Hales Street

Old Cheshire Cheese (landlord in 1851: James Kirkham): The 1851 directory is the only one which refers to this as the *Old Cheshire Cheese*; all others just call it the *Cheshire Cheese*. Situated at the corner of High Street and Cheshire Street, this half-timbered building was built in 1666. It ceased to be an inn between 1861 and 1867, and is now [2009] occupied by Lockett's opticians.

Corbet Arms Hotel (James Foden): The hotel was named after the family of the Lord of the Manor of Drayton. Prior to 1824 these premises were called the *Talbot*, after the heraldic beast of the Earls of Shrewsbury. The facade was altered in 1831 with the addition of a new portico, water spouts and iron railings; the interior was remodelled in 1844 and a new large dining room added. For just two or three years in the 1830s a Liverpool–Birmingham stagecoach called here to pick up and set down passengers and to change horses; this ceased when the Crewe–Stafford railway opened in 1837 with its connections to Liverpool, Manchester and Birmingham, the following year extended to London. Until 1850 the Petty Sessions were held at the *Corbet Arms*. For over a hundred years this was the town's premier licensed premises. It is still open, though only a shadow of its former glory.

George (Martha Barnett): The directories of 1834 and 1844 refer to this as the *George and Dragon*. It was still a pub shortly before the Second World War. The premises, which are directly opposite Church Street, have had several occupiers since then, including E & K Selby's dress shop and a travel agency; most recently they were occupied by 'Connexions' but are now empty.

Stag's Head (Robert Edge): This was the next building to the south of the *George*. It is still operating as an inn.

Red Lion (George Evans): One of the many inns which in 1851 brewed its own beer. This inn is also still open.

Stafford Street / Newcastle Road

Crown (Henry Boulton): This historic inn stands at the corner of Stafford Street and Queen Street. Photographs taken later in the 19th century show a brewery behind the *Crown*, but the 1851 directory makes no mention of it.

Unicorn (Thomas Sandells): Immediately adjacent to the *Crown*, the *Unicorn* was erected on the site of the former *Fox* inn, which was built in 1666. In 1851 it was noted as brewing its own beer. The *Unicorn* was the base for the daily coach service connecting with the trains at Whitmore Station on the Stafford–Crewe railway line from 1837 until 1863. The building ceased being used as a pub in about 1960, and is currently vacant awaiting redevelopment.

Star (John Sayers Key): Renamed the *Jack Handley* some time towards the end of the 20th century, and now called the *Salopian Star*. The 1851 landlord was also a maltster.

Lamb (James Matthews): Renamed the *Stafford Court* about 1990; still open. 'Lamb Shutt' is adjacent; the earliest record of the inn's name predates that of the alley.

Wheat Sheaf (John Barnett): This inn, adjacent to the wharf, was opened shortly after the canal was completed. It was recorded as the *Talbot* in directories of 1850 and 1856, so perhaps the 1851 directory made an error about the name. It is still open.

Queen Street (Bell Lane)

Bell: The *Bell* was an ancient inn, and gave its name to Bell Lane, now known as Queen Street. In 1834 it was recorded as the *Blue Bell*. It was not listed in the 1851 directory. The last directory to mention it was that of 1900, though the temperance hotel listed in the 1913 directory at 1 Queen Street was in the same premises — the building on the west side which was closest to High Street (and opposite the side of the *Crown*).

Cheshire Street

Royal Oak (Ann Hill): This inn was built in 1652, and the 1851 directory records it as having its own brewery. Its site was where the Information Centre now is, with the facade flush with the other buildings in Cheshire Street. The original half-timbered building was pulled down and replacement premises in brick erected in 1882. Early in the 20th century the owners of the *Royal Oak*, the Market Drayton Brewery Co Ltd, built the Town Hall alongside as a commercial venture. The *Royal Oak* was demolished in 1964, together with the Town Hall.

Shropshire Street

Grapes (William Sandbrook): This old building, dated 1653, strictly speaking was not an inn but a wine and spirit merchant's premises or 'vaults'. Only the 1861 directory gives it the name *Grapes*. It is now an inn called the *Sandbrook Vaults*. This is currently (2010) closed.

Elephant & Castle (Sarah Dale): The facade was originally brick; the jettied half-timbered facade is false. The inn was renamed the *Clive and Coffyne* in the late 1990s.

Kings Arms: This inn is shown on Malabar's 1843 map and is listed in the 1850 and 1856 directories but is omitted from the 1851 directory. It is still open.

Other inns

In the early part of the 19th century the *Phoenix Hotel* was regarded as the town's premier hostelry. It was situated in Great Hales Street opposite Phoenix Bank, the road to which it gave its name; the site later became the Phoenix Carriage Works and in the 20th century the Phoenix

The Royal Oak Inn, *Cheshire Street, before it was rebuilt in 1882*
[Drayton Museum & Resource Centre]

Garage. It was owned by the Earls of Kilmorey, whose residence was Shavington Hall — the phoenix appears in the Kilmorey crest. The hotel was still trading in 1844, but some time between then and 1851 it closed, the landlord James Foden transferring to the *Corbet Arms*.

The *Raven* was once a well-known half-timbered hostelry in Cheshire Street which in its last days was a beerhouse. It is shown on Malabar's map of 1843 but is not mentioned in any of the directories. In the latter part of the 1840s it was demolished, the site being used for Rodenhurst's 'Raven Foundry'. It was where the walkway from Cheshire Street through to the Indoor Market and Raven Square now is. A raven was on the coat of arms of the Corbet family. The name *Raven* was later reused for an inn in Station Road, a window from which is now in the Drayton Museum.

The 1851 directory did not show any inns in Little Drayton.

Beerhouses

The following people were listed in the 1851 directory as beerhouse keepers. Their other occupations are noted where appropriate.

Thomas Bresnell	Little Drayton	—
Benjamin Brookshaw	Old Wharf	blacksmith
Thomas Brown	Cheshire St	carpenter
Elizabeth Fletcher	Cheshire St	—
Thomas Hall	Shropshire St	cooper
Robert Hinton	Shropshire St	plumber/glazier
Thomas Peake	Little Drayton	plumber/glazier
John Pegg	Little Drayton	—
George Preston	Little Drayton	—
William Roden	Cheshire St	pig dealer
Elizabeth Stubbs	Queen St	—
Hill Wade	Little Drayton	—
Thomas Woodcock	Little Drayton	—
Nathanial Wright	Shropshire St	shopkeeper

One wonders whether there is any significance in the fact that only one beerhouse keeper in Little Drayton was shown as having another employment, whereas only two in Drayton Magna did not.

Except for Thomas Hall's beerhouse (see below) the exact location of the various premises cannot now be determined.

According to the article published in the *Newport & Market Drayton Advertiser* in 1901 the various beerhouses had names, but these are not shown in the directories or on any available maps. The names of 19th century beerhouses included:

Great Hales Street	*Compass & Square, Plough*
Stafford Street	*Black Horse, Cock, Cross Keys, Swan*
Tinker's Lane	*Plough & Harrow*
Cheshire Street	*Drovers' Arms, Paul Pry, Pig & Whistle, Seven Stars, Three Tuns*
Shropshire Street	*Bricklayer's Arms, Pheasant, Robin Hood & Little John* (later *Coach & Horses*)
St Mary's Street	*Rising Sun*
Little Drayton	*Barley Mow, Conquering Hero* (later *Plume of Feathers*, and then *Joiners Arms*), *Lord Hill, Wheat Sheaf*

The location of two premises mentioned in the article, *Rock in the Ocean* and *White Lion* were not stated.

Principal sources

- Directories: *Pigot* 1844, *Slater* 1850, *Bagshaw* 1851, *Kelly* 1856
- Malabar's map, 1843
- *Newport & Market Drayton Advertiser*, 2 July 1887 & 4 May 1901
- Norman Rowley, *People and Events in Market Drayton, 1770–1870*, 1985
- Sir Thomas Skyrme, *History of the Justices of the Peace*, Volume 2, 1991

The Dun Cow *in Shropshire Street is not mentioned in a directory until 1900. However, Malabar's map of 1843 shows the property as being owned by Mr Hall. The 1844 & 1851 directories list Thomas Hall as a cooper and beerhouse keeper in Shropshire Street. Nobody else named Hall is listed in either directory. It therefore seems probable that this old building was a beerhouse in 1851.*

·*[Drayton Museum & Resource Centre]*

18 : Betton

Bill Page

For a child born in the present century, 1851 would have been about six generations back to the time of their great-great-great-great-grandparents — whose parents and grandparents could still have been about. In Betton, Thomas Furnival, born 1769, was still alive aged 82. No planes or helicopters overhead then, no cars, motorbikes, lorries or tractors, but roads would have been in a worse condition for the pedestrians and horse-drawn vehicles. No radios, TVs, mobile phones or computers. No tin cans, plastics, fridges or 'electrics'. However, it was still a time of hangings, transportation, workhouses and 'Empire', with ice houses preserving food at Tunstall Hall and Betton Lodge. There was a canal, but the railway had yet to come and go.

The joint Lords of Betton Manor, Richard Corbet Esq and Peter Broughton Esq, would have been in control of most of village life. The ten or so farmers would have been working longer hours,

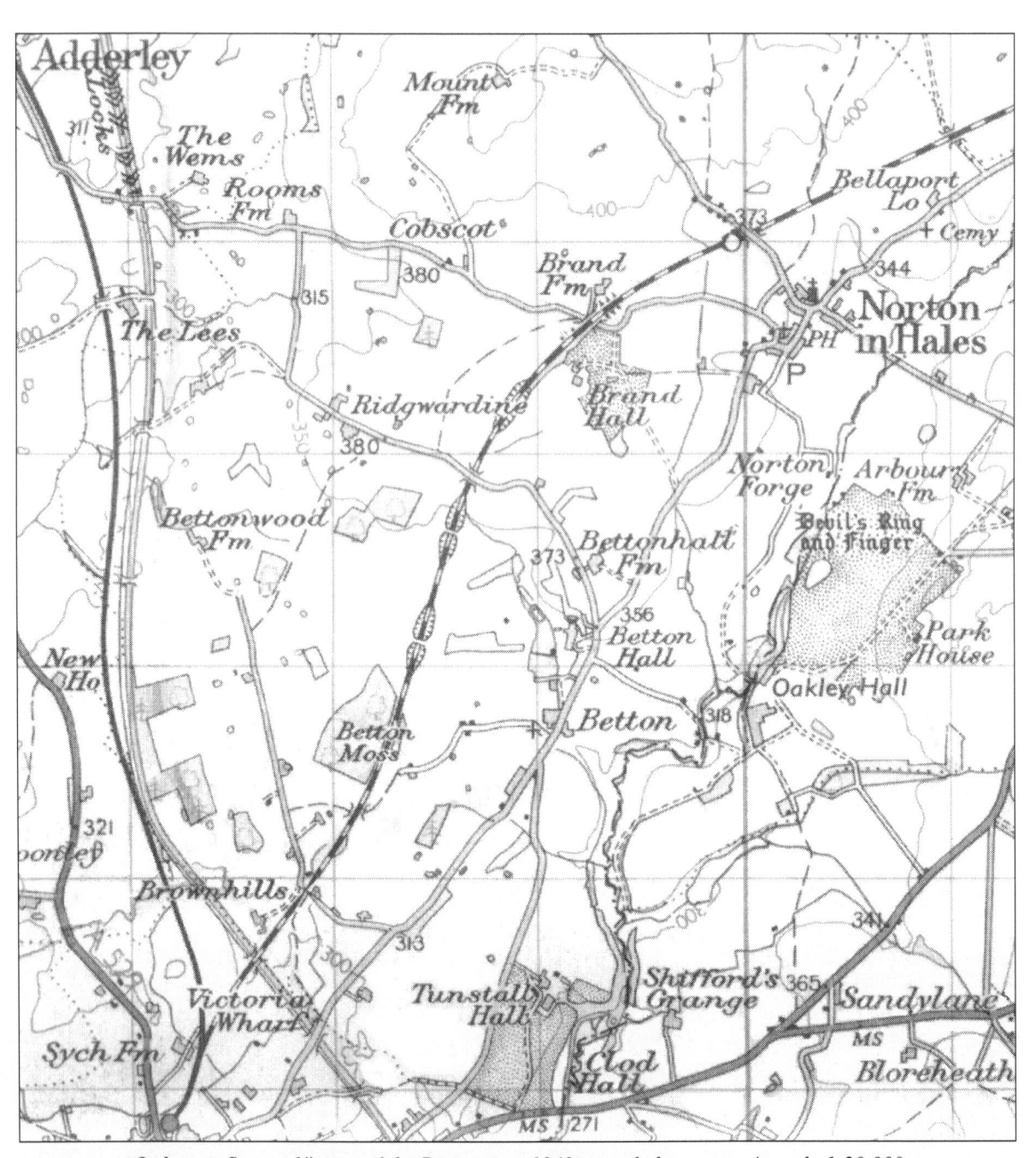

Ordnance Survey 1" map of the Betton area 1949, rescaled to approximately 1:20,000

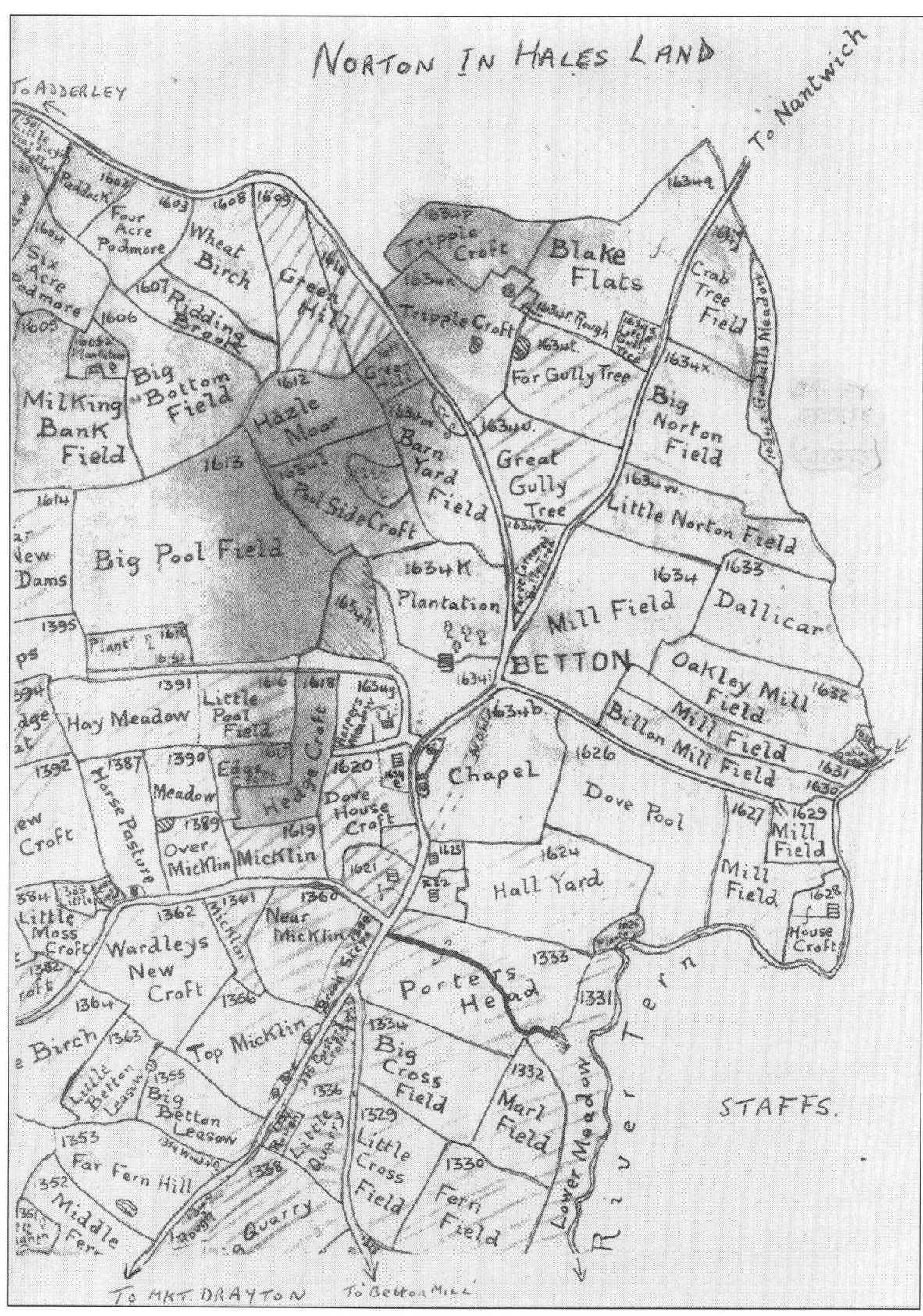

Part of H D G Foxall's field map of Betton, with additional notations by the author.
Note how the road has been diverted across Chapel Field away from Betton House (plot 1634).

usually with larger families and workforce than now. Manual work — hand milking, muck-spreading, harvesting etc — would have been more social. Although mostly dairying there were pigs and poultry too. Ditching, hedge-laying and trimming, coppice work and wall repairs would have involved more people out and about and more children playing — or working from an early age. Too much education would have put them off farming!

Skylarks, plovers and moorhens would have been about. Betton Moss would have been bigger— about 50 acres in area — with a greater variety of wild flowers and with more wildfowl and the rare Arctic willow. Betton Hall had not yet been partially demolished and it was probably more visible; possibly even looking out at its neighbours at Oakley and Tunstall from well kept grounds where the local gentry would have enjoyed garden parties, horse-drawn coach rides and boating.

Tunstall estate would have been larger. Betton Road would have led to Betton instead of stopping at the bypass. (Surely it needs renaming?) The main road, and there still is only one through road, had earlier been through the grounds of Betton House. Chapel Field was originally larger. Two properties east of the old road have now been demolished, presumably to improve the grounds where the rhododendrons brighten the roadside in spring.

Chapel Field was larger but the chapel was long gone, with only the 6ft high base of an ancient stone cross left from monastic or mediaeval times marking either a market site (c1256), a wayside preaching point, or the site of the former chapel. Fifty-year-old trees now hide the monument. The present Betton Church, a private residence converted from the former tin tabernacle in Moss Land, was not built until 1886; it was given to the village by Capt J Heathcote of Betton Hall.

Fox-hunting, shooting and fishing would have kept the Tern Valley area busier then. There was a pet cemetery in the area behind Tunstall Hall near the little man-made cave and gardens almost to the pillars left of the 'hunt bridge'. Badger baiting and poaching would have been more common. Trees isolated in many of the fields show where hedges have been removed since 1851.

There would have been at least one cottage by the working mill down Oakley Lane by the River Tern. This has now gone, as has the mill. Forge work was also carried on for a time at the mill, but probably later than 1851. The site has recently been cleared of trees. Norton Forge and Drayton metal-working firms were not far away.

Betton Cottage was two cottages in 1851. Byways 1 & 2 would not yet have been built on Custard Croft, nor Cornerways (now Hawk Lodge) by Betton Wood Lane. Ridgwardine Manor was only so named about 1841 with a Cartwright or Dobson family as tenants in the 1840s–1850s to the Church-Norcop family which later moved from Betton Hall to Brand Hall and which built (or rebuilt) Moss Lane Farm house and buildings in the 1860s.

Quarries off Tunstall and Norton roads may well have been at work and clay may have been dug from the Victoria Farm pits, though the brickworks were not set up until about 1900 on the western side of the road opposite the present fishing pool.

The black and white cottage (now Betton Old Hall) may not have been black and white in 1851 as recent work uncovered a brick and timber front under the present one (which probably replaced wattle and daub even earlier). Whether it was part of a half-timbered former Betton Hall demolished before the present Hall was built is a matter of conjecture, but Hall Yard has been the name of the field just by it and Betton Farm back to monastic times when there was a large fishpond behind a dam near the Tern Valley.

The 1851 census shows large families with servants, farm workers and/or relatives living in, and including occupations such as thatcher, miller, groom and coachman, as well as a gamekeeper. [For more about the last-named, see page 68.]

It was a relatively stable society: of the 63 heads of households and their wives recorded in the 1851 census, 37 had been born in Betton or one of the immediately adjacent parishes, 13 in Audlem or the wider Drayton area, 11 in other places in Shropshire, Cheshire or Staffordshire, and only 2 further away (Devon and Scotland).

The tenant farmers in an improving economic climate would not always have found it easy to find rent, food and clothing for their families and to keep their households running, with crop and animal health, weather and only partly drained soils setting limits to production from the varied glacial soils. Seed drills, other machines and scientific methods were arriving slowly; being near to Market Drayton's agricultural engineers was an advantage.

Excluding Tunstall Hall, there were 14 farms in Betton, totalling 1,893 acres:

Occupant	Farm	Acreage
William Norcop	Betton Hall	320
Henry Bennison	Betton Wood	176
Richard Davies	Brownhills	175
Robert Johnson	Betton House	170
John Spragg	Ridgwardine	160
John Bourne	Betton Coppice	160
Thomas Dobson	Ridgwardine Manor	155
Mrs Honor Beeston	Betton Moss	150
William Heath	—?	112
Charles Duckers	Ridgwardine	110
Edward Ryley	Betton Mill	100
John Crutchley	Brownhills	90
Henry Gidman	—?	15

The farms varied considerably. In 1840 an average of about 50% was arable, but the range was from 29% to 68%. Two examples were:

	Pasture	Meadow	Arable
Betton Moss	25%	7%	68%
Betton Hall	61%	10%	29%

Crops would have been more varied, but without maize.

Some of the red brick farm buildings were built before 1851 and more soon after. Owls were welcomed and owl holes were left in buildings at Betton Coppice Farm, Betton Lodge Farm, Betton Hall and the three Ridgwardine farms — a sign that rodents were plentiful in stockyards and barns. Few pigsties have survived but dairying by-products provided useful pig food; other cottages would have fed household scraps. Only at Betton Hall was the pigsty away from the house. Stables and carriage houses at Tunstall and Betton Halls had been built in a recent style. Other farm buildings in the area were more traditional. Metal for fencing and barns had still to arrive.

Many of Betton's houses have been extended but the overall number has not altered a great deal. Only one property was empty in 1851. Tenancies changed on four farms between 1841 and 1851 after William Church Norcop inherited from Mary Norcop, mostly because the tenants were aged 60–70. On census day 1851 Betton Moss had a female manager but it is not clear whether the farmer had left, died, or was just away for a short time. The only shepherd mentioned was at Betton Moss Farm.

With middens, primitive sanitation and without modern medical practices or medicines the ages reached by some villagers is notable:

Thomas Furnival	former blacksmith	82
Richard Davies	still farming	79
Robert Harris	farm labourer	78
Robert Beeston	retired farmer	76
Mary Holland	(the oldest female)	73
Sarah Simmins		71
Richard Hevinston	farm labourer	70
Hannah Hevinston	(wife of Richard)	70

What ages they finally reached I have not yet found out!

Of the population only Robert Beeston was living on his own though Honor Beeston, possibly his daughter, was at Betton Moss Farm. The largest family was at Betton Coppice, where John and Mary Bourne, aged 45 and 46, lived with Thomas 19, John 18, Stephen 16, Samuel 15, Sarah 12, Fanny 10, Elizabeth 7, Martha 5 and Edward 3, as well as farm servant George Holland 13 and Irish house servant Mary Eley 20 — a total of thirteen people in the household.

Only two of the family names — Ridgeway and Bourne — were still on the Betton electoral role in 1962/3.

Notes

Principal sources:
- Andrew Boden, *Tern Views*
- M Fradley, *Landscape History*, vol 25, 2006
- Judith Hoyle, *Farmsteads in north-east Shropshire c1750–1880*, unpublished PhD thesis, 2005
- N & S V Rowley, *Landed Estates and the Gentry*
- Census 1851
- Bagshaw's Directory, 1851
- Tithe map 1842

Maps:
- Roque's map of 1752 — this does not show the mill but shows Oakley Lane.
- Baugh's map of 1808 — does not show Oakley Lane.
- The first edition Ordnance Survey one-inch map, 1833, shows the mill, a building opposite the Ridgewardine turn-off, and Betton Cottage as two dwellings.

This dressed sandstone pillar, 70 metres east of Betton House, may relate to the mediaeval market and fair granted in 1256 by Henry III to the Abbot of Shrewsbury for his manor of Betton under Lyme. The market was to be held every Thursday whilst the fair was held on the vigil, day and the two following days of the feast of St Matthew the Apostle (20–23 September).

19 : Lydia Roden's mug: a detective story

Meriel Blower

The mug

The story starts in Bristol. My daughter Jessica, who runs an antique clothes stall as a hobby, was doing her usual trawl round the charity shops in Bristol when her eye was caught by a rather elaborate mug in the window of St Peter's Hospice shop. It was not the rampant floral decoration or the heavy gilding that caught her eye but the inscription: 'Lydia Roden, Market Drayton, Shropshire'. She bought it and donated it to Drayton Museum.

I was intrigued by the mug and wondered if I could investigate its history. The charity shop had no idea where it had come from. It was obviously an expensive item but there were no manufacturer's marks at all. There was no date and no clue as to why it had been given. The outside was very prettily decorated with flowers, almost certainly hand painted but it was the inside that was the great contrast and surprise! Moulded in relief and realistically painted were two frogs and a newt! I believe that these mugs are quite common and were sometimes associated with the Temperance Movement. The idea was that you drained your mug or tankard and to your horror, there was the frog in the bottom — enough to put you off alcohol for life — which was, of course, the idea.

Miranda Goodby, from the Ceramics Department of Hanley Museum was very helpful. The museum has a large collection of frog mugs but nothing that closely resembled ours. She said that the mug was fine earthenware and was almost certainly made in the Potteries. There is no maker's mark and there were a large number of small manufacturers. The mugs were produced as blanks and then customised to order. It could have been ordered anywhere in England. You could specify the decoration, including the gilt border and the inscription and the order would be sent back to the factory and then sent back to the shop in due time. Some mugs were produced already decorated with inscriptions such as 'To a friend' or with names in common use like 'Mary' or 'Henry.'

Looking at the mugs in the collection there was nothing very similar. We saw two with identical handles and another with a very similar newt. Many of the frogs were much larger and wartier and much more realistically coloured. Ugh!

There is no way of identifying the painter by their style. Stoke-on-Trent was renowned for its pottery artists. They won more art prizes than anywhere except London.

The heyday of these mugs was the first half of Victoria's reign from about 1840 to 1870. From the shape Miranda dated the mug to around 1850. After 1860 the shape became taller, narrower and more tapering.

Lydia Roden

I decided that by using census information, local directories, church records and other family history websites I would try to find out what I could about Lydia Roden and her life.

In 1841 Lydia was five years old — she had been born in 1836 and baptised at St Mary's on 27 March.

She was living with her parents, William and Jane, in Cheshire Street. We are not quite sure where — Drayton's streets weren't numbered until 1908 — but they lived next door to a farm kept by a Mr Arkinstall. We know that there was a farm where the NatWest Bank is now and the family probably lived in one of the cottages that were demolished when the bank was built. It would have been a busy and bustling house. Altogether 10 people lived there. Lydia had three elder sisters, Harriett, Elizabeth and Emma, and a younger one, Jane. Her elder brother, Richard, was not living at home. At the age of 14, he would have been considered old enough to be a live-in labourer on a farm.

As well as William and Jane and their five daughters, three other people lived in the house. One was Lydia's 77 year old paternal grandmother, Harriet. The other two were lodgers. Edward Wright was described as a pig drover and William Cliff was a labourer. William Roden, Lydia's father, was a pig dealer. There are several other Roden families in Drayton at the time and at least three of them were pig dealers. Drayton seems to have been the centre of a thriving pig trade. Lydia would probably have enjoyed the excitement of the weekly market that took place in Cheshire Street.

The next glimpse we get of Lydia is ten years later in 1851. She was now fifteen and was described as a dressmaker. She were still living on Cheshire Street but it was a much smaller household. William (Lydia's father) was not at home but as his wife, Jane is described as 'married' rather than as a 'widow', we must presume he was not dead but away somewhere, perhaps buying pigs. Of the five sisters, only Lydia and Harriett were still living at home. Jane, Lydia's mother, was supplementing the family income by selling beer. She was described as a beer-house keeper, the lowest rung of the alcohol trade. She would not have been allowed to sell spirits. Lydia's 16 year old sister Emma is the only servant with the Linscott family three doors away. Mr Linscott was an excise man and he and his wife had five children aged under eight. I should imagine that Emma was kept very busy. It was perhaps that that decided Lydia to become a dressmaker rather than go in to service.

Also in 1851 a large family called Salter were living in Shropshire Street. The head of the family was Sarah Salter, who is described as a maltster's widow. She had at least eleven children, of whom ten were living with her. Three of her sons and one of her daughters kept a draper's shop and a fourth son, Henry, aged 19, was an attorney's clerk. Another daughter was almost the same age as Lydia, who would probably have known the shop and the family.

Lydia Roden married Henry Salter in the spring of 1860 in Stoke-on-Trent. She was 24 and he was 27. We tend to imagine that people in Victorian times got married very young. This may have been true of the aristocracy but not the lower middle classes. They couldn't afford to. There was often a rather protracted courtship and it may have been at this time that Henry presented Lydia with the mug.

In 1861 Henry and Lydia were keeping the Bell Inn in Bell Lane (now Queen Street) with the help of a 14 year old girl as a servant. Much later this became a Temperance Hotel and is the building now occupied by the cobbler's and locksmith's shop.

At the time of the census the Salters had a three month old son, Henry Colley Salter. Colley was obviously a Salter family name — Henry's elder brother, Samuel, who kept the draper's shop in town, had Colley as his middle name. Henry and Lydia were still at the Bell in 1863 but by 1868 they had moved across the road to the Crown, one of Drayton's best known inns. They had a daughter, Mary Winifred, in the spring of 1865. The Salters still had their draper's shop and by 1871 three of the Salter sisters had set up as dressmakers and two were milliners. Interestingly, the 1871 census shows that all the sisters had lopped four years off their ages!

In the census of 1871 Henry Salter was described as 'innkeeper and solicitor's general clerk.' With two jobs, much of the work of running the busy Crown Inn must have devolved on Lydia. She had two children to look after but she was helped by a general servant, an ostler and a live-in barmaid.

Lydia died in early January 1873 and was buried on 14 January in the new Drayton Cemetery. She was 37 years old. I know the area of the cemetery where she is buried but the stones are so badly weathered I have been unable to find the actual grave.

Henry, her husband, gave up the Crown after his

wife's death and became a cattle dealer. He lived for a time on the corner of Victoria Road and Shropshire Street with his daughter Mary. He died in 1921, 38 years after his wife, and was buried in the same plot in the cemetery. He was 89 years old and living in Stafford Street at the time of his death.

Lydia's daughter, Mary Winifred, was living with her father in 1891 but I have been unable to track her further. Lydia's son, Henry Colley Salter, in 1891 was lodging with two Salter aunts in Marylebone in London. He was unmarried and his occupation was given as 'actor'. I cannot find him in the 1901 census but an H C Salter was listed as taking an unassisted passage to Australia between 1900 and 1906. It needs somebody with more expertise than me in finding their way round the family history websites to follow that one up.

'Lydia Roden 2'

I had asked David Asprey, who runs the Family History Group for the local U3A to help me find Lydia Roden's marriage as I was having difficulty. He succeeded in finding that it took place in 1860 in Stoke-on-Trent but then dropped a real bombshell: Market Drayton produced another Lydia Roden!

Lydia Roden 2 was born in Greenwich in 1853 to Abel Roden, who had been born in Market Drayton, and his wife Lucy. He had obviously somehow ended up in Kent because Lucy, his wife was born in Maidstone, son Benjamin and daughter Lydia in Greenwich and baby brother Henry in Gravesend. They must have moved to Market Drayton in 1860 and were living in Cheshire Street just a few doors away from Jane Roden, the beer-seller and mother of Lydia Roden 1. Abel Roden and Lydia's elder brother Ben aged 11 are described as agricultural labourers and Lucy her mother is a charwoman. I have not been able to trace a relationship between the two families but I am sure there must be one and it is entirely possible that Lydia 2 was named for Lydia 1. Roden is a common surname in North Shropshire. There is a small river and a hamlet of the same name, and according to the 1841 census there were at least four separate families in Market Drayton at that time, three of them pig dealers. Despite trawling through the IGI (the International Genealogical Index sponsored by the Mormon Church), I have been unable to establish a connection between William Roden, the father of Lydia 1 and Abel, Lydia 2's father.

Ten years later, in 1871, Lucy was a widow living now in Smithfield Road and still working as a charwoman. Lydia was at home and described as a domestic servant, her sister Phyllis was working as a horse hair weaver, and baby brother Henry now aged 11 was a scholar.

By 1881 Lydia had two illegitimate children: a son Benjamin born in 1874 and a daughter Louisa born the following year. Lydia was married to Walter Jones, a 41 year old widower with four sons and two step-children from a previous marriage. They were living on Little Drayton Common — regarded as the rougher end of the town. The family consisted of Walter and Lydia, Edward, the youngest of Walter's sons from his first marriage, Lydia's two illegitimate children Benjamin and Louisa, and Alfred, their joint baby, aged 9 months. A daughter, Annie was born in the summer of 1884 and in September of that year Walter died. Lydia was a survivor. In 1890 she married Jack Broadhurst, 12 years younger than her, and was still living on Little Drayton Common. Her daughter Annie married Edward Meadon and their son Richard Meadon is still a well-remembered name in town. His daughter still lives in town and his granddaughter acts as a steward at the museum.

Which Lydia?

We shall probably never know for certain for which Lydia the mug was made or how it ended up in a charity shop in Bristol, but it has allowed us a glimpse of very ordinary unremarkable lives that would otherwise have remained completely hidden. I say unremarkable but every life is unique and remarkable in its own way.

Although the mug ended up in a charity shop in Bristol, it had obviously been treasured at some time because it seems to have been carefully restored after a serious breakage. I am hoping to write to a local newspaper in Bristol to see if anyone can remember donating it and perhaps knows a little more about where it came from.

Miranda Goodby of Hanley Museum favours Lydia 1 as the recipient on the grounds of both date and her status. It is perhaps significant that Henry Salter, her future husband, had a brother who kept a draper's shop and sisters who kept a fancy goods shop.

I would like it to be Lydia 2 whose great-great-granddaughter is a museum steward in Market Drayton. If, as I suspect, they were related, perhaps that will please us both!

20 : The gentry houses and their landscapes

Kunigunda Gough

A small market town it may have been, in 1851, but Drayton families followed fashion with great enthusiasm. For a rural parish of modest extent, it contained a surprisingly large number of grand country houses — often by fashionable architects — set in landscaped parkland which was professionally designed. The rural parish was more extensive in 1851 than is our modern administrative district and included country estates which are now in Staffordshire, such as Oakley, Hales and Almington. The number of parklands, large and small, approached thirty.

The houses of the gentry

A look at the maps of that time will show that many villages still retained their manor houses, or the granges which were originally run by religious orders. In most cases, however, the lordship of the manor was no longer directly connected with the family which was living at the old manor house. A number of the influential titled families had moved on. By 1851 the manor house occupiers were typically local farming families of lesser status, although they were still influential in local affairs.

Where families had become wealthy, perhaps through 'good marriages', they had often invested in the 18th century building boom of grand new country houses. This created the ostentatious display which was still a key feature in the local landscape in 1851. Some of these families had strong local roots, such as the Clives at Styche, the Kilmoreys of Shavington (formerly Needhams) and the Corbets of Adderley, who had all acquired titled status over the years. The Adderley estate had two great houses in quick succession: a house in Classical style was soon demolished and rebuilt in Victorian Gothic style, revealing the Corbets to be avid followers of fashion.

Other prosperous landowners, untitled but with enough resources to build a country mansion on the grand scale, included the Mackworths and later the Tayleurs at Buntingsdale Hall. They had gradually bought and consolidated extensive land holdings.

A third category of owner was the wealthy industrialist who used his fortune to create a rural estate idyll in the traditional English landscape style. Typical of these was Purney Sillitoe, who in the early 19th century had created the Pell Wall estate through land acquisitions and then employed the eminent architect and savant Sir John Soane to build him a house in the fashionable classical style. Some of these industrialists were immigrants to the county, such as John Pemberton Heywood, a Liverpool banker whose fortune derived from the slave trade but who came to rural Shropshire to build Cloverley Hall in neo-Tudor style. This grand mansion was originally greater in extent than it is today.

On a smaller scale were the fine town houses such as The Grove, built in the 1770s by Thomas D'Avenant. The owners in 1851 were the Wilsons who had come to the area when John Wilson acted as contractor for our section of Telford's Birmingham & Liverpool Junction Canal (later becoming part of the Shropshire Union Canal). Another was The Towers, a brand new town villa completed in 1851 for Joseph Loxdale Warren, a local solicitor. Their owners followed national fashions both in interior design (the original house at the Grove School still has its fine Adam-style reception rooms) and in garden design.

The landscapes of 1851

Whether owners had a major country house or a town villa, they aspired to a fine landscape setting to complement it in style. In the Drayton area this landscape legacy includes several ornamental parklands of national significance, as recognised by their inclusion in English Heritage's 'Register of Parks and Gardens of Special Historic Interest in England'. These are Adderley, Shavington, Buntingsdale, Pell Wall, Hodnet (a 20th century garden), Tunstall and Oakley. A Grade 1 Registered Park is considered to be of international importance: Hawkstone Park has this highest status.

Deer parks

Although there had been extensive deer parks in North Shropshire from the 12th century onwards, such as the large hunting forest between Drayton and Cheswardine, they had largely been lost to farming cultivation by 1851. The tradition did remain on a very reduced scale: typically the small deer herds at Oakley, Hawkstone and Hodnet which were often kept for their ornamental value in the parkland. They sometimes formed part of the country house tradition of providing country pursuits for the family and their guests, with hunting being a continuing favourite.

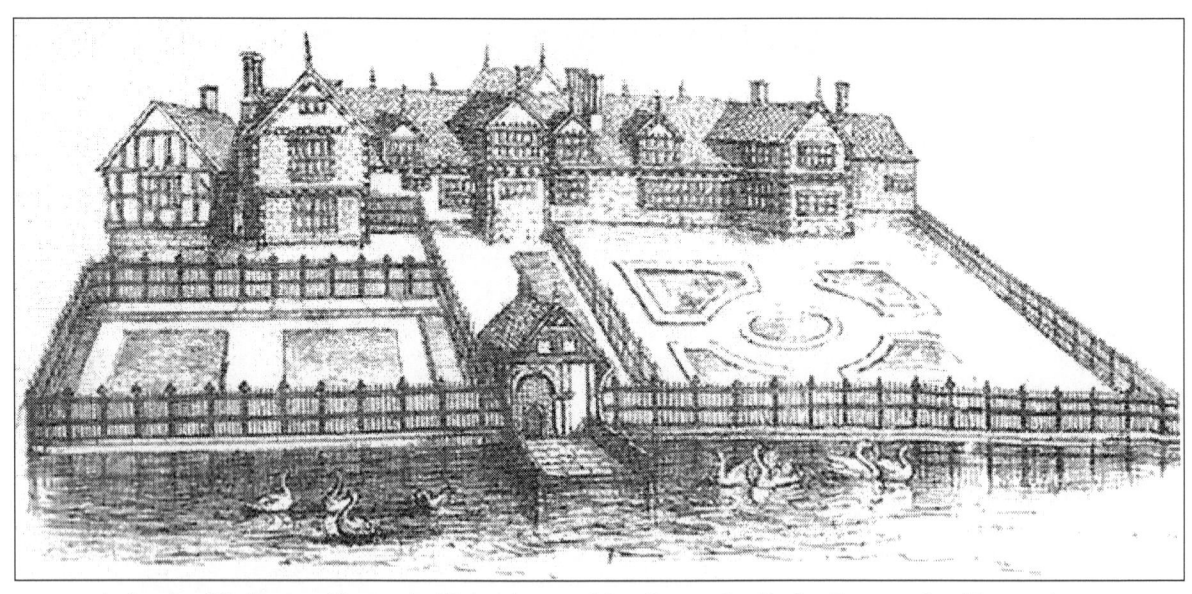

A sketch of Bellaport, Norton-in-Hales, home of the Cotton family, by Frances Stackhouse-Acton
[Reproduced from Old Country Houses in Shropshire *by Julia Ionides & Peter Howells]*

Early gardens

Throughout the scattered rural townships the heritage of the Middle Ages was still just evident, notably through the surviving half-timbered manor houses. In many cases these retained their original moats, with or without water, even though now they were kept for decorative rather than defensive purposes.

Moreton Say

An example of a moated garden was Moreton Say, where remnants of the moat had been incorporated into the new Vicarage Garden. Just as their Elizabethan predecessors had done, the Victorians enjoyed a promenade around the boundary of their ornamental gardens. Such walks often included raised viewing points from which the layout and the plantings could be admired. Moreton Say grounds were regularly open to the public for the annual village fete, and the 'beautiful grounds of the Rectory were much admired' according to contemporary accounts.

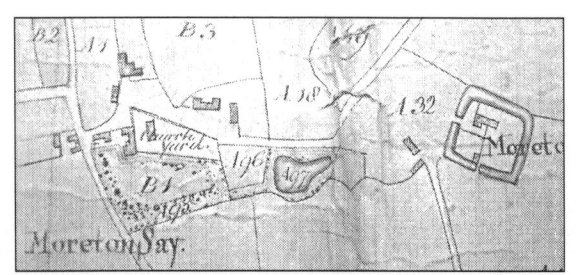

Moreton Say — estate map, 1797
[Shropshire Archives]

Bellaport

Another moated garden survived at Bellaport, built about 1520, which was later sketched by Frances Stackhouse Acton in 1868. This shows the water entrance to the garden and the formal layout of parterre beds and grass plats in front of the house.

The English Landscape Style

The English Landscape Movement in the later 18th century had produced many parklands following an idyllic pastoral vision of spacious grasslands, set with stately parkland trees, sloping down to an ornamental lake. All this was designed to be admired from the principal rooms of the house, and viewed from carefully planned carriage drive approaches. A parkland estate was often further ornamented by 'eye-catcher' garden buildings, or statuary. To enjoy these, circuit walks led the family and their visitors around the garden and park. Substantial woodland belts were usually planted inside fenced, railed or walled boundaries, to give privacy and to keep out the undesirable world. This 'English Landscape Style' was admired and copied around the world, and most of our local estate landscapes in 1851 still showed the strong, capable design character of that earlier movement. Notable examples of the English landscape style could be seen on many estates, including Adderley, Shavington, Buntingsdale, Tunstall, Oakley, Almington, Hales, Cloverley and Styche.

Adderley

At Adderley, a property of the Corbet family, a straight tree lined avenue had originally led to very

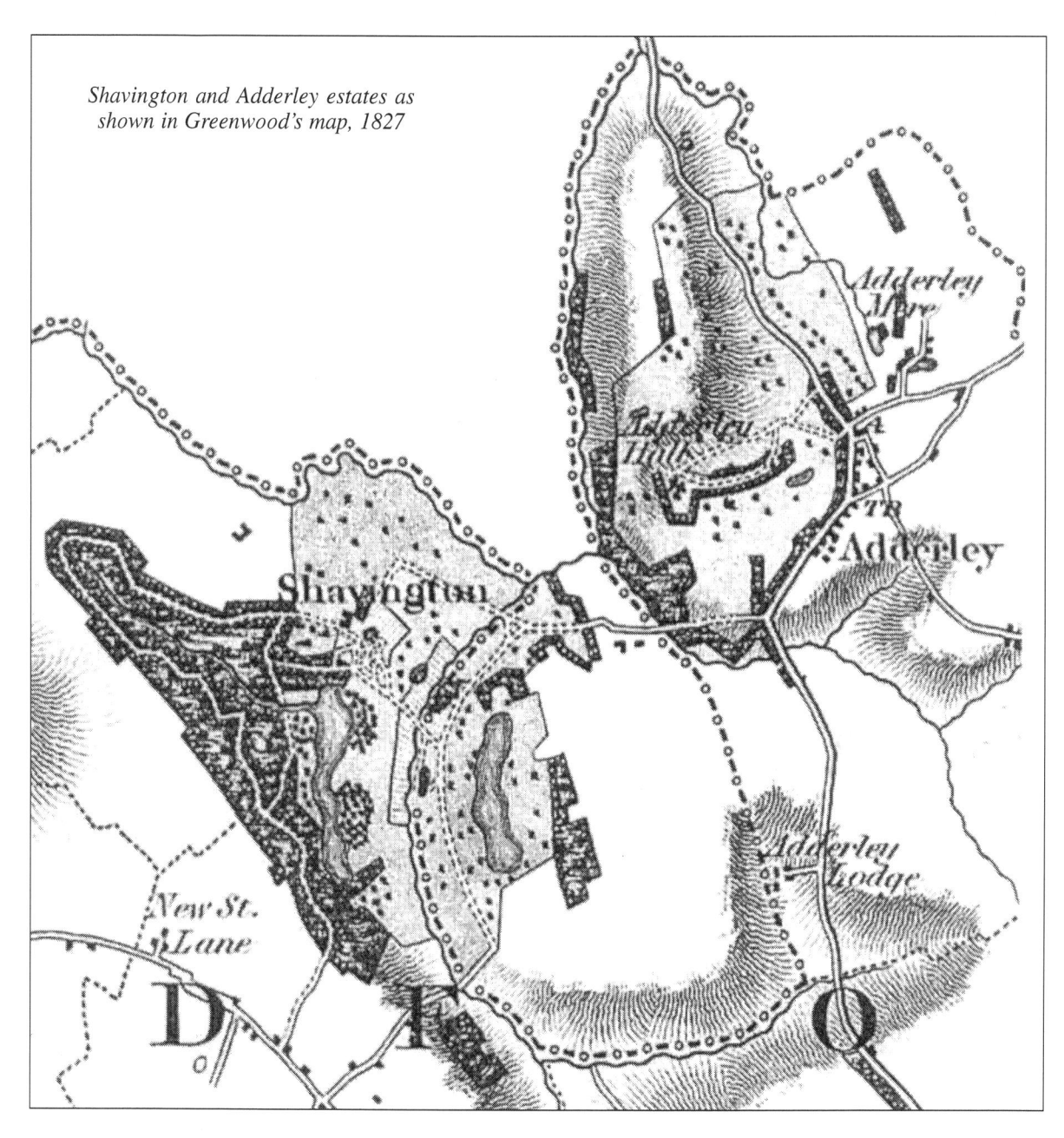

Shavington and Adderley estates as shown in Greenwood's map, 1827

formal gardens around the Hall. Built in the mid 1700s, the house in a Georgian, classical, style with 'many fine pieces of Italian sculpture' was set in a park of over 200 acres. By the early 19th century a more informal, scenic approach had been created, running between two lakes: Adderley Mere and the later lake which was formed to the south of the house. Bagshaw's Directory of 1851 described it as 'beautified with pleasure grounds and shrubberies, and stands in a well wooded park, ornamented with a fine sheet of water'.

Shavington

The neighbouring property of Shavington was originally a subsidiary holding within the manor of Adderley, but the Needham family had gradually enlarged and beautified their estate. Becoming the Earls of Kilmorey, they had in 1685 built the grandest red brick Tudor house in Shropshire, with a contemporary garden of formal geometric beds. By the early C19 however, a major period of landscape improvement had seen the old formality of gardens and straight avenues swept away in favour of the fashionable 'English Landscape Style'. Advice had first been given by William Emes (but was not implemented) who had a high reputation within the Midlands area as a landscape designer. The prestige of this great estate was such that the most eminent landscape designer in England, Humphry Repton, was then commissioned in 1793 to produce one of his famous 'Red Books' for Shavington (a design book bound in red leather which included 'before and after' sketch design proposals for remodelling a landscape according to the latest fashions). New stone bridges were built so that the scenic, curving drives which gradually revealed the beauty of the landscape now led to the Hall after passing over Long Pool, one of the ornamental lakes.

Although the extent to which his plans were followed is unclear, many key landscape elements of Shavington in the mid 19th century showed Repton's style. As well as the Long Pool, a larger Big Pool was the focus of park walks. In the pastoral grassland were dotted fine specimen trees, rounded spinneys and linear boundary plantations. Four lodges guarded the entrances. Bagshaw's Guide of 1851 recorded 'a spacious and elegant mansion of brick, surrounded with a park richly wooded & beautifully adorned with sylvan beauty, comprising upwards of fifteen hundred acres. The noble owner enlarged the park, and began to enclose the whole with a brick wall several years ago — upwards of five miles of the wall has already been built; the park is about seven miles in circumference.'

Buntingsdale

At Buntingsdale, a fine house within an existing estate had been rebuilt in 1720 for Bulkeley Mackworth by John Prince and finished by Francis Smith of Warwick, a highly reputed builder. The earlier formal gardens had been reshaped by Bulkeley Mackworth just before the house was rebuilt for him. A lake was created below the west end of the gardens, enhancing the view from the elevated site of the house westwards towards the river Tern. He also enlarged the parkland around the house. Typically, the estate included productive walled kitchen gardens to the north of the house, a gardener's cottage and a large stable block by Francis Smith. A later owner, William Tayleur, built a second lake to the south — later drained to form a dry pool. The pleasure grounds would have been explored from a circuit walk, a route carefully designed to show off the lakes, the woodland and the fine distant views.

A reminiscence by a young visitor evokes the spirit of this estate: Augustus Hare was to become a travel writer, and his childhood memories (1834–43) included visits

> to Buntingsdale, a fine old brick house of the last century standing at the end of a terraced garden, with lime avenues above the Terne, near Market Drayton. Here Mr and Mrs Tayleur lived with their four daughters ... who were very severely brought up, though their father was immensely rich ... [M]any of my childish pleasures came from Buntingsdale and I was always glad when we turned out of the road and across some turnip-fields, which were then the odd approach to the lime avenue on the steep bank above

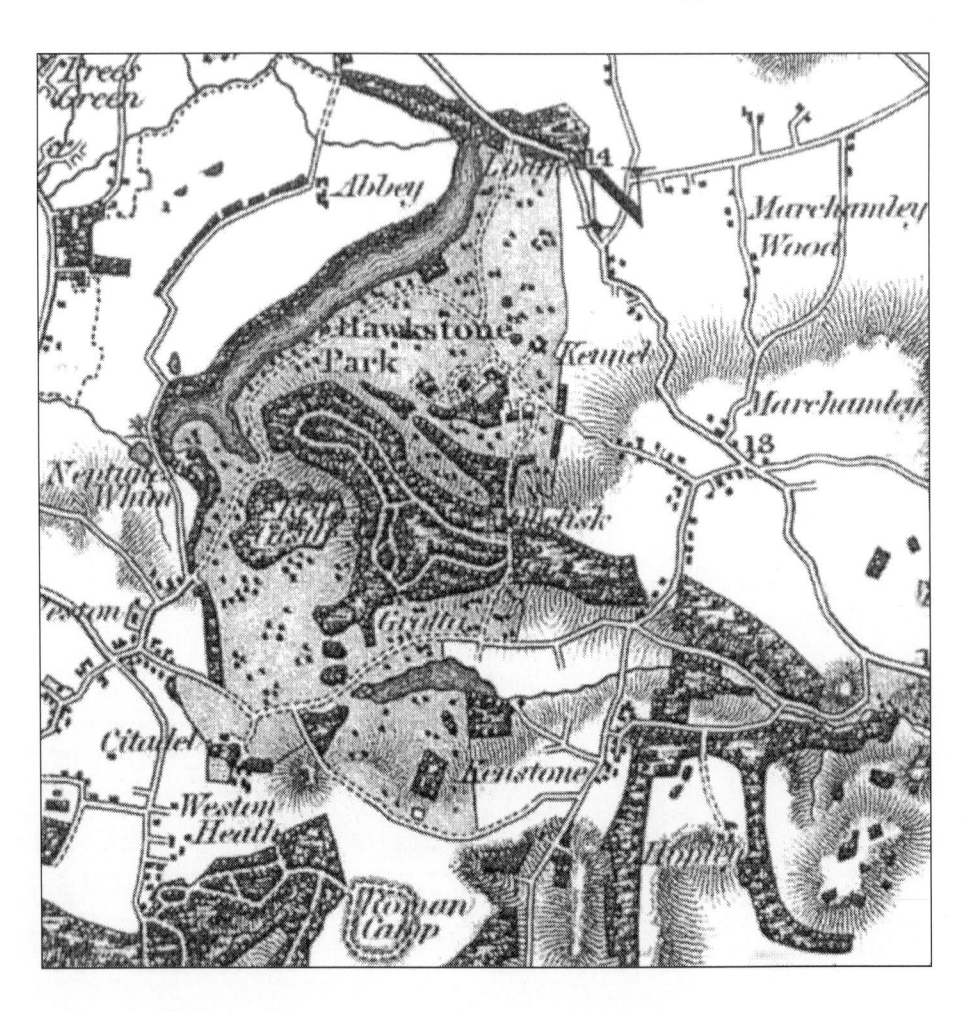

Hawkstone Hall and Park, as shown in Greenwood's map. 1827

Lithograph c1850 of the grotto at Hawkstone Hall

[From A History of Hawkstone *by Denis McBride]*

the shining Terne, and to see the brilliant border of crocuses under the old garden wall as we drove up to the house.

The Picturesque legacy: Hawkstone

Hare was also a frequent visitor to the Hill family of Hawkstone. Included in the Market Drayton administrative area in 1851, it was — and still is — famed as perhaps the greatest example of the Picturesque landscape movement in England. In its original undivided form the extensive landscape park swept around both sides of a dramatic sandstone ridge which offered fine prospects over the countryside. The tall monument to Sir Rowland Hill which stands on the ridge could be seen from a long distance.

Emerging in the later 18th century, soon after the English Landscape movement, the Picturesque style had also replaced the earlier fashion of formal gardens with naturalistic landscapes. The key feature of the Picturesque, however, was an emphasis on ruggedness, not tranquillity, and the desire to inspire awe and perhaps a little fear in visitors. In this objective Hawkstone definitely succeeded! Dr. Johnson had written about

> its prospects, the awfulness of its shades, the horrors of its precipices, the verdure of its hollows and the loftiness of its rocks…above is inaccessible altitude, below is horrible profundity.

From the time that its owners, the Hills of Hawkstone, first admitted tourist visitors into the park in the C18, this 'sublime' landscape of craggy rock faces, precipitous paths, scary bridges and dark tunnels and caverns fascinated visitors.

Hawkstone Hall in 1854, when a ball was held to celebrate the coming of age of Sir Rowland Hill's son, Rowland Clegg Hill [*From* A History of Hawkstone *by Denis McBride*]

Augustus Hare wrote:

Hawkestone was and is one of the most enchanting places in England. There, the commonplace hedges and fields of Shropshire are broken by a ridge of high red sandstone cliffs most picturesque in form and colour, and overgrown by old trees with a deep valley between them, where great herds of deer feed in the shadow. On one side is a grotto, and a marvellous cavern — 'the Druid's Cave' — in which I used to think a live Druid, a guide dressed up in white with a wreath, appearing through the yellow light, most bewildering and mysterious. On the other side of the valley rise some castellated ruins called 'The Red Castle'. ... Over one of the deep ravines which ran through the cliff near the Red Castle was 'the Swiss Bridge' — Aunt Kitty painted it in oils. Beneath it, in a conical summer-house — 'the Temple of Health' — an old woman used to sit and sell packets of ginger-bread — 'Drayton ginger-bread' — of which I have often bought a packet since for association's sake.

In 1851 the park would have been seen at its peak, and the Hills were still enlarging it, converting fields behind the mansion and its immediate pleasure grounds into further parkland. The approach from Marchamley followed the Terrace Walk which Sir Rowland Hill (1800–75) had extended. By the 1840s it stretched for three quarters of a mile along the high ridge, giving outstanding long views and crossing two gorges via wrought iron bridges. New plant introductions from around the world now ornamented the pleasure gardens and the Terrace Walk, including the newly fashionable exotic conifers. These helped to restore the tree cover which had been depleted by some 1,100 trees which were lost in severe gales in 1839 and a hurricane in 1850.

Although some of the 18th century elements of the landscape had vanished, such as the once-fashionable Chinese temple and Turkish tent, and an automaton had replaced the 'live hermit' in his cave, new elements had replaced them in the first half of the 19th century. Boating had become the rage, and short break visitors often enjoyed sailing as part of a two or three day stay at the enlarged Inn (now the Hawkstone Park Hotel). Various tableaux formed points of interest on the walking tour which began at the Inn, such as 'the scene at Otaheite' reflecting contemporary interest in South Sea discoveries. Hothouses and menageries could be visited, and in the 1850s the eland, or South African antelope, were introduced to the park. However the continuing highlights of the visit were still the contrasting experiences: the narrow clefts and the dark tunnels suddenly opening out onto cliff top viewpoints above precipitous drops. In 1834 the visitor Edward Sidney had described the network of truly awesome grotto caverns as 'incrusted with shells and minerals, sparkling in a thousand hues, shed on them through coloured lights placed in the fissures of the rock above.'

It is no wonder that Hawkstone was one of the principal landscape attractions in England, a nationally renowned 'sublime' garden intended to inspire thoughts of eternity .

Nineteenth century villa landscapes

From the early part of the 19th century, the growing prosperity of middle class professional and business men enabled them to built new houses in spacious grounds. Their substantial villas on the edge of town were often set in a scaled-down version of a country park: their houses, overlooking a rural prospect, were set above mown lawns planted with fine specimen trees. The grounds often included a lake or pool, as at Peatswood, Old Springs and The Grove, and perhaps a traditional ha-ha boundary to the pleasure grounds. Pell Wall, just outside the town, included all these landscape elements within an undulating landscape which was screened from public roads by a traditionally wooded perimeter, as in larger country estates. The newer elements of these landscapes would, by 1851, have reflected the blossoming of floral interest in Victorian gardens, the importing of exotic conifers, and the sporting pursuits suited to smaller gardens, such as croquet lawns. Flowers rioted in formal beds near the house and in heated conservatories, while tender fruits such as peaches and vines were raised in heated glasshouses. Early photographs and postcards illustrate these town garden fashions.

Pell Wall

Pell Wall was completed in 1828 for Purney Sillitoe. The family's wealth was based on trading in London as iron merchants, but his grandfather, mother and wife all came from Market Drayton. Having built up an estate south of the town, he employed Sir John Soane to design a country villa (to be his last), a coach house and several lodges, including the ornate triangular gate lodge. The brick walled kitchen gardens were built in 1822–8 and included glasshouses, a gardener's house, and the usual range of sheds and bothies for garden staff.

By 1845 the Pell Wall estate extended to 452 acres, and Sillitoe had extended his ornamental planting as far as the river Tern and also Salisbury Hill. After the house was completed Sillitoe wrote to Soane, who had become a friend, that 'the foliage of the place was now in very high order'.

Pell Wall: entrance front, 1821
[Fo.vi.4, reproduced with permission from the Sir John Soane Museum]

By 1851 four new approaches had been made, three having lodges. The north-east forecourt included a carriage sweep around a central circular bed: a typical feature of Victorian villas. The old field name 'Pell Wall' is believed to have meant 'a spring in the hollow'. The focus of the pleasure grounds was indeed a series of improved ponds lying in a dingle which drained to the river Tern. A sandstone viewing platform (and possibly a lost garden house) were built from which the scenic prospect over the Dingle could be admired. Its woods and ornamental shrubberies could also be enjoyed from a network of pathways, while still remaining is a rustic summerhouse — certainly documented in 1860 — made of cedar boards with a heather thatched cladding. It had both internal and external seating, and a black and white pebble path ran around the outside.

An ice house and a thatched boathouse had also been recorded. This rustic style of construction was very popular in Victorian times and many pattern books were published encouraging owners to build rustic arbours, benches, fencing and trelliswork. The planting was typical of the time: it included Wellingtonias and other exotic conifers which were being introduced by plant hunters, as were the newly fashionable azaleas and rhododendrons. Examples of these were commonly found in villa gardens, just as in larger parklands.

Grove House

Grove House was another property where the lifestyle resembled that described in the larger estates. In 1851 the Wilson family employed a large number of servants to manage their mansion and its spacious grounds, seven of them 'living in' the main house, five with their families in Grove Cottages, in the grounds, while others came from the town. An undated photograph shows household staff posed against the background of a ferny dell: a passion for ferns and rockwork being another Victorian garden obsession. Another shows family members by a grotto, some younger members being perched on its walls and roof. A 'Plan of the Grove Premises at Market Drayton' dated 1850 shows the line of the ha-ha bounding the garden, perimeter planting, a lake in a wooded hollow and a treed walk to the walled kitchen garden (to the north of the main road). The form of this walk resembles the little 'wilderness gardens' of the 18th century: not really wild, but with geometric paths running through tree planting. This small example illustrates how the fashions in gardening, as in

Pell Wall, rustic summerhouse
[Author]

architecture, were coming full circle, with a revived interest in the irregularity of the English Gothick and a vogue for the re-creation of gardens from earlier historic periods.

Town plots

Even where dwellings were clustered at high density in the centre of town, the desire for a patch of green space for relaxation was so strong that detached pleasure gardens were a feature of Market Drayton, as of other towns. Although laid out in strip plots, as are today's vegetable garden allotments, the original character of these gardens was far more decorative. Families often built little summerhouses: places for tea and quiet relaxation, from which they surveyed their flower-filled green sanctuaries. Even today occasional narrow footpaths survive from the days when they were used as wheelbarrow paths to these gardens, although the pleasure garden strips themselves have gone.

Principal sources

Publications:
- English Heritage, *Register of Parks and Gardens of Special Historic Interest in England*
- Bagshaw's *Directory of Shropshire 1851*
- Andor Gomme, *Smith of Warwick*, 2001
- Frances Stackhouse Acton, *Castles and Old Mansions of Shropshire*, 1868
- F Leach, *The County Seats of Shropshire*, 1891
- Julia Ionides & Peter Howell, *The Old Houses of Shropshire in the Nineteenth Century: The Watercolour Albums of Frances Stackhouse Acton*
- Denis McBride, *A History of Hawkstone*
- Walding Associates, *Hawkstone: A Short History and Guide*
- Emma Gieben-Gamal & Andrea Wulf, *This Other Eden: Seven Great Gardens and 300 years of English History 2005*
- David Lambert: unpublished notes on Pell Wall gardens
- John Udall: unpublished notes on Pell Wall gardens
- Census of England and Wales, 1851

Maps:
- C&J Greenwood, *Map of Shropshire 1827*
- Ordnance Survey Maps: various editions
- Plan of Moreton Say & Bletchley, 1797: Shropshire Archives

Archives:
- Shropshire Archives, Shrewsbury
- William Salt Library, Stafford
- Drayton Museum

On-line sources:
- www.francisfrith.com: 'Historic Photograph Collection'
- www.discovershropshire.org.uk

Pell Wall: the rustic bridge — although the photograph was taken much later in the 19th century, all the 'rustic' features in the grounds are thought to have been in place by the 1850s [John Udell]

Supplement

The Shropshire Rifle Volunteers
2nd (Market Drayton) Company 1860–1908

David Jenkins

Introduction

The creation, from to time, of volunteer units to support the British army, has followed an established procedure since 1558 and this will be described.

To understand the reasons underlying the establishment of the Rifle Volunteers, it is necessary to outline the development of facets of British and French history in the 18th and 19th centuries and to identify the perceived threats that rose to a climax in 1859, that the Rifle Volunteers were intended to help combat. The formation of the Rifle Volunteers, on a national basis, was not an initiative from the War Office, who opposed the concept, but was the result of public demand, to which the Government eventually acceded and much later, eventually supported.

The Rifle Volunteers were different from previous volunteer units in that they were armed with a modern, sophisticated, accurate weapon, capable of making combat take place at a considerable distance. The need to acquire a skill at using the rifle necessitated a new approach to arming and training the volunteers than had hitherto been the practice.

The historical background to volunteers

There has, in Britain, since the late 16th century, been, at times, the need for the established army to be aided by volunteers, engaged for a specific limited purpose for service in the home country. These volunteers were known as yeomanry if they were mounted on horses or as militia if they were foot soldiers. Sometimes these volunteers were mobilised to assist in curbing civil unrest and at other times volunteers were assembled to counter a perceived threat of invasion.

These volunteers are not to be confused with 'fencibles' (a contraction of defensibles) who were regular troops of either infantry or cavalry that were recruited at times of specific emergency, particularly in the latter half of the 18th century.

In 1556 Queen Mary created the post of Lord Lieutenant in each county of England. A Lord Lieutenant's duties included the role of raising and commanding militia in his county. Since the need for militia was intermittent and a militiaman was a volunteer, formal and disciplined training was also likely to be non-continuous. Nevertheless the structure existed for many centuries, which enabled militia to be mobilised by the Lord Lieutenant on several occasions at short notice.

Britain's involvement in warfare with France from the 17th century

From the time of Charles II, the seeds of what would be the British Empire were starting to grow, together with a great increase in international trade and the naval forces to protect that trade. Competition and rivalry with European monarchs, who were generally more despotic than a British monarch could be, led in the 18th century to at least forty years of intermittent warfare in Europe, North America, the Caribbean and India, in which Britain was always involved and in which France was always one of the enemy. After 1800 there was yet another fifteen years of war against Napoleonic France.

The only attempts the French made to invade the British Isles were at Bantry Bay in Southern Ireland in 1796 and Fishguard in Wales in 1797; both attacks were on a small scale and were unsuccessful. However in 1803, Napoleon Bonaparte created a large assembly of military force of some 130,000 troops and 6,000 horses and many naval vessels and barges at Boulogne, obviously intended to be used to invade England. This force remained as a threat until 1805 when the French, having lost the naval battle at Cape Finisterre in July and, being thus unable to protect their invasion fleet, were obliged to give up their attempt at invasion. Following the battle of Trafalgar in October 1805, there was no prospect of an invasion being threatened again for the foreseeable future. The British had enrolled 400,000 yeomanry and militiamen to help defend the homeland in the period 1803–5.

France between 1815 and 1848

The losses at the battles of Trafalgar and Waterloo and the exile of Napoleon Bonaparte to St Helena were bitter pills for the French to swallow, as were the terms of the peace treaty of 1815. In one respect however the French were treated leniently, in that they were required to pay only the equivalent of £28 million for the expenses of the war, which had cost the British Exchequer £572 million!

Louis XVIII was monarch of France from 1814 until his death in 1824. After 1815 his rule was stable and he established parliamentary government. He was succeeded by his brother Charles X, who was expelled in 1830, as he was thought to be repressive. It was during the reign of Charles X that Britain and France fought as allies with Russia against Turkey and they jointly won the naval battle of Navarino in 1827.

Louis Philippe, the Duke of Orleans, was elected monarch in 1830 and ruled until 1848. He had given some initial support to the revolutionaries and his rule was described as the 'bourgeois monarchy'. Notwithstanding the revolutionary pressures in France and the fear in Britain that these would give encouragement to the Chartist movement that began in Britain in 1837, the relations between the French and British governments were good. Indeed the term 'entente cordiale' was first used, not as usually thought in 1904 in the reign of Edward VII, but in the period 1843–6, when Britain supported France diplomatically, whilst France was subject to coldness from Prussia, Austria and Russia. However Louis Philippe was unable to contain the aspirations of the Bonapartist revolutionary party who were belligerent and anxious to avenge the humiliations of 1805 and 1815. Eventually Louis Philippe fled to exile in England in 1848.

The reign of Louis Napoleon: the Second Republic and Second Empire, 1848–70

1848 was noted as the 'Year of Revolution' in that revolutions took place that year in Belgium, Holland, Hungary, Austria and the states of the German Confederation, including Prussia, as well as in France. It is not surprising that the British government was most anxious that the 'revolutionary fever' did not cross the Channel.

Louis Philippe's passage to exile in England was coincident with Louis Napoleon's return to France from exile in England. Louis Napoleon was nephew to Napoleon I and he subsequently became President and, in 1852, Emperor of the 2nd French Empire with the title of Napoleon III. (Napoleon II was not an emperor of France but the son of Napoleon I and King of Rome 1811–32.)

Napoleon III was clearly anxious to emulate his uncle and to restore to France the glory that had once been hers. The British were concerned that he might yield to French popular desire for war with Britain to avenge Trafalgar and Waterloo. Napoleon III was certainly bellicose. In 1848 he sent an expedition to Rome to unseat the revolutionary government there and restore the Pope. The Emperor Napoleon's perceived aggressiveness alarmed the British people and Parliament responded by passing a Militia Act in 1852 and ordering a review of Britain's defences.

In 1853 Turkey declared war against Russia and as a consequence France and Britain became Turkey's allies in the Crimean War of 1853–6. It was in this war that Napoleon III ordered that the French battleships bombarding Sebastopol were to be clad in iron plates to make them invulnerable to the cannon of the day. This initiative alarmed the British Admiralty and led to the launch in 1860 of the first British ironclad battleship, HMS Warrior. Other innovations introduced to the French navy were the screw propeller and steam-powered propulsion.

During 1857–60 France and Britain were allies in a localised war against China to protect their trading interests. In 1859 France, Piedmont and Sardinia went to war with Austria to free parts of what is now northern Italy from Austrian control. This expedition was short and successful and was one where Napoleon III sought to emulate his uncle by being near the front line. He was however unskilled in the art of war and did not interfere with his generals. It was this campaign of Napoleon III in northern Italy and his subsequent annexation of Nice and Savoy for France that alarmed the British Parliament and the British newspapers which both had a great fear that Britain would be drawn into another continental war.

In 1859 France became very belligerent towards Britain as a consequence of the unsuccessful Orsini conspiracy to assassinate Louis Napoleon. Orsini was an Italian who with others had planned the assassination in London. The French, on discovering the plot and claiming that Orsini's bomb had been made in Birmingham, thought that the British Government had supported Orsini and, if it had not, it should not have given Orsini asylum.

The following are verbatim extracts from *Eddowes Shrewsbury Journal* of 1859, which are quoted to convey a sense of the perceived French threat.

> February 9th: 'The maintenance of the maritime power of this country is vitally important, especially when such extraordinary preparations for war are taking place on the other side of the Channel.'
>
> April 20th: 'There is little doubt that the prime mover and instigator is Louis Napoleon whose conduct of late years has diminished very materially his reputation for sagacity and forethought which he previously enjoyed. Since the Orsini affair the French Emperor seems to have lost his head.'
>
> 'The use of arms has been encouraged by the state among three generations of Frenchmen.'
>
> 'In England there is a violent panic every two years about a French invasion.'

'The French believe they will avenge the loss of Canada and India and the fall of Napoleon.'

July 27th: 'There is concern in Parliament about the undefended state of the South Coast.'

'The French fleet is being armed with rifled cannon.'

August 3rd: 'The French army has been reduced to a peacetime establishment of 650,000!'

'The British army in England is only 30,000!'

September 14th: 'The French navy is building twenty new iron plated frigates.'

October 26th: 'Every dockyard in France is in full work and within a few weeks France will have a Mediterranean fleet twice the size of the British fleet.'

'The present French government is determined to deprive England of naval supremacy.'

November 23rd: 'The Times of London is quoted as reporting, "War with England is the aspiration of every Frenchman".'

'In these days of steam, not to be prepared is to be ready to surrender ourselves to the buccaneering propensities of a man who has already proved that with him honour and conscience are as naught.'

Napoleon III had an aggressive foreign policy that included a six-year intervention in Mexico from 1861–7. He thought that Louis XIV was right to believe that the natural boundary of France should be the Rhine and to this end he sought to annex Luxembourg and Belgium, but neither monarch achieved their goal. This belief eventually led to the Franco-Prussian war of 1870. This conflict against the rising tide of Prussian imperialism, despite the great expenditure on soldiers and weapons, led in a few months to the defeat of the French, the loss of Alsace-Lorraine and the indignity of Napoleon III having to surrender personally to the Prussians at Sedan, before he once again sought sanctuary in England.

To summarise: Napoleon III did not appear to act aggressively against Britain. His bellicosity and anxiety to once again make France a formidable power in Europe was a worry to Britain and particularly his modernising and rebuilding of the French navy could only be seen as a threat to Britain, when a navy was of much less relevance to Continental expansion.

In conclusion of this brief note on Napoleon III, it is apposite to note that he was given the nickname of 'rantipole' meaning 'a wild and reckless person'.

The Royal Commission of 1859 to Enquire into the State of British Fortifications

This Royal Commission reported in 1860 and recommended the expenditure of over £11 million on defensive forts and batteries to protect royal dockyards and arsenals. There was concern that the French could invade by landing on an unprotected stretch of the south coast and then march overland to attack naval bases like Portsmouth and Plymouth from the rear. Eventually this perceived threat was met by the construction of a ring of fortresses around each naval base.

In the period 1860–70, seventy-four additional forts and coastal defence works were built as follows:

Plymouth	25
Portland	4
Isle of Wight	12
Portsmouth	12
Dover, Thames and Medway	9
Other locations not on south coast	12

In addition to the fortresses built on land, four forts were built in the sea across the Solent between Portsmouth and the Isle of Wight. These forts were some 150 feet in diameter with walls of great thickness and clad in three inches of wrought iron to withstand naval bombardment. The forts were built to mount nine 12.5 inch bore, rifled, muzzle-loading guns.

The coastal defence forts were substantially complete by 1870, when the Franco-Prussian war had caused any threat of French invasion to have totally vanished, if indeed there had ever been a real threat. With the benefit of hindsight, these coastal fortifications were labelled 'Palmerston's follies' since Palmerston had been the Liberal Prime Minister in 1855–58 and 1859–65.

The formation of the Rifle Volunteers

The desire for a volunteer force arose from popular demand. It was not actively supported by the Regular Army, who saw volunteers as part-time amateurs, who would be unequal to the hardship of combat. The Government was also a reluctant supporter, as it did not want the proposed volunteers to be a cause of further public expenditure.

As a consequence of public pressure, encouraged by some newspapers, particularly *The Times*, the War Office wrote on 12 May 1859 to the Lords Lieutenant of all British counties asking for their proposals for the formation of Rifle Volunteer units in their respective counties. This initiative by the Government, in passing responsibility to the Lords Lieutenant, resurrected the authority given to Lords Lieutenant by Queen Mary in 1556 and absolved the Government from any responsibility for the outcome.

The basic requirements that were laid down by the War Office for a county force of Rifle Volunteers were as follows.

1 Any officer must receive his commission from the Lord Lieutenant.

2 All volunteers must take an oath of allegiance to the Crown.
3 The volunteers were liable to be called out in the event of invasion or of a related rebellion.
4 While under arms, volunteers were to be subject to military law and they were entitled to be billeted and to receive pay in like manner to the regular army.
5 Volunteers could not quit while on active service and only at fourteen days notice othcrwise.
6 Volunteers were expected to present themselves for drill and training for twenty-four days in a year.
7 Volunteers undertook to supply their own arms, equipment and uniform, all of which were to be to the approval of the Lord Lieutenant. However since the War Office undertook to provide the ammunition, *at cost*, it was essential that the rifles provided by the volunteers were of a standard and consistent barrel diameter to match the ammunition.
8 The establishment of officers and non-commissioned officers was to be fixed by the War Office but the Lord Lieutenant was to specify the number of separate units forming the county force.
9 The Lord Lieutenant was responsible for the Rifle Volunteer units in his county and for the nomination of the necessary officers.

Subsequent circulars from the War Office offered:
- Rifle training courses at the infantry rifle range at Hythe, Kent, the cost to be borne by the trainees' volunteer unit.
- The provision of regular army instructors to attend units and provide training in drill and musketry. The cost of the instructors' pay, their travel subsistence and lodging was to be met by the volunteer unit.
- A training manual entitled *Drill and Rifle Instruction for Volunteer Rifle Corps* at a cost of sixpence per copy.
- Targets for ranges at cost price.

Each unit of volunteers was required to provide, at its own expense, a safe rifle range of at least 200 yards length and a safe place of custody for its arms, together with an armourer responsible for the maintenance and care of the arms. All arrangements were subject to inspection and approval by the War Office, without which the unit could not continue to exist.

Volunteer units were permitted their own bands (at their own expense), which were often engaged to support non-military events. Units were not allowed to have their own colours.

The experience of forming volunteer units was not unfamiliar to Lords Lieutenant in the 18th & 19th centuries. In Shropshire, for example, during the Napoleonic wars of 1793–1815, cavalry, infantry and artillery regiments were raised, but these were not expected to serve far from their home area. Some examples were the Loyal Ludlow Infantry and the Oswestry Volunteer Infantry. The writer has found no evidence of the creation of a Market Drayton unit in the Napoleonic period.

One important development that had taken place since the Napoleonic period, when volunteer units would not be expected to serve in areas far from their home county, was the development of the railway system, which by 1859 would enable the rapid transportation of units to a scene of potential conflict. Though Market Drayton was not served by rail in 1859, Whitmore station, only ten miles from Drayton, was on the London–Crewe line and would have enabled rapid access to the south coast.

In one respect the meanness of the War Office relaxed. On 1 July 1859 a new administration headed by Palmerston was formed and they offered to make a free supply of 25 rifles per 100 volunteers. This issue was raised to 50 rifles per 100 on 14 October 1859 and then to a complete issue on 20 December 1859.

Viscount Hill, the Lord Lieutenant of Shropshire convened a meeting of his deputy lieutenants in mid July to consider their reaction to the War Office letter of 12 May, and the conclusion of the meeting was favourable. On 27 August the Lord Lieutenant held a meeting designed to gather funds to meet the expenses of forming a Rifle Volunteer company in Shrewsbury and he set an example by donating £50. By December the 1st Company of the Shropshire Rifle Volunteers was established with War Office approval of their arrangements and facilities.

The procedure to establish a company of Rifle Volunteers

Members of the public in a town who were desirous of forming a company of Rifle Volunteers would begin by calling a public meeting to ascertain the amount of public support, the potential active membership (which would aim to be about 60–100), and the ability to raise the necessary funds for the establishment and equipping of the company and for its future outgoings.

Members would be of two kinds: those older men who wished only to support the company financially and be honorary members, and those who wished to be active, enrolled members and undertake training. Since the proposed company had to provide its own uniform and equipment, armoury, armourer and rifle range, the need to be confident of raising sufficient finance was the most important objective in establishing a company.

An honorary member, who was entitled to wear the company's uniform, would be expected to pay a life subscription of about ten guineas and an annual subscription of 1–3 guineas. An enrolled or active member would be expected to pay an annual subscription of one half to one guinea. If a unit wished to have a band, and many did, then this would require an additional and dedicated subscription. Some units might be prepared to subsidise the subscriptions and the cost of uniforms for some members, so as not to be unattractive to poorer working class potential members.

Once a potential unit had satisfied itself of sufficient local support in terms of active members and of sufficient fund-raising ability, it would then make a proposal to the Lord Lieutenant outlining details of its intended formation, giving nominations for officers (one captain, one lieutenant and one ensign for a company of 60-100 men), their proposals for an armoury for the safe storage and maintenance of weapons, and their proposed range site.

If these particulars were satisfactory to the Lord Lieutenant then the unit could be formed. In order to be formally established, it would have to be inspected and its arrangements formally approved by a Regular Army officer appointed by the War Office, who would subsequently provide formal approval or rejection of the unit's proposals.

On receiving approval from the War Office, the unit would then seek the consent of the Lord Lieutenant to the proposed details of their uniform. The uniform colour was usually required to be drab, that is, grey, dark green or blue, to avoid the conspicuous red of the regular army. It was the Lord Lieutenant's duty to maintain a consistency of colour and style in the uniforms of the different volunteer units in his county. Thus each county, if not each unit, could have its own design and colour of uniform.

Since each unit was formed from a relatively small community there was much less social division between the officers and men, and indeed the management of the unit was by means of a committee containing both officers and men. Discipline would be exercised by a scale of fines for offences. Officers were not necessarily appointed for military skill but were often nominated or elected by the men.

The creation of the Market Drayton Company of Rifle Volunteers

An inaugural meeting was held in Mr Gordon Warren's office (now the offices of Graham Withers and Co) in Cheshire Street on 8 December 1859. One hundred potential supporters attended this meeting. The meeting nominated and approved the appointment of the following officers, subject to the approval of the Lord Lieutenant:.

Captain	Alfred Hill (a former captain in the 68th Foot)
Lieutenant	William Manly Wilkinson
Ensign	George Gordon Warren
Hon Surgeon	Foliot James Sandford

The Committee of Management comprised Dr Saxton as the Honorary Treasurer and Mr Gordon Warren as the Honorary Secretary, the three officers and three nominated members of the company.

The potential unit enlisted many honorary members and finance appeared to present no difficulty. The Old Workhouse in Shropshire Street, which was owned by the churchwardens and parish of St Mary, was selected as being suitable as an armoury (hence the building's subsequent name). Mr Warren claimed to have found a ground for rifle practice, though the location was not revealed.

Gordon Warren proposed a uniform that would be a light grey colour, that would cost between £3.15s. and £4.5s. but the uniform design had yet to be approved by the Lord Lieutenant.

Formal approval of the Market Drayton Company's proposals was received in February 1860 and the Market Drayton Company was formally known as the 2nd Company of the Shropshire Volunteer Rifles. The Company had an active strength of 90 men and its drills were held three times a week.

Although the national Rifle Volunteers had a motto 'Defence not Defiance', the Market Drayton Company wanted its own motto as follows: 'Decus et decorum est pre patria mori' which translates as 'Honour and glory to die for one's country'.

Subsequently the Shropshire Rifle Volunteers were organised in two administrative battalions as follows, together with the dates of the commission of the first officer in each company. Thus Market Drayton was the first company in the county, after Shrewsbury, to respond to the call for volunteers.

1st Administrative Battalion

1.	Shrewsbury 1st	14.12.1859
4.	Bridgnorth	13.2.1860
5.	Condover	5.3.1860
6.	Ironbridge	13.2.1860
9.	Shrewsbury 2nd	2.3.1860
10.	Ludlow	2.3.1860
11.	Cleobury Mortimer	4.5.1860
12.	Shifnal	21.4.1860
16.	Munslow	24.5.1860
17.	Shrewsbury 3rd	8.1.1861

2nd Administrative Battallion
2.	Market Drayton	15.2.1860
3.	Whitchurch	18.2.1860
7.	Wellington	27.2.1860
8.	Hodnet	2.3.1860
12.	Wem	3.5.1860
13.	Ellesmere	2.6.1860
15.	Oswestry	28.4.1860
18.	Newport	17.1.1862

Notable events in the history of the Market Drayton Company of the Shropshire Volunteer Rifles

On 7 March 1860, 2,000 officers of the Volunteer Rifles attended a special levee at St James Palace, at which they were presented to Queen Victoria and Prince Albert. The Market Drayton Company was represented by Lt W M Wilkinson, Ensign G G Warren and Hon Assistant Surgeon F J Sandford. After the levee the officers dined in St James Hall and this was followed by a ball in the Floral Hall at Covent Garden, to which, it was reported, 4,000–5,000 officers and their ladies were invited. This was a grand occasion held very soon after the launch of the Volunteer Rifles, which helps to demonstrate the rapid rate of recruitment. This levee was never repeated, probably because Prince Albert died in 1861 and for a long time after Queen Victoria withdrew from social engagements.

It was reported in *Eddowes Journal* of 14 March 1860 that 'The 7th March 1860 will long be remembered as the day which terminated the periodical fancies of foreign invasion'. This odd observation was perhaps linked with the news that by June 1860 the overall national strength of the Rifle Volunteers had reached 120,000.

On 20 June 1860 the Market Drayton Company held their first church parade at Christchurch, Little Drayton, at which the service was conducted by the Reverend Edward Cheere, vicar of Christchurch, who was commissioned as the chaplain to the 2nd Company SRV in July 1860.

On 23 June 1860 there was a grand review of 21,000 Volunteers, with their bands, in Hyde Park, on the site of the Great Exhibition. It appears that not one of the Shropshire companies was represented.

In July 1860. the Market Drayton Company had an inauguration banquet, given by the officers, at the Corbet Arms. This must have been a very memorable occasion as the report in *Eddowes Journal* on 18 July ran to 44 column inches! Captain Heber Percy and Lieutenant Corbet were guests. There were very many speeches congratulating the Company and it seemed that they were all reported verbatim. It was noted that the Company had a 'practice ground within five minutes of the town centre' but its location was not revealed, except to say that the site was jointly owned by Messrs Corbet and Twemlow.

The Volunteer Rifles trained initially with an Enfield rifle, which was replaced by a Snyder breech-loading rifle in 1863. This was followed

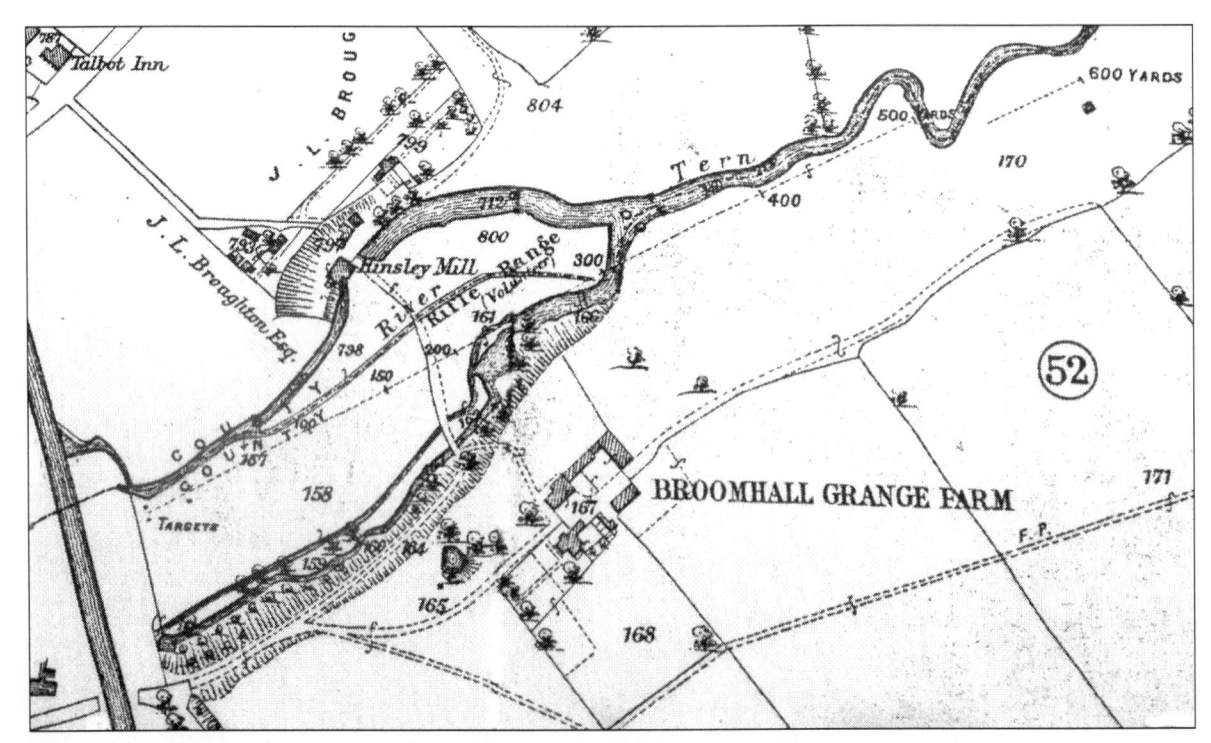

The rifle range at Broomhall Grange, as shown on the 1900 Ordnance survey map

The Market Drayton Rifle Volunteers firing a celebratory salute on the occasion of Queen Victoria's Diamond Jubilee, June 1897. The Company was under the command of Captain A R F Exham and Lieutenant Huntbach
[Newport & Market Drayton Advertiser, 26 June 1897]

in 1881 by a Martini-Henry breech-loading rifle, and finally in 1895 a Lee Metford magazine rifle was issued and this had an increased range. These increasingly sophisticated weapons meant that range training became ever more important than proficiency at drill.

A notable training event was a camp of all the companies in the 2nd Battalion, held at Shiffords Grange for six days in August 1884. An average of 476 Volunteers per day attended over the six-day period and they were accommodated in 90 bell tents! The guest units arrived, mainly by train, from Whitchurch, Wellington, Hodnet, Wem, Oswestry and Newport, accompanied by the bands of the companies from Market Drayton, Whitchurch, Wellington and Oswestry. The whole event must have required a considerable amount of finance and organisation, in which the War Office would have played no part. However the camaraderie would have been excellent.

It appears that the Market Drayton Company had, in the course of its history, a number of rifle ranges around the town. The only one that can now be positively identified was at Broomhall Grange; this is marked on the 1900 Ordnance Survey 1:2,500 map. This range was 600 yards long and had its butts (that is, the target end) in the embankment carrying the Shropshire Union Canal, which was a safe location. Most of the firing points at 600, 500, 400, 300 and 200 yards distance were adjacent to the river Tern. The use of this site had been given to the Rifle Volunteers by Marten Harcourt Griffin, who was the owner of Pell Wall Hall from 1861 to 1902. Harcourt Griffin had bought the Broomhall Grange estate in 1878 and presumably the Rifle Volunteers had the use of the range between 1878 and 1902. This facility was no doubt the reason for the choice of the Shiffords Grange site for the 1884 camp, which was only 300 yards from the range and up-range.

Harcourt Griffin was a benefactor of the Market Drayton Rifle Volunteers and their band was invited to play at Pell Wall Hall on a number of occasions.

The Market Drayton Volunteers paraded in the town in June 1897 as part of the celebrations of Queen Victoria's Diamond Jubilee and they fired a celebratory salute in the air with their rifles, when assembled at the head of the High Street.

The subsequent growth of the Rifle Volunteers

The national strength of enrolled volunteers continued to grow throughout the life of the movement as follows:

June 1860	120,000
1861	161,000
1870	193,000
1887	228,000
1901	288,000

This growth is remarkable having regard to the original opposition of the War Office to the volunteer movement. This lack of interest gradually waned as the War Office found that by not providing any financial incentive, they had little influence in the management of the volunteers. In 1860 the total expenditure by the War Office on the Volunteer Rifles was £3,000! However by 1897 the annual cost to the taxpayer had risen to £627,000 and the Government then had a greater opportunity to exercise control.

The Volunteers never mounted a political lobby in Parliament and they remained quite apolitical.

However notwithstanding the disappearance of any real threat from France after 1870, War Offices throughout Europe had to practice the solution of theoretical problems and in the 1890s both the German and French general staffs were using the invasion of Britain as a subject for their planning exercises!

Conclusions

1. At a distance of nearly 150 years, it is difficult to appreciate the alarm that was felt by the public in 1859 at a perceived threat of invasion by the French. Why else would they want such a large army and more particularly, such a large modern navy?
2. The Rifle Volunteers were created by the people as a consequence of public demand, fuelled and encouraged by some elements of the press, and as a response to the unpredictable bellicosity of Louis Napoleon.
3. The British Government also had this concern, which was evident from the huge programme of strengthening the defences around Britain's naval bases in the period 1860–70.
4. Notwithstanding its appreciation of the threat of invasion, the War Office was opposed to the creation of the Rifle Volunteers and the Government was passive, leaving the Lords Lieutenant of the counties to ascertain the actual level of support, which had to be self-financing, and then to encourage its mobilisation.
5. The enthusiasm of the middle class and upper working class particularly, ensured an immediate and substantial support for the Volunteer movement, which must have surprised both the War Office and the Government.
6. The meanness of the Government in failing to meet any of the expenses of providing uniforms, equipment, armouries and rifle ranges was astonishing and only reluctantly and in instalments, did they provide rifles on free issue.
7. The fact that the Rifle Volunteer movement grew in strength progressively throughout the last forty years of the 19th century, despite the disappearance of any perceived threat from the French after 1870, showed that the Rifle Volunteers, as well as being a patriotic response met a need for social camaraderie that had less rigidity than that in the Regular Army.
8. In Shropshire sixteen companies of the eventual eighteen were formed in the first six months from the launch of the Rifle Volunteers, and the Market Drayton Company was the second to be formed after Shrewsbury. With the help of local landowners and the churchwardens of St Mary, the Market Drayton Company obtained the facilities it required to develop its training. It was as strong when it became part of the Territorial Army in 1908 as it was after the first year of its existence. The band that the Market Drayton Company created, at their own expense, was a popular asset to the social life of the town.
9. The positive response to the Volunteer movement and its increasing support with time, enabled the nation to respond positively to a call for volunteers in the Boer War and particularly the Great War, thus enabling the Government to delay conscription until January 1916.

Sources

- J Cannon (Ed), *The Oxford Companion to British History*
- J H Jackson (Ed), *A Short History of France to the Present Day*, 1959
- I V Hogg, *Fortress: A History of Military Defence*, 1975
- M H Brice, *Stronghold*, 1984
- I F W Beckett, *Riflemen Form: A Study of the Rifle Volunteer Movement, 1859–1908* (Unfortunately, Beckett uses no sources from Shropshire)
- N Rowley, *People and Events, 1770–1870*, p10
- 'Shropshire Rifle Volunteers' on website, www.discovershropshire.org.uk
- *Eddowes Shrewsbury Journal*, 1859–1860
- *Newport & Market Drayton Advertiser*, 9 August 1884 & 9 April 1904

Index

People

Andrews, George	62
Arkinstall, Misses	59
Baggaley, Maria	67
Barnett, John	74
Barnett, Martha	73
Bayley, Edward	47
Beech, John	68
Beeston, Robert	79
Bennion, Thomas	61
Bickerton, Henry	68
Bratton, Mrs	59
Bonell, Samuel	21
Boulton, Henry	73
Bourne family	79
Bratton, George	67
Bratton, Mary	59
Broughton, Peter	25, 32, 51, 61, 65, 66, 68, 76
Brown, Thomas	67
Buchanan, Rev Alexander	25, 51, 61, 65
Butler, George	67
Calow, William	20
Chetwode, Sir John	51, 68
Clive, Henry	25
Collier, Joseph	58
Cooke, Charles	58
Cooper, Edward	68
Corbet, Mrs	61
Corbet, Richard	65, 76
Crewe, Willoughby	51
Crutchley, John	68, 78
Crutchley, William	45, 61
Dale, Sarah	74
Dawes, Colonel	51
Dawson, George	71
Dod, Elizabeth	67
Eaton, George	59
Edge, Robert	73
Efford, John	67
Elcock, Mrs	59
Evans, George	73
Foden, James	73
Ford, Judith	58
Fullwood, Thomas	67
Furnival, Thomas	76, 79
Gee, John	68
Gladstone, Rev John	38
Godwin, William	20, 38
Goodhall, Thomas	67
Gower, Andrew	8, 15, 21, 26, 67
Griffiths, Thomas	67
Gromley, Henry	26
Hall, Thomas	75
Hand, Elizabeth	59
Harding, Egerton	51
Hare, Augustus	86–88
Haslam, Joseph	20–21
Heber Percy, Algernon	25, 26, 65, 66, 96
Hemming, William	66
Henry, Thomas	67
Hewett, George	58
Highfield, Samuel	68
Higgins, Elizabeth	58
Hill, Ann	74
Hill, George	25, 65
Hill, Viscount	25, 51, 64–65, 88, 94
Hoben, Thomas	67
Hopkins, John	26, 47, 62
Horner, Capt John	62
Hudson, Thomas	51
Hunt, John	67
James, Richard	66
Johnson, Mrs	62
Johnson, Richard	68
Johnson, William	68
Jones, Frances	59
Jones, Hannah	67
Justice, Henry & Mrs	25, 51, 61, 65
Key, John	74
Kilmorey, Earl of	74–75
Kirkham, James	73
Lee, Rev James	9–10, 11, 35, 58
Lewis, Thomas	36
Lloyd, Ann	67
Macaulay, Rev Samuel	51
Machin, Jeremiah	73
Matthews, James	74
Miles, Charles	58
Miller, Rev Charles	59
Minor, Samuel	30
Montford, Richard	68
Moore, John	67
Norcop, William Church	51, 68, 78
Onions, John	62
Palmer, Elizabeth	59
Palmer, John	68
Parker, John	38
Peplow, Thomas	67
Pigott, Creswell	26, 62
Porter, Elizabeth	68
Porter, Thomas	68
Pimlott, Joshua	20
Ray, Susan	59
Reynolds, William	68
Roberts, Thomas	47
Roden, Adam	71
Roden, Lydia and family	80–82
Rodenhurst, John	8, 21
Salter, Henry and family	81–82
Sandalls, Thomas	70, 73
Sandbrook, William	20, 26, 71, 74
Saxton, William	47
Scott, William	58
Sillitoe, Purney	16, 25, 51, 65, 88
Simmonds, George	68
Tayleur, Frances	62
Tayleur, John	25, 30, 61
Taylor, Mary	67
Tillery, Sarah	59

Tomkinson, William	71	Old Springs	16
Twemlow, Thomas	25, 45, 51, 61, 65	Ollerton	36, 37, 38, 42, 43, 59
Upton, Rev Robert	38	Pell Wall	83, 88–90
Wainright, John	68	Peplow	37, 59
Warren, Charles	26, 65	Shavington	83, 85–86
Warren, Gordon	95	Stoke Heath	37, 42, 43, 59
Warren, Joseph Loxdale	26, 62, 65	Stoke-on-Tern	16, 36, 37, 38, 40
Webb, William	68	Tern Hill	9, 37, 38, 43
Whittingham, Mary	59	Wistanswick	37, 43, 59
Whittel, John	68	Wollerton	36, 37
Wilkinson, William	26, 62, 95, 96	Woodseaves	59
Wilson, Ann	26, 27, 88	Woore	37, 40, 43, 58, 59, 66
Wilson, John	26, 27, 51, 62		
Wormsley, John	47		
Wright, John	67		

Places

Other

Adderley	37, 40, 85	Canal	9, 22, 87–72
Ashley	36, 40, 41, 42, 55, 58, 66	Carriers	5, 70–71
Betton	76–79	Census	19–27
Buntingsdale Hall	83, 86–87	Churches & chapels	see Religion
Cheswardine	36, 37, 40, 58, 59	Clothing trades	21
Child's Ercall	16, 37, 40, 58	Court Leet	11, 65
Eaton-upon-Tern	37, 41, 59	Crime and justice	12, 64–68
Great Soudley	37, 41, 42, 59	Education	10–11, 15, 57–60
Hales	40	Fairs	12–13
Hawkstone Hall	83, 86–88	Farming	5, 9, 16, 19–20, 77–79
Hinstock	16, 36, 37, 40, 41, 43, 58, 59, 66	Felons, associations for the prosecution of	66
Hodnet	16, 36, 37, 40, 58, 60, 66	Friendly Societies	49–56
Hookgate	41	Health	12, 14–15, 22–23
Kenstone	37, 41	Horse-hair weaving	8, 20, 24, 60
Knighton	41, 42	Housing	6
Little Drayton:		Illegitimacy	18
Baptist Chapel	41	Industry (generally)	5, 8, 20–21
Christchurch	37, 39, 40, 59	Inns and beerhouses	22, 73–75
Common	13, 28–35	Iron-founding	8, 21
Inns and beerhouses	75	Life expectancy	18
National School	58	Market	10, 70
Wesleyan Methodist Ch	41, 42, 59	Market Drayton Becher Provident Society	51–53
Workhouse	11–12, 45	Market Drayton Book Society	61–63
Longford	36, 37	Market Drayton Society for the Acquisition of Useful Knowledge	61
Market Drayton:			
Congregationalist Ch	41, 42, 59	Migration	15
Corbet Hotel	64, 73	Milling	8, 20
Courtroom	12, 64	Names	16
Grammar School	58	Oddfellows, Independent Order of	50–55, 67
Grove, The	27, 83, 89–90		
Inns and beerhouses	71, 73–75	Police	12, 65–67
National School	58	Poor Law	11–12, 44–48
Phoenix Inn	70, 74	Population	8, 14, 17
Police Station	12, 66	Railways	5, 9, 73
Primitive Methodist Ch	41, 59	Religion	9–10, 23, 36–43, 59
St Mary's Church	9–10, 37, 38, 40, 59	Rifle Volunteers, The	91–98
Workhouse / Armoury	11, 44–47, 95	Roads & road transport	5, 22, 32, 69–71
Moreton Say	16, 37, 38, 39, 40, 59, 60, 84	Servants	23, 25–27
		Stage coaches	70
Mucklestone	40	Shops	22, 24
Norton-in-Hales	37, 40, 42, 43, 58, 59, 60, 84	Water supply	9

Printed in Great Britain
by Amazon.co.uk, Ltd.,
Marston Gate.